THE GRAMERCY PARK HOTEL

• A NEW YORK ICON •

MAX WEISSBERG

Published by The History Press
An imprint of Arcadia Publishing
Charleston, SC
www.historypress.com

The images in this book are the author's own unless otherwise stated.

This book contains sensitive material, including descriptions of drug use, suicide, and explicit sexual content.

First published 2026

Manufactured in the United States

ISBN 9781467158848
Hardcover ISBN 9781540299925

Library of Congress Control Number: 2025943124

Notice: The information in this book is true and complete to the best of our knowledge. It is offered without guarantee on the part of the author or The History Press. The author and The History Press disclaim all liability in connection with the use of this book.

CONTENTS

David Bowie at the Gramercy in 1973. *Photo by J. Stevens, Zuma.*

INTRODUCTION

It all began with David Bowie. Candy-colored hair. A lightning bolt across his cream-painted face. A mysterious backstory that he was a "messenger from Mars." It was February 1973, and Bowie had come to New York to promote *The Rise and Fall of Ziggy Stardust and the Spiders from Mars* and his upcoming *Aladdin Sane.* Because Bowie's first American tour had been a money-losing operation, RCA Records booked the Gramercy Park Hotel for him instead of the Plaza. For his two-week stay, Bowie and his one-hundred-plus-person crew took over the third floor of the Gramercy, turning the place into a dormitory with "copious coke," as his tour photographer Leee Black Childers put it, and groupies circling in and out of Bowie's hotel room.

It might seem strange that a star would rent rooms on a low floor rather than one with a better view, but Bowie had a fear of heights. And there was another possible reason: Bowie's management company had instituted a policy in which no one, aside from specially designated individuals, was allowed to take Bowie's picture. Everywhere Bowie went, two bodyguards followed him. According to the late Childers, the whole thing had been a cheeky publicity stunt, since it would only *help* Bowie if people circulated his image. The effect, of course, was to make people try harder to take his picture. Eventually, a cherry picker appeared outside Bowie's window to snap a photo—which was only possible because Bowie was on a low floor.

The scheme worked: the press went wild. The lobby filled up with teenage girls, Polaroid and Kodak Instamatics in hand, desperate to record a glimpse of the star. Among the attendees at his sold-out February 14, 1973 Radio

City Music Hall show were Andy Warhol, Truman Capote, and Salvador Dalí. Bowie didn't disappoint. There were smoke machines, stage risers, half a dozen costume changes, and a backup band as big as a football team. During his last number, "Rock 'n' Roll Suicide," Bowie fainted and was dramatically whisked offstage by one of his bodyguards. The ensuing debate over whether the collapse was real or fake added to the sensation. (The official explanation was that Bowie's makeup had clogged his pores and caused him to pass out.)

After Bowie checked out of the Gramercy, some of the glitter remained. His visit cemented the hotel's reputation as a top-tier party spot among bands. The two-week residency even led to a new nickname, the "Glamercy," and word quickly spread that it was a place where you could *get away with anything*. At the height of the Gramercy's popularity, through the birth of punk and new wave, its guest list became a social register of rock history, including everyone from Jerry Garcia and Bob Dylan to Aerosmith, U2, and the Clash. The hotel's history, however, has seldom been given the credit it deserves. For many of these artists, their time at the Gramercy coincided with crucial moments in their creative lives. It was more than just a party spot—it was a reliable muse.

"We like this place, the Gramercy Park Hotel," Clash lead singer Joe Strummer once said. "It's economically viable to stay here, not like uptown somewhere. That means five nights of hotel rooms ain't no problem. And we like to get some vibe of New York, you know, because we'll put that information onto a record."

The Gramercy had large, cheap rooms with thicker walls than most Manhattan accommodations. It was one of the only places you could call up room service to order a pick or a guitar string. But its tolerant atmosphere, more than anything, is what made the place what it was. That atmosphere was owed almost entirely to one person, my grandfather Herbert R. Weissberg, who owned the hotel for nearly forty years. As long as guests (or the record company) paid the bill, he let them do whatever they wanted. The Gramercy Park Hotel was his kingdom, and everything from its wobbly tables to the low prices in its bar reflected his vision of what a hotel should be. When a guest needed attention, the employees gave it, and when a guest wanted to be ignored, they did that, too. One thing a guest could not do, however, was sit at the best table. That was always reserved for the Weissbergs, of course.

Under my grandfather's proprietorship, the hotel maintained many of the features from its construction in 1925. Dim chandeliers. Bloodred carpet. A feeling halfway between *Casablanca* and the *Titanic*. Herbert's approach to

Herbert Weissberg and his grandson Michael. *Photo by David Weissberg.*

décor was that of a museum curator, albeit a museum where the furniture always had cigarette burns and the TVs might be missing a knob or two. The atmosphere prevailed so deeply that a guest arriving in 1998 could hardly notice anything different from when they had arrived in 1958; their luggage was even carried by the same jockey-sized Irish bellhop, Pinky, who had, years before, opened the door for Babe Ruth. Something deeply ingrained in Herbert made him want to hold time in check. At the Gramercy Park Hotel, that wish magically held true.

International guidebooks invariably described the Gramercy as a quirky hostelry that approached the platonic ideal of "old New York." It had 18 floors and 509 hotel rooms, along with a rooftop terrace, a restaurant, a bar, a lounge, a newsstand, and a beauty salon. But it was also a home. Herbert lived there with his wife, Ruth, whom everyone called "Danny." And everyone in the family—four sons, three daughters-in-law, and nine grandchildren—lived in the hotel at one point or another. I lived in the Gramercy as a baby and later averaged around three months a year there in between semesters at boarding school. Though my own father, Robert, a college professor, played no role in the business, Herbert's other three sons, Marty, Steven, and David, were dependent on the hotel for their livelihoods, with Steven, being the heir apparent, groomed for eventual succession. The

Hotel Gramercy Park (later the Gramercy Park Hotel), circa 1932. *Photo by Ewing Galloway (1880–1953).*

Gramercy was the site of many of our family events and happy memories—birthdays, bar mitzvahs, weddings. But the permissive atmosphere, which we had prided ourselves on, took its toll. It turned out there was a price to pay for living in a rock star's paradise.

Other than the Glamercy, the hotel had a second nickname: the "Gram." Guests could order a "Telegram at the Gram," meaning a doorman or a bellhop (never Pinky, mind you) would deliver cocaine to their room like a pepperoni pizza. Police interference was rare, maybe because of the good relationship Herbert had with the off-duty officers he employed as security. When busts did happen, the flow of drugs slowed only temporarily. Eventually, bellhops were selling drugs, desk clerks were selling drugs, and even maids, aided by their boyfriends, found a way to profit from the drug culture that was so prevalent in New York at the time.

My uncles moved into the hotel in the mid-1970s, right when the party scene was really hitting its stride. My uncle David, an aspiring photographer, took a suite on the seventh floor with a large terrace overlooking the park, a pack of Doberman/black Lab mixes as his roommates. David had developed a heroin addiction as a teenager in Brooklyn, and the hotel's drug culture made it hard for him to stay clean.

Temptation was everywhere, and evidence of the "anything goes" atmosphere had a way of seeping into the hotel's public spaces. When Bob Marley stayed, my uncle Steven remembered, "The hallway looked like the smoke detectors were gonna go off." One time, a drunken Englishman came down from his room stark naked and took a seat at the bar. It was Pinky's job to find a sheet to wrap him in, which he was happy to do until he realized that naked people don't tip (no pockets). As a kid, I remember going down to the lobby late one night to find a guy with boxy glasses in the middle of a drug overdose, foaming at the mouth and marching in circles, knocking things over like he was possessed. The night doorman who was guarding the perimeter shouted at me like a farmer fleeing a tornado, "Don't come here! Turn around! *Turn around*!"

For a while, acid guru Timothy Leary lived in the hotel, as did *Rolling Stone* journalist Hunter S. Thompson, who hosted drug orgies in his room. According to a former guest, at one party, Thompson used a dildo to mash cocaine. Another remembers a sign outside his door that read, "BEWARE!! Do not knock! If a throat must be slit here today, why not yours?" As a sidenote, Thompson added in the corner, "Except for Room Service."

High Times magazine even had its founding party at the Gramercy in 1974. "We got these five-foot-high tanks of nitrous oxide and *High Times* balloons that had a mushroom on them," remembered Andy Kowl, one of the magazine's cofounders. "This was great press....From CBS and NBC to the *Daily News*, everybody loved it....All of the journalists did look askance at the nitrous oxide balloons at first. It was very weird, because people had to line up with their balloon to get it refilled. My clearest memory is that by the end of the night, almost every single one of [the journalists] had a balloon in their hand and was in line."

The late Nat Finkelstein once told me, "Everybody knew about the hotel." Finkelstein was a rock photographer whose career thrived in Andy Warhol's Factory, and he moved to the hotel in 1985. "You could get away with anything," he said. "And it was classier than the Chelsea. The Stones had stayed there and I think [Keith Richards's then-wife] Anita Pallenberg. Actually, I was there because Anita told me to go there. She said, 'They'll carry you.' I had no bank account. I had nothing. But they let me come into the place and take one of the high-rise suites."

"In New York, during our reign of terror in the '70s," Childers, Bowie's photographer, recalled, "depending on how much you could hoodwink the record company for, you went from the Chelsea to the Gramercy to the Plaza." Alan Vega, one-half of the punk duo Suicide, put it more bluntly: The Gramercy, he said, was where bands went "on the way up or on the way down." Of course, that was something everyone used to say, and at this point, no one knows its source.

◇◇◇◇◇◇◇◇◇◇◇◇◇◇◇◇

THE GRAMERCY SAW A lot of turning points in a lot of careers. One night, in the wee hours, Steven got a call from security downstairs. A loud group of hotel guests had just come in from a night on the town and wanted a drink at the bar, which had already locked up for the night. It was Bob Dylan. He'd been staying at the Gramercy for several weeks with his band, gearing up for his 1975 Rolling Thunder Revue Tour, which included, among others, folk legend Ramblin' Jack Elliott, ex–Byrds guitarist Roger McGuinn, Joan Baez, and former Bowie guitarist Mick Ronson.

Dylan's previous trek, in 1974, had been a big commercial arena tour. With Rolling Thunder, he was getting back to his roots. He looked for inspiration in the scene where his career started: Greenwich Village. He used the hotel as his base while he recruited musicians from the Bleecker Street club the Bitter End (then briefly known as the Other End). The first rehearsals were held in the hotel, until the band got so big they had to transfer to a studio. Dylan had also just separated from his wife, Sara, and spent many late nights in his room writing lyrics that eventually became part of the album *Desire*.

The night before the band's departure to Plymouth, Massachusetts, for their first gig, they celebrated the twenty-fifth birthday of guitarist Steven Soles in the hotel's bar. Lou Reed, who was then living in the hotel, appeared and bumped into his old colleague from the *Transformer* album Mick Ronson. Along with his dark trans muse, Rachel, Reed joined Ronson's table to discuss "gore photos," as writer Larry Sloman later described. Feeling out of place among the folk rockers, Reed suggested to Ronson that they head to a party around the corner, but the glam guitarist didn't budge. At another table, Ramblin' Jack Elliott strummed a lazy tune on his acoustic guitar and, in his cowboy drawl, mused about learning to play the electric guitar. "I'm tired of Jerry Garcia picking circles around me 'cause he's got $12 million," he complained bitterly.

Steven remembered helplessly fumbling with the liquor cabinet lock until guitarist Richard Bowden suggested they break it open. "Go ahead, give it a shot," Steven shrugged, and a couple of jabs later, Bowden busted off the cabinet's hinges. The band cheered wildly. Everyone ordered drinks, including Dylan, who had five Rémy Martins, enough to last him the night. Steven proudly served them.

After he finished pouring, Steven politely asked for the money.

"He's charging for these fuckin' drinks?" Ronson groaned. The conversation died down. The sound of strumming guitars suddenly quieted.

Steven straightened his spine. "Look, that's not bar prices, it's a substantial discount," he explained, adding that the money would go to fix the lock and tip the bartender who would clean up the mess. That sounded reasonable enough to the musicians. The aura of hospitality endured. Steven had saved the day.

Steven Weissberg. *Photo by David Weissberg.*

According to *Rolling Stone* writer Larry Sloman's book *On the Road with Bob Dylan*, Chesley Millikin, Elliott's manager, asked Dylan that night why he called the tour the Rolling Thunder Revue. "I was just sitting outside my house one day," Dylan said, "thinking about a name for this tour, when all of a sudden, I look up into the sky and I hear a *boom*.

Then *boom, boom, boom, boom*, rolling from west to east." Dylan punched into the air, like a prizefighter. "Then I figured that should be the name."

Dylan ordered another drink.

Millikin posed a second question: "You know what Rolling Thunder means to the Indians?"

"No. What?" Dylan asked.

"Speaking truth," Millikin replied.

"Well, I'm glad to hear that. I'm real glad to hear that, man." (Dylan always says things twice.)

Camped out at the Gramercy at the same time as Dylan was Lou Reed. He lived in room 605 with his androgynous trans muse, Rachel, on an allowance of fifteen dollars a day from the record company. Despite being unhappy with his situation, he declined Dylan's offer to join his tour, preferring instead to continue working on *Coney Island Baby*, his comeback record after the experimental noise assault album *Metal Machine Music*. Drinking carrot juice, working out, and indulging in a bit of speed, he found a routine that enabled him to finish the album, which reached number 41 on the *Billboard*'s Hot 100.

In the spring of 1982, John Phillips, formerly of The Mamas & the Papas, checked into the hotel with some other musicians. He had recently overcome a heroin habit and had been working as a drug counselor, but he was also trying to relaunch his music career. The comeback did not go quite as planned, however, and he ran up a large debt with the hotel. My grandfather saw an opportunity. He contacted Phillips about taking David under his wing; my uncle had been in and out of rehab and had even been arrested. Phillips agreed, and he and David, along with Steven, began playing music together. (I lived with my family down the hall, and my mother would leave the door cracked so we could hear them practicing.) The sessions were "calming" for David, Steven recalled. Eventually, the maids smelled marijuana coming from the band's rooms, so Herbert gave them the boot. David, meanwhile, continued to wrestle with his addiction.

Many of the legends who passed through the Gramercy's doors came *before* they were legends. In December 1980, the budding college radio band U2 had just released their debut album, *Boy*, and were on a club tour to promote it. For most of the group, this was their first time in the United States. Bono once remembered:

> *We landed in JFK, and we were picked up in a limousine. We had never been in a limousine before, and with the din of punk rock not yet faded from*

> *our ears, there was a sort of guilty pleasure as we stepped into the limousine. Followed by a sly grin, as you admit to yourself this is fun. We crossed Triborough Bridge and saw the Manhattan skyline. The limo driver was Black, and he had the radio tuned to WBLS, a Black music station. Billie Holiday was singing. And there it was, city of blinding lights, neon hearts. They were advertising in the skies for people like us.... We pulled up at the Gramercy Park Hotel, and everyone went in.*

Bono later immortalized these first impressions of New York on *Rattle and Hum*'s "Angel of Harlem."

U2's stay at the Gramercy was also the first time they met their idols, the Clash. Bono recalled it to music journalist Michka Assayas:

> *The Clash were staying there, the Slits. It was like an American bohemia. I remember the Slits hadn't got guitar straps. They were so punk. Their guitars, they were around their necks by strings. I think Edge put out his hand to shake one of their hands, and the singer, Ari Up, slapped it. She said, "We don't do that."...*
>
> *We saw the Clash in the lobby. They were just so cool, and we knew we weren't. I had a fur coat, which was funny. I remember I walked out to the street. It was snowing in America. I just wanted to take it all in, standing at the corner in my fur coat and my crap haircut. And this unusual looking man just stops on a bicycle beside me and says, "Hey, honey, where are you going? How are you sweetheart?" And I was like, "Urrggh! Not so bohemian after all. I want my mother!"*

IN THE EARLY 1980s, the club Danceteria moved in around the corner, at 30 West 21st Street. It was a hangout for artists Keith Haring and Jean-Michel Basquiat, along with Duran Duran, Billy Idol, and the Smiths. Madonna worked there as a hat check girl. Parties that began in the club often ended in the Gramercy.

Madonna's manager at the time, Camille Barbone, had a business partner, Adam Alter, who happened to do the hotel's penthouse landscaping. Alter was also friends with my uncle Steven, who was himself an accomplished musician. Steven remembered meeting Madonna at Gotham Records:

> *I met her in a recording studio that was owned by my friend Adam.... She had some great songs, but her voice didn't project at the time. Because she didn't have the exercise. She didn't have the stamina. She didn't have the vocal training. She didn't have the muscles, nothing. She didn't have the figure. She was bottom-heavy. They had to work her, get her into shape, vocal lessons. She was made. She was created. She was a very hard worker. She wanted it and was going to do whatever it took. And she never let up.*

Later, the group came back to the hotel, and Steven invited his wife, Madalyn, to join them. Steven grabbed a key for room 1202, facing Gramercy Park. There, Madonna started stroking Madalyn's back and offered a threesome with Steven. Steven thought she was joking—"She did that to everybody!"—but Madalyn took it seriously and jumped up and went to a different couch. (Madonna didn't respond to requests for comment on this anecdote.) In the months that followed, Madalyn liked to tell her story of the girl who called herself "Madonna" and offered a threesome with Steven. Madonna, meanwhile, got a big break when the DJ at the Danceteria played her tape. After Madonna became famous, Madalyn stopped telling her story because nobody believed her anymore.

Debbie Harry, also known as Blondie. *Photo by Martyn Goddard.*

Debbie Harry, Chris Stein, and London hairdresser Gregor Schumi. *Photo by Martyn Goddard.*

During Blondie's recording of their commercial breakthrough, *Parallel Lines*, Debbie Harry and Chris Stein lived in a small, dark room in the hotel's annex. After finding commercial success, they upgraded to room 502, facing the park. Jerry Lee Lewis stayed and enjoyed himself at the bar so much that he was three songs late to his gig at Tramp's. Elvis Costello told Steven he had his first martini at the Gramercy just after he was kicked off *Saturday Night Live*. When punk became popular, the Squeeze, the Buzzcocks, and Siouxsie and the Banshees all stopped by. According to the hotel's former general manager, the late Tom O'Brien, Sid Vicious stayed but was permanently banned after he threw a television out the window. Sometime later, O'Brien told me, when Sid wanted to book the Gramercy a second time, my grandfather refused him. Fatefully, Sid chose the Chelsea Hotel instead, where his girlfriend Nancy Spungen was later murdered.

The stories are endless. And beyond rock stars, the Gramercy attracted artists of all kinds—writers, photographers, filmmakers. In 1975, during the show's first season, part of the cast of *Saturday Night Live* took up residence at the hotel, including John Belushi, Dan Aykroyd, and Gilda Radner. (After Steven procured Belushi some rolling papers, he was offered a ticket to the first episode of *Saturday Night Live*, hosted by George Carlin, and the premiere party that followed.) Once, when some of the writers had a maintenance problem in their rooms, it was fixed by Boris, a Czech painter, and his assistant, both known in the hotel for their wild dance moves and frequent Studio 54 visits. According to Steven, this incident later spawned the creation of the "Wild and Crazy Guys" sketch.

Martin Scorsese used the hotel for rehearsals and preproduction when he made *Mean Streets*, and a few years later, he filmed a scene from *Raging Bull* in room 1501 and cut the film there. Like U2, Scorsese was a fan of the Clash, and he first met them at the Gramercy. The director wanted the Clash to work on the soundtrack for a film he was planning called *Gangs of New York*, but when the movie was delayed (by a couple of decades), he offered them a small part in *The King of Comedy* instead. Scorsese and Robert De Niro attended one of the Clash's legendary concerts in Times Square at Bond's International Casino in 1981. The Clash stayed at the Gramercy during what became a seventeen-show residency at Bond's, and their presence made the hotel's bar scene buzz even more than usual. Some years ago, I asked Scorsese about his time in the hotel, and with a bit of nostalgic glee, he said he visited "when all the rock bands were there."

In the '90s, the hotel's golden era waned, but bands continued to pay visits and collect free drinks from my family members. The bar had changed little since the 1930s—mirrors lined the walls, and a musty scent mixed with cigarette smoke. There were always Goldfish crackers on offer and candles lit inside cherry-colored glasses. The bar's clientele, like the hotel's guests, were so loyal that only the wallpaper had been there longer. The Harvey sisters, a pair of octogenarian martini drinkers, had been coming since the '60s. Another regular was the librettist Ira Gasman, who would often sit in the bar with a rhyming dictionary and compose his lyrics. (When I asked him about this, he said, "*Everybody* uses one.") Harmonica legend Paul Butterfield became a hotel resident and lived hand to mouth on what the record company would give him. My personal favorite was Lionel George, a dapper Swiss polyglot who claimed to have an inheritance from a grandfather who invented the automobile clutch. Less frequent but still regular patrons were the director John Waters, the Carradines, and hotel resident Matt Dillon, who always had a group of girls waiting for him in the lobby. No matter what celebrity was at the bar, however, the best seat was always reserved for Herbert R. Weissberg.

But signs of decline began to appear everywhere. The elevators filled up with graffiti. The waiters looked like they slept in their uniforms. The chandelier light bulbs burned out and were ever so slowly replaced. The colorful world my grandfather had created began to dim. What followed were tragic events—my cousin overdosed; my uncle David jumped off the roof and landed in front of his wife; my sister disappeared. Other grim tales emerged, followed by a story of hope.

In 2006, the new Gramercy Park Hotel opened, a manifesto of modern design made possible by the artist Julian Schnabel, who decorated much of the interior. Within weeks of the hotel's opening, it hosted a glitzy Marc Jacobs party that famously denied Paris Hilton entry. The Rose Bar, filled with high-profile works of art, soon became a top party spot, and *Page Six* and *TMZ* regularly camped outside on Lexington Avenue to snap photos of the many stars who visited. Rock 'n' rollers who had been regulars in the Gramercy's heyday, like Madonna and Steven Tyler, came back.

Far from being a shabby establishment, the hotel brought in guests like former presidents Bill Clinton, celebrating his sixtieth birthday, and Barack Obama, who ate at Maialino, the hotel's restaurant, operated by Danny Meyer. Among the new residents in the remodeled annex (now called 50 Gramercy Park North) were (supposedly) Jennifer Aniston, Karl Lagerfeld, and an Icelandic billionaire couple who provoked a lawsuit by remodeling their John Pawson–designed kitchen with IKEA. The hotel's intense hype briefly died down after Schrager sold his stake to Rosen, though the Rose Bar's elegance did not wane. After closing during the COVID pandemic, the hotel reopened in 2025 under the stewardship of MCR Hotels, a family-run hotel chain headed by billionaire Tyler Morse.

At the center of the glossy new Gramercy, the heart of the old hotel still beats inside. To me, the hotel is a special place, not just because my family once owned it but because it was a home to so many, including me. The story of the Gramercy, with its long, stubborn traditions and its eventual surrender to change, in many ways mirrors the history of New York City itself. Its rises and falls, and its role as both a muse and occasional enabler of self-destruction, continue to attract people from all over the world. It's a tradition that I think will live on no matter who is in charge. As Leee Black Childers once said, "The Gramercy Park Hotel is New York's soul."

This book includes as many stories as I could cram in. We begin with the stories of others who stayed in the Gramercy and end with the Rose Bar. Along the way is the story of my tragic family and me, who some believe became cursed as a result of living in the hotel.

1

IN THEIR OWN WORDS

Hotel sign, circa World War II: Keep Cool, Do Not Scream, Walk, Don't Run.

Tom O'Brien (manager): At one time, they had manual elevators in the 1960s. There was one [operator] named Murphy, and [bellhop] Pinky told the story that he would go on top of the elevator and sleep on top of the elevator so no one could find him.

Steven Weissberg (heir): The dining room in the 1960s actually had Italian and German and French waiters. The banquet manager was French and named "Petite." That was his last name. I never knew his first name. He would click his heels when you said his name. He said all the dishes in French.

Tom O'Brien: [In the 1970s,] we would buy furniture from the Drake, the Regency, when they were renovating and getting rid of furniture. I thought it was better than what they were putting in. Gradually, we renovated everything.

Steven Weissberg: The Gramercy [cost] twenty-eight dollars [a night] in the '70s. By '76, the Democratic Convention comes in town. The rate goes up to forty dollars. Nobody got mugged, and everybody loved New York.

Alan Vega (musician): It was expensive. It was really expensive. But lo and behold, I went down to pay the second month, and they said, "No, no." And they gave me back all this money that I had paid them because I automatically became a full-time resident.

Leee Black Childers (photographer): In every city, the bands had a piece of paper with the hotel's name and address and phone number written on it, so if they got lost, they could show it to a taxi driver. In New York, it would say "Gramercy Park Hotel," and that address and the people at the desk obviously could take it from there if you were delivered to the front door.

Nat Finkelstein (photographer): The Gramercy Park Hotel was in my own worst days. Everybody knew about the hotel. You could get away with anything. And it was classier than the Chelsea. And the Stones had stayed there and, I think, Anita Pallenberg. Actually, I was there because Anita told me to go there. She said, "They'll carry you."

Me: Sorry, who is Anita?

Nat Finkelstein: Anita Pallenberg was Keith Richard's wife. Anita was the only woman who fucked all five Rolling Stones. And she was a great lady.

Leee Black Childers: In New York, during our reign of terror in the '70s, there was, depending on how much you could hoodwink the record company for, you went from the Chelsea to the Gramercy to the Plaza. The Chelsea was the bottom. The Gramercy was one step up. If they stayed in the Gramercy, then they felt that the company was investing more in [them] as a serious musician.

Nat Finkelstein: Physically, the hotel was much nicer than the Chelsea. It was much more discreet than the Chelsea was. I hate to down the Chelsea, but you knew what hotel worker you could buy your drugs from in the Chelsea. The Gramercy was not that way.

Top: John Mayall and Maggie Parker on December 2, 1979. *Ebet Roberts.*

Bottom: Joni Mitchell and editor/photographer Debby Chesher on December 2, 1979. *Ebet Roberts.*

Alan Vega: It was like a ritual of life or something. You had to go through the Gramercy Park Hotel, whether on the way up or on the way down.

Tony Zanetta (Bowie's manager): It was a faded elegance. It had an elegant feeling about it, but it was definitely beyond its glory days. That section between those two parts of the hotel. There were always a lot of old ladies who lived there. They kind of hanged there.

Paul Shaffer (musician): The place was the essence of shabby gentility. The carpets were musty, the furniture was in disrepair, and a distinct funk hung in the air when you walked down the hallways. I loved it.

Gary Lucas (musician): It was one of my favorite hotels of the world. It had this vibe—better than the Chelsea. The Chelsea was more living off the legend. The OD's. This guy, that guy. The Gramercy was nicer. That's why I'd use it for affairs.

Paul Shaffer on the hotel's roof on June 29, 1983. *Ebet Roberts.*

Steve McQueen (actor): I lived on the brew and cocaine, along with acid, pot, and fuck-flings. Yes, I attended bisexual orgies, one of them taped by the FBI at the Gramercy Park Hotel in Manhattan. I bet that ugly old queer J. Edgar Hoover got an eyeful watching the sex tapes of me in action.

Leee Black Childers: There was a lot of drugs. A lot of illicit sex. Copious coke. But it really was handled in a more discreet fashion. In one place [the Chelsea,] you threw the TV out the window. In the other place, [the Gramercy,] you still destroyed your TV, but you left it in your room so no one knew.

Nat Finkelstein: So I was there I think for a month without paying anything. My tab came to over $3,500, and then one night or one early morning, we ran out of coke. This is about three o'clock in the morning. We are out of our coke-addled heads. We imagine that there must be a plastic bag in the wash basin, remember those wash basins. Did you ever see them?

Me: Yeah.

Nat Finkelstein: Well, underneath them, there were these two holes where the cast iron had been sprued, so there's a little hollow space. Cyrinda [Foxe], myself, some friends of Yoko's, everybody stuck their finger in, and we thought we felt the bag. Every time you stuck your finger in it, the bag got a little farther away. So at one point, Terry said—

Me: Wait, did you put the bag in there? Was this something you knew about or were you surprised to find it?

Nat Finkelstein: This was the last-chance desperation. The girls are gonna put their clothing on and leave. We had to stop this one way or another or there'd be disaster. It was just the imagination running rampant. So Terry said, "Listen, I think I have a small crowbar at home. And maybe we can get this crowbar into one of the holes and push the bag into the other side."

So Terry, who lived nearby, came back and we dismantled the water basin as best we could, and then the water basin broke in half. The entire fucking wash basin broke in half. And I said, "Oh my God. I think it's time for us to part." But Terry said, "No, no, we don't do that. We repair the wash basin." The idea of how insane this whole thing is. "We were gonna repair—OK fine." Then we were gonna get some epoxy and glue it back together.

So sometime around five o'clock in the morning Cyrinda says, uh, "Don't worry, I can get industrial epoxy." Where she was gonna get industrial epoxy God only knows. But you have to understand that Cyrinda was the absolutely highest-class cocaine whore. And she could find anything. You could go to sleep with your last $300 in your hand and your hand underneath the table, and you would wake up and Cyrinda would be gone, as would be the money. And she would come back an hour later with the coke. So, sure enough, she comes back with the industrial epoxy and was really in a frenzy because the chambermaids were gonna come around ten o'clock, so we gotta get out. Like that Steely Dan song "Kid Charlemagne," "Pack up the test tubes and the scale, or we'll all wind up in jail." I don't know how we managed to get that thing to stick together. We reassembled it. And at eight o' clock in the morning, before the staff came in, I checked out, leaving behind a bill of about $3,500 or $4,000.

Me: Did you ever pay it?

Nat Finkelstein: Never.

Herbie Flowers (Bowie musician): That was the one time in my life when I thought I could get by with artificial support [cocaine]. For a week, I stayed locked in my room at the Gramercy Park Hotel with a married couple looking after me. Then they put me on the SS *France*, with someone else traveling with me to look after me.

Leee Black Childers: By then, RCA had decided to put Bowie in his proper place at the Gramercy Park Hotel. David had decided to put himself in his proper place, which was [with] groupies going in and out all the time and quite a lot of drugs, which he would not deny. That's not speaking out of turn at all. That was his period. That was his period of a lot of cocaine. Roadies were entirely wild. There was a cherry picker outside. It was wild times. A lot of going from room to room.

Tony Zanetta: Girls would just show up in the hotel and hang out in the bar, go up to the floor. They'd roam the hall.

Ava Cherry (model): David [Bowie] was a really smart man, and I was very taken with him. I was really falling for him. He obviously felt the same, so he invited me back to the Gramercy Park Hotel, where we had some drinks, listened to *Aladdin Sane*, and then one thing led to another. But then, next morning, the doorbell rings, and it was Angie [Bowie's wife]. She was very bombastic, like, "Hello, darling!" I said, "Who is this?" And she said, "Oh, I'm David's wife! I'm Angie." Then she goes just as quickly as she arrived. "Goodbye, see you!" Just like it was nothing. David sees the look on my face and says they have an open marriage.

Bebe Buell (model): [I] was staying at the Gramercy Park Hotel, and I would go rushing over there at four or five o'clock in the morning. Every time I got there, there would be someone leaving and someone arriving. I remember him going, "Ah, let's put on silk robes and play with makeup!" So that's what we did. We put on silk robes, and we put makeup on, and played with different ideas on our faces for like four hours. So that was my big sex with David Bowie.

David Johansen (musician): Me and [Bowie musician Mick] Ronson met at the Gramercy Park Hotel when Bowie came over. We both enjoyed a cocktail.

Suzi Ronson (Mick Ronson's wife): It was the classy rock and roll hotel. It was where the rooms were big. One suite at the end was for the star. And the other suite was for the big party before everyone went to sleep. And we had guards on the elevators. It wasn't its best days. The carpets were worn. The elevators still worked. Everything was a bit dusty and faded. It was fantastic.

Joe Perry (Aerosmith musician): Back at the Gramercy Park Hotel, I was still buzzing from the speed and grateful that New York television, unlike Boston television, is an all-night affair.

Leee Black Childers: I think it was Aerosmith that destroyed a few rooms there. It was '74 because I was on the road then with Mott the Hoople. Aerosmith and I were crossing paths. We stayed at the Gramercy on that tour. And I thought, "Boy, is this meant to be. Here are rock stars, and they can trash the rooms." So in the living room, part of the couch was in splinters. The legs and railings torn off of it. All ripped up and all that kind of stuff. The TV was broken—that was a rule. And so forth. Broken lamps and ripped lampshades. All the bands did it. It was a traditional Led Zeppelin imitation. If they wanted to show that they were as successful as Led Zeppelin, they did it.

Axl Rose (musician): We stay at the Gramercy hotel here, and—the, uh—one of our friends, West Arkeen…his dad had a heart attack, and they didn't give him the message. And then when he yelled at the [clerk], [West] jumped over the counter and he hit him. And then the other guys [who worked there] jumped [West]. So then [West] came up and got me. I went downstairs, and…two big [employees] come up to me real close. I grabbed a huge metal sign. You know, it was like a showdown. They backed off. The cops came.

Rick Cusick (*High Times* editor): In 1978, I needed a place to go have a honeymoon. I got this suite. It was the only suite that was available. I got there at two o'clock in the morning. I kept saying, "It was a rock and roll hotel." [In the room] there was this huge scorch mark, twenty feet long, across the wall, like they had taken some kind of fire and just sprayed it across the wall. So I called up [the front desk], and I said, "My wife wants to know what this scorch thing is." And he said, "Oh, we had a punk rock band in here, and we had to throw them out."

Tom O'Brien: Sid Vicious created a scene—a real bad scene. They were throwing things out the window. They were making a racket. He had a feeling that he was not obliged to live by the rules. After the incident with him, they wanted to come back, and I said, "No way."

Leee Black Childers: [Sid] wasn't the rowdy type. It might have been Nancy who got 86-ed. She was the rowdy type. She would scream in public. And that they didn't allow in the lobby of the Gramercy Park Hotel. You didn't make scenes in there. You could have freedom in your room, but the lobby was well maintained.

Steven Weissberg: I remember Bob Marley was in the hotel. He sold his guitar to a friend of mine. I almost bought his guitar. It was a Les Paul Junior, single pickup. They put him on the seventh floor, facing the park. The hallway looked like the smoke detectors were gonna go off before he checked out.

Tom O'Brien: They [Rita Marley and the other band members] were passing out literature in the lobby, advocating marijuana legalization. If they wanted to do it out in the street, that's one thing, but if it's in the lobby, that's a whole another thing.

Roman Kozak (writer): There is something faintly bizarre about going into a hotel lobby and asking for the Stranglers. But it's part of the job, and anyway, the clerk at the Gramercy Park Hotel in New York wasn't surprised. They're used to bands with funny-sounding names there.

Guest: The lobby was the scene of skeletal chain-smokers with stringy hair and bad teeth carrying guitars and sound equipment.

Billy Gibbons (ZZ Top musician): I remember walking into New York's Gramercy Park Hotel and seeing a guy in crushed velvet hot pants, lace-up knee boots, and a feather boa, with multicolored streaks and tips in his hair, and thinking, "Why are we the ones tagged weirdos?"

Theresa Kereakes (photographer): We were all in one suite, and then, eventually, we picked the lock on the door that joined our suite to the room next door. [We] got ourselves an extra bed, couch, and bathroom at no extra charge. There were always people coming and going...and I even spent a week at someone's loft while the suite at the Gramercy was crawling and overflowing with punk rockers. We had done a few shows with the Ramones, and Dee Dee was a frequent visitor to the crazy suite.

Patti Smith (musician): Toward the end of the '70s, I was preparing to leave the city for Detroit when I bumped into [Lou Reed] by the elevator in the old Gramercy Park Hotel. I was carrying a book of poems by Rupert Brooke. He took the book out of my hand, and we looked at the poet's photograph together. "So beautiful," he said. "So sad." It was a moment of complete peace.

Lou Reed (musician): There was just me and Rachel living at the fucking Gramercy Park Hotel on fifteen dollars a day while the lawyers figured out what to do with me.

Godfrey Diamond (music producer): I went to the Gramercy. This was a trip, man. [Lou Reed] had these people hanging around, and they were so strange to me—and I knew some weird people. These people were this beautiful array of homeless, degenerate-looking, brilliant, weird-as-shit [characters]. I walk in, and he's got a camera on me right away doing an Andy thing. He said, "I'm recording everybody who comes in." It's like a party. Rachel was gorgeous for a guy. Jesus! I guess he was a transvestite. God, he was just gorgeous looking.

Mick Farren (writer): The Gramercy Park Hotel is generally thought of as a rock 'n' roll hotel. It even upped its prices by ten bucks just after Bob Dylan had been a resident during a pre-conversion bout of drinking and fornicating.

Ronee Blakley (musician): I first met Bob [Dylan] at The Other End in Greenwich Village in October 1975. Bob invited me to join his tour, but I told him I couldn't because I was headed out the next morning for Muscle Shoals to prepare for my own tour. The party kept going at the Gramercy Park Hotel. Bob tried to convince me again, but I needed to catch the flight to JFK. As I left, he held the elevator door open and said, "You should have caught me in my prime." I said, "I think I have."

Al Aronowitz (writer): Once, as we were leaving for the night, Bob [Dylan] looked at himself in the full-length mirror of his Gramercy Park suite, broke into a grin and asked, "Well? Do I look like Billy the Kid?"

Bob Dylan and Suze Rotolo outside Gramercy Park. *Barry Feinstein.*

Steven Weissberg: [During a citywide blackout in 1977,] we put rifles with the doormen and kept them on guard. Somebody left a dozen rifles in the room when they checked out, so we had extras. Nobody checked out. Nobody moved. Everybody went to the bar and had room service. Everybody was just floating around, drinking.

Debbie Harry (musician): We checked into the Gramercy Park Hotel completely exhausted and disoriented.

James Sliman (rock manager): I had a party at that time, and Debbie Harry and Chris Stein showed up. [Debbie Harry] and Chris pulled me into a bathroom and opened up a big sandwich bag full of blow. The guy from the record company or radio interview had given it to them. Debbie said, "We have tons of it back at the hotel. This is nothing."

Debbie Harry: Back at the Gramercy Park Hotel, we were getting ready to make *Parallel Lines*. Chris wrote "Sunday Girl" one afternoon when he missed me and [our cat] Sunday Man.

Michael Chapman (music producer): I first met Chris and Debbie at the Gramercy Park Hotel. They played me tapes of new songs from their album. The music was great, but I wanted a song that would really pop. I asked if they had anything else. They said, "Well, we have this song we call 'The Disco Song.'" When they played it, I thought it was quite good, but the song wasn't 100 percent there yet.

James Sliman: [Debbie] said, "They give this stuff to us just to keep us stoned. I don't even want it. You fucking take it. They just keep giving it to us! That's all these fucking guys give us! They want, they want, they want, and for that, they give us this shit! James, this is for you. I don't even want it. My hotel room is full of it." So I kept it. It was like a couple thousand dollars' worth of cocaine.

Leee Black Childers: [A music producer] had two suites adjoined, and he had all this space. All he did was drink Coca-Cola and sniff cocaine. It was the Coke and coke suite. He was always in a dressing robe, and his skin was gray, and he weighed four pounds.

Andy Kowl (*High Times* editor): Hunter [S. Thompson] was coming to town, and we were paying his way. Now, I had never met the man before. So I called the hotel again, and finally, he had checked in. And he picks up the phone, and I hear, "*Rrr! Rrr!*" And he was saying, "Hi, Hunter, this is Andy, I hope you got in, blah, blah." And I couldn't really understand half of what he

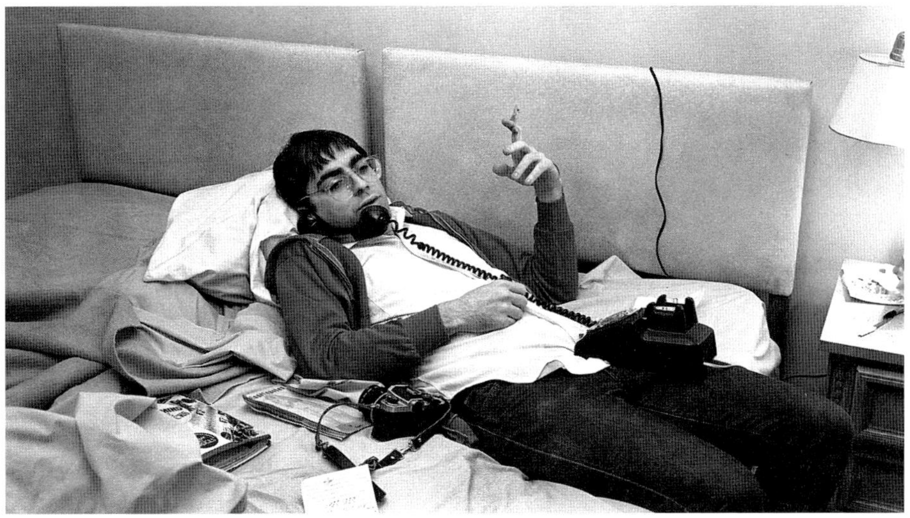

Chris Stein of Blondie. *Martyn Goddard.*

was saying. And—I'll never forget—I had the impression that I had just woke him up out of a horrible nightmare, or he was in the middle of a knife fight. And I said, "Look, call me. You have my number." So a few minutes later, my roommate calls me and says, "I just got the strangest call. This guy was looking for you and he said his name was John Belushi." So I called Hunter up at the Gramercy, and Belushi picked up. He said, "Oh, Andy, I'm really sorry. I was practicing my Hunter Thompson imitation when you called. I felt terrible." He felt like he had blown some business deal.

Guest: [Hunter S. Thompson] was staying at the Gramercy Park Hotel, and I ended up staying there with him for about two weeks. I hadn't quite got the hang of his humor, so it was tense—because I was scared sometimes. We were sitting in the bedroom talking, and every now and again, he would go into the living room and I'd hear these weird screams—lamenting, hideous, agony-filled screams. Then he'd come back into the bedroom and pick up right where we'd left off and act like nothing happened. I thought, "He's insane, and I have to get out of here." The third time he went out and screamed, I said, "Stop that! Why are you doing that?" Hunter started laughing, and he said, "I can't find my lighter."

Hunter S. Thompson. *Lynn Goldsmith.*

Marianne Faithfull (musician): I ran away [from my boyfriend]. But all I did was move myself and my drugs into the Gramercy Park Hotel.

Tom O'Brien: David Mamet lived there before he became a hotshot. His first play that he had when he was living there was *American Buffalo*. I asked him if I could get tickets. He smiled and said it's no problem—I could go to the theater and pay for them myself.

Alan Vega: So the guy from Motörhead, Lemmy, "Ace of Bass" was his hit song. I remember scoring speed for this guy. He'd stay there, and we'd be up all night talking. He was a smart guy. When you looked out the window, it was like watching a movie—like you were looking out on a quiet ocean.

Phil Taylor (Motörhead musician): I'm lying in my bed, just trying to get some sleep, and the night operator calls me up and tells me she's going off duty and settle my phone bill. I ask her, "What phone bill?" And she says, "The $700 call to Tokyo."

Charlie Martin (Bond's general manager): One day, the door of my office opened, and Bernard Rhodes [Clash manager] was standing there. The pitch I gave him was: "You go to Madison Square Garden and maybe sell three-quarters of it, or you can come to our joint and do eight shows in seven days. You'll have the entire attention of the media for a week." We went over to his room at the Gramercy Park Hotel, drank a bottle of Scotch, and came to an agreement. The contract was written on a napkin.

Joe Strummer (musician): We arrived in the city, the trouble went down, and the whole thing seemed to take off. The Gramercy was overrun with our thing. It was good fun. A real golden time.

Sabotage Times: When the Clash had played at Bond's, I had observed that the Gramercy Park bedrooms of both Joe and Paul each contained rows of plastic containers of Nature's Plus-brand vitamins, all mega-strength. The yin, presumably, to the yang of the bottles of Rémy Martin brandy that each of them also had on display.

Joe Strummer: We love this place, the Gramercy Park Hotel. Talk about faded grandeur. We stayed there in the heyday, and I don't think one fitting in the whole hotel has changed since '78. I just love that. You would've thought some yuppie developer would've swept through and changed it. The fronts fall off the AC units, and the plastic bits fall off the phone. I'm more at home in a situation like that.

Nat Finkelstein: Joe Strummer came in to be interviewed for a book I was working on and he announced that he was off all drugs, and I just put a base pipe in front of him and I was just getting stoned off cocaine base while I was interviewing Joe.

Tymon Dogg (musician): [Clash guitarist Mick Jones] played me some of the new material they'd recorded at Electric Lady, and he said, "What d'ya reckon?" He had just changed his hotel room to this really plush one [at the Gramercy Park Hotel]. I said, "It sounds like your hotel room looks."

Mick Jones (The Clash musician): We always ended up with a few kids coming back to our hotel to sleep. The floor of my room would always have people asleep on it. But so would Joe's, unless he had a woman with him, which was fair dos.

Bono (musician): I remember when we were a baby band, we were staying at the Gramercy Park Hotel in New York City, and the Clash, our idols, walked through the door. Paul Simonon, the bassist, looked like somebody out of *West Side Story* crossed with an axe murderer. He had this jacket, and on the back was the name of a local gang. They had been hanging out with some of the gangs, listening to early scratch hip-hop. Then they came up with "This Is Radio Clash," finding in New York that sort of interface between Black and white music that they'd found in London.

Guest: I was probably the first, along with my sister, U2 "groupie" (sort of) in the United States. I slept at Bono's feet at Gramercy Park Hotel in New York City in a room with the Edge as well.

The Edge: We got out of the car and walked straight into the lobby. I looked out the window and saw the two guitars where we'd left them and two guys walking across the street about to grab them, so I ran out and got there first. But we were so close to being taken out by a sucker punch. A bunch of kids from Dublin arrive and immediately have their guitars stolen. It would have been sad.

Tom O'Brien: Pinky [the bellhop] would say, "You don't think I can carry this myself, do you? You'll have to help me."

Steven Weissberg: It's amazing that the bellmen were so small they fit perfectly in the bell stand, but they would carry these huge pieces of luggage that were so big, you would just see their hands—that was it.

Guest: There was not a waiter in the place taller than five feet. They were all short, round men in faded red jackets with slick black hair. The room had the faint smell of mold mingled with aroma of Goldfish crackers from the bar. For as long as I recalled, there was always a "Reserved" card on the small booth nearest the bar.

Guest: I "met" [John Lennon] at the Gramercy Park Hotel bar in [New York City] in '77, when I was playing bass with a guy named Billy Swan. Wimpy handshake, etc. Said the wife was driving him nuts and just ran into the bar for a quick drink.

Gary Lucas: We walked into that bar, and there was John Carradine. He played Frankenstein, and he was there holding court with his Shakespearean voice. Carradine had a hat on. And the bartender, you know, said, "Hey, John Carradine, can I try on your hat?" And he put the hat on his head to model it, and John Carradine snatched it back and said, "You, sir, look like a fool. Whereas when I walk down the street, all the people say, 'There goes there that very distinguished looking Mr. Carradine.'"

Alan Vega: And then the bar was like everybody who was passing through New York, you know. Matt Dillon was there for a while. I befriended him. David Johansen would show up every now and then. I just liked living there. I liked the style.

The bar, circa 1934, at the end of Prohibition. *Photo taken from the hotel's magazine.*

John Moore (musician): One night, Alan Vega invited [me] up to his room, and [he] played all his new songs. He had the backing tracks all on a cassette, and Alan Vega proceeded to go through all his songs, doing his act—but in his underpants, jumping up and down on the bed. But all the songs were kind of the same. All like [impersonating Alan Vega] "woah baby," "ooooh," "new rock 'n' roll."

Gary Lucas: Another time, Captain Beefheart was staying there, and XTC was there. And they claimed they saw Andy Partridge [of XTC] buying a porno magazine in the gift shop.

Bono: I recall exactly when "the scourge" lifted from me. I was in the bath at the old Gramercy Park Hotel in downtown Manhattan, and the Grammy Awards were on television in the next room. I could see the TV through the doorway. Of course, having, at that point, absolutely no chance of being nominated, I was blowing bubbles through the acceptance speeches. If I had not been naked and submerged, I would have pulled the plug. And then the Staple Singers came on.

Kit Harington (actor): My stay at the Gramercy Park Hotel in New York was wonderful.

Marilyn (singer): I can't stay there. [Boy] George and I ran up tremendous bills during our last stay and never paid them.

Alan Vega: It was so easy, you know. So convenient. You paid the rent downstairs. They cleaned your room. They don't clean your room if you don't want them to. That was so I could sleep late.

Tom O'Brien: One time, I was walking through the lobby [with a keyboard], and I saw Paul Shaffer in the lobby. And he said, "What are you doing?" And I said, "I got my daughter a keyboard for her birthday." And he said, "You want me to show her how to play?" I said, "Yeah." He came up and Paul taught her how to play a jam, and she was thrilled.

Mark Knopfler of Dire Straits on February 25, 1980. *Ebet Roberts.*

Paul Shaffer: Room service was superb. The hamburger was excellent, the fries crispy and salted to my exact taste. When I caught a cold, the house doctor was there in a flash, happy to dispense whatever antibiotics were needed. The doorman would fetch my medicine from the drugstore. I looked forward to getting sick. Riding the elevator was always an adventure. One evening, the door opened, and there was Debbie Harry. She told me that she'd decided to live in the hotel. Passing through the lobby, I saw Paul Butterfield at the bar. I stopped to say hello. We struck up a friendship that resulted in my playing on his last album.

Tom O'Brien: Paul Butterfield was always borrowing ten dollars from the bartender to pay for the drinks he was going to have because we didn't let him charge anything.

Marvin Weissberg (hotel executive): Gramercy Park became like the family institution. We stayed there. Everybody stayed there. It was the hotel everybody came up to.

Juan Correa (waiter): I remember when Hillary Clinton was there. I was the server. The Weissbergs were there. Your grandfather was there [meeting with her]. At that time, Hillary Clinton came there, and it was for brunch. And we saw Secret Service coming in, and we had to close half the dining room. She was just having a little appetizer.

Steven Weissberg: David [Weissberg] had a big fight with his wife in front of Peter O'Toole. He loved it. He raved about it. He told me [he] saw my brother having this big fight with his girlfriend in the elevator. "It just put so much passion in me." He was studying [my brother] for his acting.

Rick Cusick: In November 1999. It's the twenty-fifth *High Times* anniversary, and this is the biggest party we've ever had. We rented two suites and three extra rooms. Because it was the anniversary, everyone brought their best pot. Jack Kerouac was the first one to show up. I was very nervous about it. Wow, dude, I'm partying with Jack Kerouac. This was the type of *High Times* party where the only goal is don't be arrested in the morning. Packed, every room, bathrooms, both suites. You couldn't see from one end of the room to the other. And so then, it's 1:30 in the morning. And someone comes up to me and says, "Rick, you got a problem. The police are at the door." So I push through the crowd, and I open the door a crack. A cloud of smoke pours out the crack. I slip through the crack and close the door behind me. So the police officer said, "We're not interested in arresting anybody. We're not interested in making any trouble. We just want it to stop." So I went back into the room and closed the door behind me. The next words out of my mouth were the words nobody wanted to hear. As I'm talking, there are maybe a dozen major pot dealers scrambling for open windows. They're pulling drunks off the toilet. It just kicked in like mice in a cage. There were three cops. We just walked by. There was smoke pouring out into the hall. And they had to walk the perp walk. We walked straight to the elevator. Everyone was waiting for an "Excuse me!" And you could actually see the trail of urine all the way to the elevator.

Jimmy Fallon (comedian): We were at the Gramercy Park Hotel once. And [Karl Lagerfeld's] like, "I'm buying an apartment here." And I go, "I want to live here!" He goes, "You want to be neighbors?" I'm thinking we'll watch *Jeopardy!* together, borrow sugar. He's like, "I'll get a deal for you." Next day, he calls me and tells me the deal. $19 million. I'm like, "Karl, we're definitely not going to be neighbors."

2
GRAMERCY PARK
1641–1904

I know most people came here to read about the cocaine and parties. But for a few moments, at least, let's look at how this whole thing began.

The First Settlers

In the days of the Lenape Natives, the area of Gramercy Park was a wide parcel of grassy marshes and low-lying hills. Legend says that the area's foliage had a rosy color, likely due to its scarlet oak or red maple trees. Other than trees and bushes, its first residents included deer, squirrels, and the occasional rabbit or turkey. Its man-made border was the old Lenape footpath on its western edge, which eventually became Bloomingdale Road and then Broadway. Perhaps the Natives of Manhatta ("island of the hills" in Lenape) hunted game in the vicinity of Gramercy Park and drank from its freshwater stream.

After Peter Minuit purchased Manhattan from the Natives in 1624 for sixty guilders, the area became a fertile farm managed by the Dutch West India Company, called the De Grote Bouwerij, which translates as "the great farm." Its southern end reached Canal Street, and its northern border was present-day 21st Street. The property was, in effect, under the magistrate of Peter Stuyvesant, the tough, one-legged governor of New Amsterdam and a director in the Dutch West India Company. De Grote Bouwerij produced mostly wheat and corn, which was shipped south to the colony on the southern tip of Manhattan.

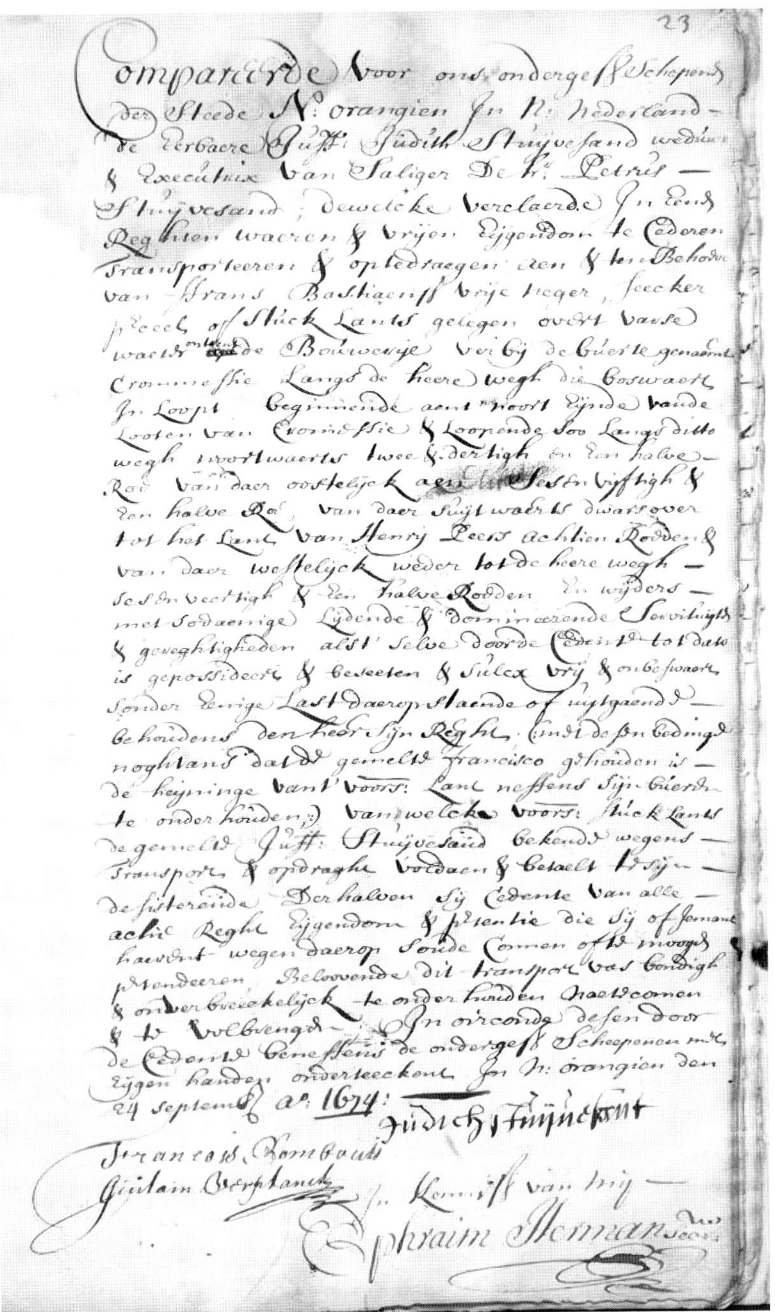

23

Compareerde voor ons ondergess: Schepenen
der Steede N: orangien In N: Nederland –
de eerbaere Juff: Judith Stuyvesand weduwe
& executrix van Saliger De Hr: Petrus –
Stuyvesand; dewelcke verclaerde In eene
Reghten waeren & vrijen Eijgendom te Cederen
transporteeren & opteedraegen aen & ten Behoeve
van Frans Bastiaenss vrije neger, seecker
perceel of Stuck Lants gelegen over 't vaerse
waeter ontrent de Bouwerije ver bij de buerte genaemt
Crommeshie Langs de heere wegh die boswaert
In Loopt beginnende aent noort eijnde vande
Looten van Crommessie & Loopende soo Langs ditto
wegh noortwaerts twee & dertigh en een halve
Roe van daer oostelijck [illegible] Sesen vijftigh &
een halve Roe van daer suijtwaerts dwars over
tot het Lant van Henry Peers achtien Rodden &
van daer westelijck weder tot de heere wegh –
Sesen veertigh & een halve Rodden en wijders –
met sodaenige Lijdende & dominerende Servituyten
& gereghtigheden alst selve door de Cedent tot dato
is gepossideert & beseeten & sulcx vrij & onbeswaert
sonder eenige Last daerop staende of uytgaende –
behoudens den heer sijn Reght, [illegible] bedinge
noghtans dat de gemelte Francisco gehouden is –
de heyninge vant voors: Lant neffens sijn buerde –
te onderhouden;) van welcke voors: Stuck Lants
de gemelte Juff: Stuyvesand bekende wegens –
transport & opdraghe voldaen & betaelt te sijn –
desisteerende derhalven sij Cedente van alle –
actie Reght Eijgendom & pretentie die sij of iemant
haerent wegen daerop soude connen of te moogen
pretendeeren, Beloovende dit transport vast bondigh
& onverbreeckelijck te onderhouden naecomen
& te volbrengen; In oirconde desen door
de Cedente beneffens de ondergess: Schepenen met
eijgen handen onderteeckent In N: orangien den
24 septemb: ao: 1674:

Judith Stuyvesant

Francois Rombouts
Guilain Verplanck

In kennisse van mij –
Ephraim Herman Secr:

The "Crommessie" contract, signed in 1674 by Judith Stuyvesant and Franciscus Bastianse. *Collection of the New York Historical Society.*

The new colony was mostly dedicated to the beaver trade, as the beaver hat had become a major fashion item in Europe. The best source of beaver pelts at the time was North America, and settlers spent months away from their New Amsterdam homes hunting beaver in Canada and the Midwest.

On March 12, 1651, with the help of his sneaky agent Jan Jansen Damen, Stuyvesant officially took over the land from the Dutch West India Company, purchasing it for 6,400 guilders, or about $340,000 today. By then, the property included a dwelling house, barns, woods, six cows, two horses, and two enslaved Africans.

Historians agree that the first reference to Gramercy was in a September 24, 1674 deed made out by Stuyvesant's widow, Judith. The document describes "a parcel of land lying beyond the fresh water [a pond near present-day Worth Street] nigh the Bowery, beyond the neighborhood of *Crommessie*." The new owner was Franciscus Bastianse, a free Black man married to Barbara Emanuel, a free Black woman.

You may be surprised that the first residents of Gramercy Park were Black farmers. Allow me to backtrack a bit. The incredible story of their freedom began a generation earlier, in January 1641, after a man enslaved by the Dutch West India Company, Jan Premero, was murdered. Nine enslaved people confessed to the crime. To eliminate the confusion, the investigators interrogated each one individually. But the detained all responded that they did not know who did the deed, except that they "committed the deed together." It's possible the enslaved assumed the colony would not execute any of them, since there were only thirty enslaved laborers total in all of New Amsterdam. But the authorities needed to punish *someone*. So they made the enslaved draw lots. Manuel of Gerrit de Reus, or "Giant Manuel," selected the short straw. His punishment was to be hanged.

On January 24, 1641, a crowd gathered to watch the execution. Manuel's neck was tied to two ropes. Then he was ceremonially pushed off a ladder. Miraculously, both ropes snapped. Manuel landed on the ground. The crowd shouted for mercy. The provincial council agreed, and all nine of the enslaved prisoners were acquitted. Three years later, these nine enslaved laborers (plus two more) petitioned for their freedom. They were granted a "half freedom," along with their wives. (This odd designation meant they could be called back into service at any time.) The group settled north of the city in the area "Beyond the Fresh Water."

Manuel later had a daughter, Barbara Emanuel, who married Franciscus Bastianse, the aforementioned first resident of Gramercy Park. Bastianse was the son of Bastien de Britto, the "captain of the blacks," who probably got his name from managing work quotas.

Over the years, Franciscus, Gramercy's first tenant, grew his family and expanded the number of his farms, spreading out to what is now Madison Square and Greenwich Village. His family was one of the many prosperous Black families making the best of a difficult situation in the early eighteenth century. For white settlers, Black farms helped create a buffer zone from Native attacks, which was especially important when white settlers went beaver hunting. The freed Black settlers also paid an annual tax of thirty schepels of wheat and one fat pig.

By the time of his death in 1712, Bastianse was the last Black landowner left in New Amsterdam. In the years prior, the British had imposed their laws on the city. In 1712, the year of Bastianse's death, the authorities passed a law preventing Black individuals from inheriting property. Left with no choice, Bastianse's heirs sold the property back to the Stuyvesants. Was Gramercy Park stolen from a Black family? I'll let the reader be the judge.

Years passed, and the Stuyvesants slowly sold off their land in parcels. Stuyvesant's grandson Gerardus was left in charge, and he sold the land in 1671 to James Duane. He renamed Crommessie "Gramercy Seat," and the Gramercy moniker stuck. James Duane was only twenty-eight and an up-and-comer himself. He wrote a letter to his father-in-law sometime after the purchase: "I must keep a number of horses or expect no good of my farm, as the land is very poor. I have got a good stock of dung this winter, so that I have a prospect of reaping the fruits of my expenses very soon."

This may sound like an inauspicious beginning for the young lawyer, but the farm thrived and so did his career. He built a house, a well, and gardens on what is now Gramercy Park West. By 1774, he had been elected to the Continental Congress and, following the Revolution, became the first mayor of New York. Despite his conservative, cautious outlook in revolutionary times, Duane never lost the trust of the people.

During New York's occupation in the Revolutionary War, two British officers, Major General Daniel Jones and Admiral Robert, took over the Gramercy Seat property. Though most of New York was trashed by the enemy army, Gramercy Park was spared. The two officers added two rooms to Duane's house, new stoves, and a gazebo, among other improvements. The property was in such great shape that some questioned if Duane had been given special favors thanks to his conservative political outlook before the war.

THE ORIGIN OF "GRAMERCY"

Most historians think that because Crommessie sounds like *krom mesje*, Dutch for "crooked (small) knife," the name must come from the crooked knife shape of the creek, as it was drawn on old maps. The creek was also called Crumme Vly, or winding creek, at least according to a 1697 deed written by Gerard Stuyvesant. It was also later called Cedar Creek. Creating further problems for the crooked knife explanation, the first deed clearly spelled the property as "Crommessie," without any K, which one would expect if the name had come from krom mesje or some derivation thereof. As a counterargument, spellings in Dutch, like in English, were not standardized at the time.

In the 1930s, a pamphlet in the National Arts Club argued that Crommessie instead originated from *cramoisy*, a word meaning "red" in English, Dutch, and French. Since the clay and foliage in the district were known to be red, cramoisy probably evolved to become Crommessie over time. Supporting this theory is a 1746 land deed from James Duane to his brother-in-law James Watts that mentions a "Rose Hill," in reference to a plot of land between present-day 21st and 30th Streets.

There is yet a third explanation. Crommessie, so the theory goes, was the Native name for "the marsh," as the land was sometimes called. To the Lenape Natives, the place could have been described as *gowa-massa-assisku*, meaning the "hedged-in great marsh." Then it could have morphed through the continued mispronunciation to Gowamassisku, then Gwamassi, then Gramassi, and so on until it became Gramercy. The source for this theory was a pamphlet issued by the Gramercy Park Hotel in the 1930s, so believe what you wish.

NEW YORK BOOMS

In 1825, the Erie Canal opened, linking New York to the Great Lakes, and from there, it traveled to Canada and the cornfields of Illinois and Ohio. This increase in interconnectivity was all the more significant to New York City before the construction of nationwide railroads. Following the opening of the canal, New York soon surpassed Boston and Philadelphia as the premier commercial city in America.

Given that corn was cumbersome to transfer, even by boat, the invention of corn whiskey in the late 1700s helped remote farmers obtain a better price for their corn by selling it as whiskey in New York.

Before corn whiskey's appearance, the average person drank approximately 5.8 gallons of pure alcohol per year (compared to 2 gallons today). By the 1830s, that number reached 7 gallons per person, and the proportion of alcohol consumed in distilled spirits (as opposed to beer and wine) increased by 50 percent. It became common for men and children to start their day with a glass of whiskey. Employers provided alcohol during break times, leading to the term "the elevens." Cheap alcohol upset the social order so much that the first "bar" originated in New York after a tavern owner enclosed his serving table inside a barred cage so it could be locked up after hours.

Public drunkenness, coupled with an increase in crime, sent the first waves of people fleeing from the city. Magazines and newspapers lamented that "the living problem"—the ability to inhabit an urban environment without noise, traffic, and drunks—was unsolvable. The suburbs developed as the first alternative.

Two individuals were determined to solve this problem *inside* the city: the founder of Gramercy Park, Samuel Ruggles, and the future builder of the Gramercy Park Hotel, Alexander M. Bing.

Samuel Ruggles Buys the Land

Samuel Ruggles (1799–1881).

Samuel B. Ruggles, a Connecticut native, had an impressive résumé. After graduating Yale at only fourteen, he soon became a successful lawyer and real estate magnet. He donated land to create Union Square and then set his sights north toward Gramercy Park. By 1830, Ruggles had succeeded in acquiring the various lots held by Duane's heirs. Then he officially founded Gramercy Park a year later.

In 1831, Gramercy Park was a swamp with a winding creek running through it. The creek began at the Rose Hill duck pond in what is today Madison Square and then meandered east until it reached the East River near 18th Street. At some points, the creek formed gullies with "bold and rocky" walls almost forty feet deep, according to records. When it reached Lexington Avenue, the creek split in two, and the shallower, marshier finger flowed where the Gramercy Park Hotel now sits.

To eliminate the nettlesome creek, Ruggles acquired nearby Bowery Hill, which was twenty-five feet above sea level, and then used its dirt to fill in Gramercy Park. All this digging required three million loads of dirt at a cost of $180,000. Ruggles succeeded in burying the creek, transforming the marshland into an area suitable for the construction of multistory buildings.

But in subsequent years, Crumme Vly reappeared. It first emerged during the construction of Peter Cooper's house on the southeast corner of Lexington Avenue and 22nd Street. Cooper, the world-famous engineer, piled more wood and dirt atop the marsh, sending the creek farther underground. When faced with a similar problem over the years, other residents copied Cooper's rudimentary method of reburying the creek.

Today, this burrowed creek flows underneath the Gramercy Park Hotel. Its significance cannot be overstated. British scholar Paul Devereux's research revealed that Native and ancient groups often built their sacred worship sites on top of underground streams, similar to the present-day Crumme Vly. For example, both Stonehenge and Chichén Itzá were built on top of underground streams, as were many rock structures left by the Hopewell Natives in America. In various parts of the United States, rock cairns (piles of rocks) are still left at the intersections of these underground rivers. Devereux speculated that ancient peoples found these sites through dowsing and that they used them for healing purposes.

As Gramercy Creek, also known as Crumme Vly, became farther submerged, its nooks and crannies became filled with various minerals, including Rochelle salt crystals and perhaps even quartz crystals. Over time, the weight of the Gramercy's heavy structure has slowly crushed these crystals. This crushing produces piezoelectricity and releases small amounts of plasma, which sometimes rises to the surface. So strong is the piezoelectric effect, one occasionally gets a shock when entering the lobby of the Gramercy Park Hotel.

Perhaps this is why they come to the Gramercy—to feel some of the magic, the energy, the inspiration, and some of the electricity.

RUGGLES FORMS GRAMERCY PARK

After leveling the land, the park's founder, Samuel Ruggles, divided Gramercy Seat into eighty-eight lots, with twenty-two used for the park. This left sixty-six lots to surround the park, which he offered for sale. He then appointed gardener James Virtue to landscape the place, with instructions to plant one hundred trees and one thousand plants in the park. Ruggles also created two new avenues, which he hoped would prevent the city from eventually confiscating the park via eminent domain.

Ruggles named the southward avenue Irving Place after one of his friends, author Washington Irving (of "Rip Van Winkle" fame). On the northern side, Ruggles created Lexington Avenue, named after the first Revolutionary battle where blood was shed, between 3rd and 4th Avenues. To ensure maintenance of the park, Ruggles charged Gramercy residents a ten-dollar annual fee. A few things were forbidden in the park: "any livery stable, slaughter house, smith shop, forge, furnace, steam engine, brass foundry, nail or other iron factory, or any manufactory of gunpowder, glue, varnish, vitriol, ink or skins, hides or leather, or any brewery, distillery, public museum, theater, circus, place for the exhibition of animals, or any other trade or business dangerous or offensive to the neighboring inhabitants."

By 1832, the park had a wooden fence, replaced the following year by an "elegant iron fence." In 1842, Ruggles hosted a grand ball that Charles Dickens attended. As the story goes, the *Tale of Two Cities* author admired Gramercy Park, which he found to be similar to London.

One evening in the 1830s, while surveying his new square with his friend Dr. Hawks, Ruggles proclaimed, "Come what will, our open squares will remain forever imperishable. Buildings, towers, palaces, may molder and crumble beneath the touch of time; but space—free glorious, open space—will remain to bless this city forever."

"And do you not perceive the reason?" Dr. Hawks replied. "Man makes buildings, but God makes space."

By May 1844, the gates and other decorations were completed. The park has been under lock and key ever since. Until the late 1800s, keys to the park were available to anyone in the general area who was willing to pay a fee, and as many as 1,500 families had keys. But by the early twentieth century, the only keyholders were the immediate residents of Gramercy Park, along with the members of the Players and National Arts Clubs.

Over the years, Gramercy Park has had many threats to its privacy. During the draft riots in July 1863, the greens were nearly demolished when the governor stationed a military detachment in Gramercy Park. The final battle of the riots took place at the northeast corner of Gramercy Park, where the army's twin cannons fired in the direction of 3rd Avenue. Thirteen people, mostly Irish New Yorkers, died in the gunfire. The park's foliage was completely devastated after the military operation. Two years later, the trustees sued the state government to recoup the costs of the army's occupation, but they were unsuccessful.

In 1890, the city almost divided Gramercy Park in two so a cable car could pass from 14th Street up Lexington Avenue, but the trustees were victorious this time. In 1912, the Lexington subway line (the 4, 5, and 6) was set to pass through Gramercy Park, but the park's residents had it rerouted along Park Avenue. In the 1930s, the city wanted to add a bus line around the park, but even that ended thanks to powerful interests. In 1975, Gramercy Park's residents (led by Mike Burke, a hotel resident and Madison Square Garden CEO) even prevented a McDonald's from opening too close to the park.

In the Charlton Heston dystopian flick *Soylent Green* (1973), which is set in 2022, Gramercy Park is the last park remaining in a dirty and crowded city. Though most of the film's predictions turned out to be wrong, they were right that Gramercy Park will always remain.

Inside Gramercy Park, there are three benches with the name Weissberg written on them. These belong to Madalyn Weissberg, my aunt; Rose Weissberg, my great-grandmother; and Max Weissberg, my great-grandfather. More on them later.

Before moving on, I should mention that there was a Gramercy Park Hotel in the nineteenth century that occupied the entire eastern side of Gramercy Park. Built in 1853, the place was originally called Sanderson's Family Hotel. But the owners went bankrupt within the first year, and the new owners immediately renamed it the Gramercy Park House. Most people referred to it as the Gramercy Park Hotel, however. The place was known to be a "resort for actors" and once hosted the musical writing duo Gilbert and Sullivan. The two had traveled from the United Kingdom to the Gramercy because their works were so frequently pirated in the United States that they "decided to come here and do something about it." During their stay, perhaps inspired by their copyright predicament, they wrote *The Pirates of Penzance.* The legendary musical premiered in New York on New Year's Eve 1879.

For many years, the first Gramercy Park Hotel was managed by Curtis Judson, who forever changed the hotel industry by introducing room service to America. The story is fascinating. Like all American hotels, the Gramercy initially had no room service. This was because early Americans prided themselves on their sense of equality. At hotels, meals were shared at buffet-style tables, and no one was allowed to dine by themselves. Room service was also forbidden. European travel journals at the time were filled with

Left: View of Gramercy Park from the hotel's rooftop in 1982. *Photo by Georgeanne Hume.*

Below: *Photo by Max Weissberg.*

complaints about America's barbaric ways. Yet the young republic wanted to hold on to its ideals.

At the Gramercy, before the invention of room service, if a guest wanted to sit at an empty table, the waiter would reply with something to the effect of, "That one's engaged. Won't you dine with the lady?" Since the dining room had only round tables that sat six people each, there was plenty of opportunity for guests to meet each other. Newspapers as far away as New Zealand recorded how couples met and married as a result of the Gramercy's dining rules. So perhaps early America's ideals weren't so bad.

One incident changed this practice at the Gramercy and in hotels across the country. Sometime in the early 1870s, a pregnant bride visited the hotel for two weeks while her new house and furniture were being readied, a gift from her father. At breakfast, the waiters sat her next to a man and his three daughters, all of whom had cleft lips. The seating arrangement caused her to panic. She feared her unborn child would be born with a cleft lip. Months later, the mother actually gave birth to a cleft-lipped baby.

This bizarre story, retold by the woman's physician, Dr. Fordyce Barker, found its way into numerous science journals. Soon it formed the basis of a new scientific theory. To be clear, the theory was not that the cleft trait was communicable; rather, it said that the psychological condition of the mother

The first Gramercy Park Hotel, also known as the Gramercy Park House.

during pregnancy influenced the physical characteristics of the baby. That is, if the mother saw something like a cleft lip, the mere sight of it could impact the unborn baby.

After this, Curtis Judson and the Gramercy Park Hotel quietly introduced room service. Today, the only remnant of the old hotel is 38 Gramercy Park East, located at the corner of 21st Street. All its other buildings had been destroyed by 1904.

3

HOMES FOR IMMORTALS

1925–1958

In September 1925, Hotel Gramercy Park opened its doors on the northern side of Gramercy Park. The hotel was designed by architect Robert T. Lyons and built by the Bing brothers, Leo and Alexander M., and its construction cost $1 million. The first advertisement for the hotel boldly announced: "The Living Problem *Solved*." This was far from being a mere sales pitch; the new owners were indeed preoccupied with the "living room" as much as Samuel Ruggles had been a century earlier. The Bing brothers owned over thirty buildings and seven hotels at the time, including the St. George Hotel in Brooklyn, the largest hotel in the city. In 1925, Alexander M. Bing, the more prominent of the two brothers, was less concerned with the Gramercy, however, than the construction of the Sunnyside Queens development, which was supposed to be a working-class version of Gramercy Park. Like the hotel, the new development was supposed to solve the living problem. More on that later.

Alexander M. Bing (1878–1959).

A New Hotel

The Gramercy building had a Neo-Renaissance façade with camel-colored brick, faux Roman balconies, and a balustrade lined with smiling gargoyles. The building's first marquee was a sleek, lightbulb-lined iron awning.

Inside, the hotel's lobby had Art Deco chandeliers, Persian rugs, and ornate chestnut paneling. To the right of the marble-topped front desk, through a pair of French doors, was the dining room, Le Parc, a mirage of white tablecloths over coffee-colored Chinese Chippendale tables and chairs. The wallpaper initially depicted a painting of a Chinese legend with scenes of men drinking tea, fighting, and shooting arrows into the air, created by the legendary firm Desfossé & Karth in Paris. Though alcohol was still prohibited, the hotel's construction included a bar tucked away in the corner of the building, just in case things should change.

The new hotel had elevator operators, shoeshine boys in the lobby, a library on the second floor, a kids' playroom, boiling hot and ice water faucets in the rooms, and a coal oven in the basement. In the hotel's basement laundromat, one employee pressed the guests' clothes while another ironed the newspapers. Upstairs, the doormen and bellhops wore bleached ivory shirts and black ties underneath fine-pressed uniforms with the hotel colors of forest green and gold—a modern look in 1925. The manager, William H. Barse, who had come from the Waldorf Astoria, had different whistles for the bellhops, doormen, and clerks.

The Gramercy Park Hotel's Footprint

The actual construction of the Gramercy led to the destruction of several brownstones, including the former home of Robert Ingersoll, the famed nineteenth-century agnostic orator. Two months after the hotel opened, three hundred of Ingersoll's devotees gathered on the outside corner of the hotel to ceremonially hang a plaque in his honor. In fur coats and black hats, the distinguished crowd took turns giving speeches in the cold, misty weather.

One "Mrs. Blatch" thanked Ingersoll for rescuing the world from our "old, sour Puritan hypocrisies." Then a "Senator Thomas" argued that Ingersoll's morals were superior to those of a "sullen priesthood and a raving crowd." Others got up and sang Ingersoll's praises or recited his poetry. Finally, the plaque was unveiled. The inscription read: "On this site was the home of Robert Ingersoll. He knew no fear but the fear of doing wrong. Born 1833. Died 1899."

Following the ceremony, some of Ingersoll's original manuscripts were handed off to the hotel's manager to be stored for the Ingersoll Memorial Library, which was to be located on the hotel's roof and available to guests. The next day, the *New York Times* predicted the hotel would soon become a "shrine to agnostics." Not only was the new hotel the former location of the Ingersoll Museum, but it was also the site where Ingersoll famously stopped an assassination attempt by reasoning with his would-be killer. There's no telling if any Ingersoll fans really came to the shrine, but he was certainly not forgotten.

Alas, someone stole Ingersoll's plaque a few months later. It was replaced, then stolen again, and then replaced ad infinitum. Most recently, in 2005, Ian Schrager and Aby Rosen had the plaque removed during major renovations.

Along with Ingersoll, architect Stanford White was mentioned in press releases to boost the hotel's prestige. His brownstone had been located at the corner of 21st Street and Lexington Avenue, and during the construction of the hotel, six of White's fireplaces were incorporated into the hotel's upper floors.

It's hard to overstate Stanford White's impact on taste and architecture in the nineteenth century. Two decades prior to the hotel's construction, he had been the most famous architect in America. Among his feats were the arch in Washington Square Park and a White House renovation on behalf of Theodore Roosevelt. White also came up with the idea of having a girl jump out of a paper birthday cake. Despite his long architectural career, he is perhaps best remembered for his sensational murder atop Madison Square Garden by his jealous rival, Harry K. Thaw, in 1906. Thaw later got off thanks to the first ever "temporary insanity" defense. Following White's death, his house was sold to the Princeton Club and then torn down to make way for the hotel.

Both Ingersoll and White helped the hotel tell its story and linked it with stardom. Soon after its opening, however, a crisis struck. One of the new maids, Mary Maher, started stealing after being on the job for only three hours. First, she took a guest's $1,000 sealskin coat and left her own cheap coat in its place. Then she robbed a few more rooms and skedaddled upstate. Police had an easy time catching the woman, however, as she was wearing a flashy coat.

The hotel was profiled by *Wallpaper* magazine in 1925 for its unusual wallpaper.

The First Famous People

Coinciding with its launch, the hotel aggressively advertised its amenities and connection to the park:

> *Homes for Immortals.*
>
> *The lovely old trees of Gramercy Park whisper tales of Edwin Booth, Cyrus Field, John Bigelow—all that host of immortals who lived there during the past century. In the years to come other immortal names will be added and the homes of many of them will be* 52 Gramercy Park North.

Among the first of these immortals was the famous actress Helen Menken, who married a then-unknown actor, Humphrey Bogart, on May 20, 1926. Bogart and Menken had gotten their marriage license in 1922, but Bogart himself was reluctant to follow through. Menken was certainly very pretty, thin, and famous enough to be considered an A-list actor. But he wasn't that into her. Also, she was ten years older, though their marriage certificate stated they were the same age. At one point, Bogart admitted to a friend that he didn't want to marry Menken but needed the publicity. So, after four years of his career going nowhere, Bogart decided to take the plunge.

For the ceremony, 126 guests—the who's who of the theater world—crammed into Helen Menken's parents' Gramercy Park Hotel apartment to hear their vows. Because Menken's parents were deaf and mute, the entire ceremony was conducted in sign language and led by a deaf officiator, Reverend John H. Kent. From the start, the guests were lost. They couldn't read sign language, and they could barely understand the officiator. When Bogart said, "I do," the officiator got so confused, the wedding guests had to step in. This was the wedding ceremony from hell—never mind that the press was watching along with some of the most famous people in America.

After the ceremony, Helen Menken was so distraught that she fled into a neighboring room, locked the door, and cried. Of course, the show had to go on. Bogart pleaded at the door to be allowed in. Privately, he calmed Helen down so she could do the interviews. After having been forced to wait, the press enquired about the couple's four-year delay in getting married. "I've been so frightfully occupied, you know, I just haven't found time to marry," Helen said, tears in her eyes.

Humphrey Bogart and Helen Menken in a photo released for the press in 1926.

As planned, the couple's wedding pictures made the front pages (in some cases, only Menken's photos were printed). The press mostly wrote about the faulty ceremony and the delay, however. Clearly, their marriage was off to a bad start. They never took a honeymoon either due to their busy acting schedules.

Less than a year later, they divorced. But both the hotel and Bogart were on the map, linked with stardom. For Bogart, this marriage would lead to bigger theater roles and then a movie career. Like it did for so many guests, the hotel helped him on the way up.

Only a year after the Bogart-Menken marriage ceremony, in the summer of 1927, the Kennedy family moved onto the second floor of the hotel for three months. There, they awaited the remodeling of their new home in Riverdale, the Bronx. At the time, Joe Kennedy (John F. Kennedy's father) was making a fortune importing whiskey to the United States, taking advantage of a permit that allowed alcohol to be imported for religious use. He also owned a film studio, RKO Pictures, which didn't earn much money but led to a steamy affair with actress Gloria Swanson. Things were looking up, and Kennedy could afford to put his family in a four-star hotel for months at a time.

For the Kennedys, life at the hotel was a moment for them to spend time together in more intimate quarters. Every day, ten-year-old John Fitzgerald played with his older brother, Joe Jr., inside Gramercy Park. Most nights, the entire family ate in Le Parc, where Mrs. Kennedy instructed her young children on dining etiquette, as the hotel's telephone operator later remembered. One can imagine what impression the busy cosmopolitan hotel made on a young John F. Kennedy, who later received high marks in current events while a teenager in boarding school. Such early interests, fostered by the encounters with other "immortals" in the Gramercy Hotel, perhaps pointed him toward the presidency.

In 1929, the Bing brothers, who owned thirty other buildings, decided to expand the hotel westward to 50 Gramercy Park North, adding a new structure at a cost of $375,000. After the completion of its construction, the hotel nearly doubled in size. The new tower was connected to the old on six of its seventeen floors. For many, this part of the hotel became known as the annex.

The hotel's business subsidiary, Gresham Realty, soon faced major financing problems following the collapse of the stock market, however. The Bing brothers began foreclosing, handing their properties back to the banks and insurance companies. A new company, Gramercy Park Hotel Corporation, took over the hotel property.

Alexander M. Bing, meanwhile, was having bigger problems than the Gramercy with his Sunnyside Queens development. The development had been built off an ideology to solve the city's "living problem." Bing promised to limit the company's profit in the venture to 6 percent while building a development that was so well-designed residents could shop or go to school without "crossing any single street." What resulted was the cul-de-sac. Among its charitable-minded investors were Eleanor Roosevelt and John D. Rockefeller Jr. But now that the values of the homes had collapsed along with the stock market, the do-gooder Bing was being sued by everyone.

Over at the Gramercy, guests did not immediately notice any difference following the crash. In March 1930, Professor Max Winkler held an event in the dining room and explained that "while economic crises may develop in our country, they cannot but be of short duration." The room nodded in agreement.

By 1931, however, the Depression was inescapable in New York. Every day, men crowded around the Fulton docks to get a job. Women and children waited outside churches for scraps and went wherever a new job was posted. In Union Square, socialists gave speeches and handed out pamphlets. In Central Park, shacks and huts filled with the unhoused made up "Hooverville." Unemployment was above 15 percent in New York and more than one-third in industries like construction.

In Gramercy Park, however, the local residents, led by the hotel's silver-haired manager, W.D. Mesenzahl, circulated petitions to end the "bus nuisance" that was disturbing the neighborhood. Above the hotel's canopies and marquee, an electric sign that read "Quiet Please" was added. The park association then successfully got a new city law passed to prohibit trucks from circling the park at night. As the hotel's magazine elegantly described it, the park remained "a little private oasis in a desert of concrete and steel."

In 1933, President Roosevelt ordered all of the banks closed to review the "failures of our banking system," which paralyzed the economy's cash flow.

Above: The dining room, Le Parc.

Left: The lobby.

Amid the crisis, however, the hotel's magazine proclaimed, "Cash Shortage a Joke." "So little did the bank 'holiday' inconvenience guests at the Hotel Gramercy Park," the hotel's magazine wrote, "that indeed something of the festive spirit commonly connoted by the word did animate them all." The clerks gave out credit to guests, relieving them of the burden of hoarding cash, an unseemly affair for a "respectable" person. One patron passed out IOUs, which he promised to redeem in gold once the banks reopened. Another borrowed a dime from the bellhop. One guest received a wire from a friend asking him for a small loan just after he had sent that same friend a similar wire. This caused the clerks to have a laugh. As if to show the Depression would not interrupt any party at the hotel, its magazine printed a photo of a children's birthday party with the caption "No Depression worries here."

During the peak years of the Depression, the hotel had a healthy 90 percent occupancy rate—that is, at least, what it claimed in its magazine. When asked by a journalist if the hotel had cut its rates, manager J. Edgar Muir laughed and said, "Why should we? We are doing fine. Business must be picking up, for a great many people who formerly lived here but who moved out when things went bad, are back again."

Maybe it was all a lie. But if the Depression was really hurting the Gramercy's business, the staff and PR people did a good job of hiding it.

More Famous Guests

While visiting New York in 1929, the English philosopher Bertrand Russell stayed in the Gramercy. He was in town to debate American philosopher Will Durant for entertainment purposes. Sitting comfortably sans martini in his hotel suite, Russell told a journalist, "I know America from pre-Prohibition days. Now the transformation is hardly believable. I never saw such drunkenness. It appears stolen apples are the sweetest. It seems Prohibition simply does not prohibit." He then called for a repeal of the Nineteenth Amendment. Since he was visiting the Gramercy without its legendary bar, I can understand the frustration.

After Prohibition ended on December 5, 1934, the bar business boomed. The bar and cocktail lounge became so popular that management renovated it to accommodate more people. Babe Ruth was among its first patrons.

Still earning $40,000 a year in the 1930s, the Babe was known in the hotel for his rowdiness. But he was also known to occasionally give out a $100 tip for something like a $0.30 drink—though only when he was on a hitting streak. After a series in which he hit four home runs, he visited the Gramercy and drunkenly threw a $100 bill out on his table without designating its recipient. Two torn uniforms later, the staff agreed to divide the money five ways.

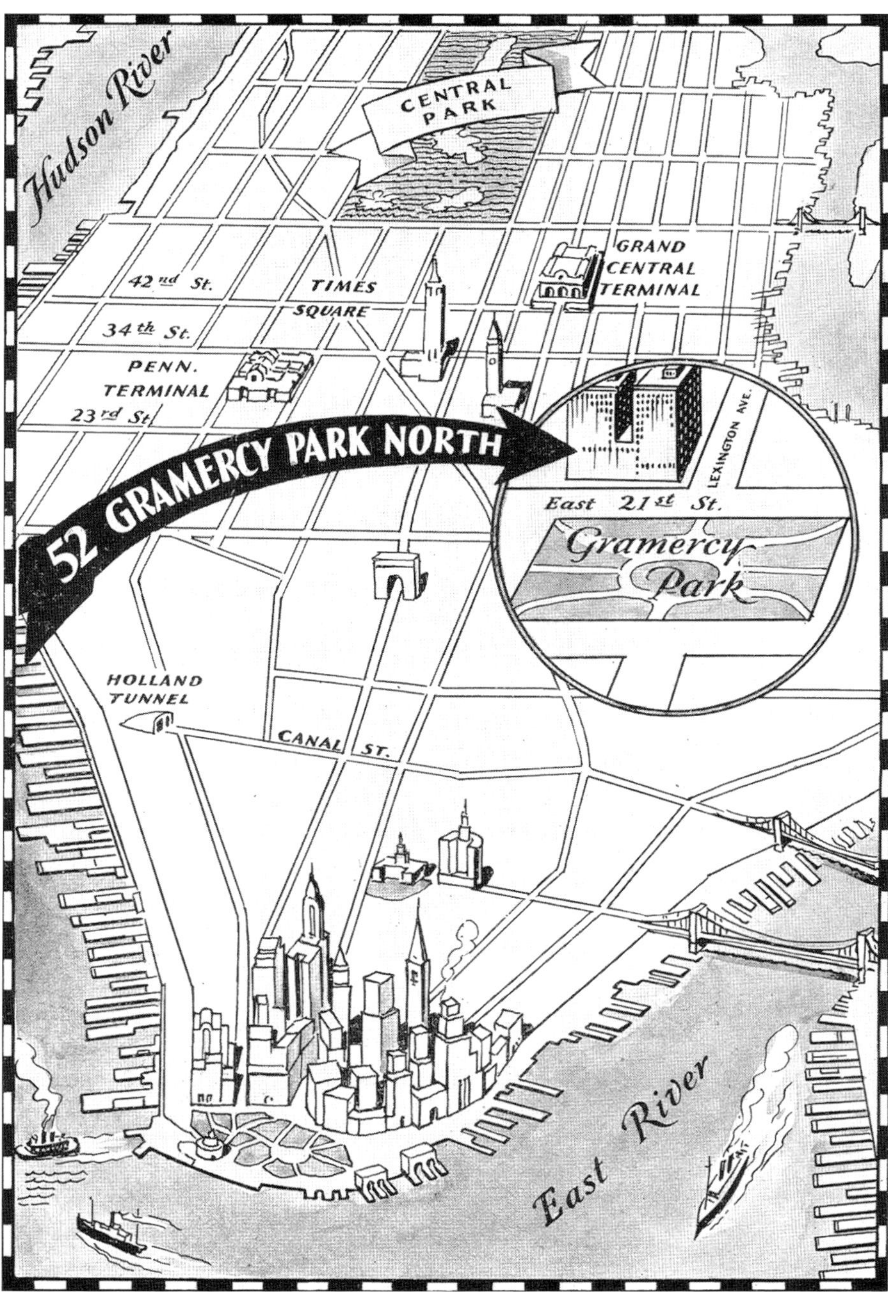

An advertisement from the hotel's magazine.

Babe Ruth also liked to get his hair trimmed at Ralph's Beauty and Barbershop, located in the hotel's annex. The hair salon's guests appreciated the tight-lipped environment Ralph maintained, something he had acquired during his upbringing in Sicily, where keeping your mouth shut was a means of survival. It was fine to schmooze at Ralph's, but gossip was discouraged. Its former clients included several New York power brokers, including Mayor Vincent Impellitteri, hotel residents Senator Robert Wagner Sr. and Mayor Robert Wagner Jr., Mayor Bill O'Dwyer, and city planner Robert Moses. These were men whose faces regularly graced the front pages of the city's newspapers.

John Barrymore also got his hair cut in the hotel. Moving from the stage to the silver screen, he had recently played an out-of-luck baron who becomes a jewel thief in *The Grand Hotel*. The hotel's emblem with a top hat and cane, created in the 1940s, was taken from a silhouette of John Barrymore shortly after he passed. Supposedly, the hotel did not publicly announce this connection because it did not want to pay a royalty.

Another major actor of the time, James Cagney, visited the hotel often and had a sister who lived there. When James Cagney got his hair cut at the Gramercy, the desk clerks asked the barber to save some of the clippings as a souvenir. At the same time, the hotel was hosting real gangsters like Jimmy Hines, who stayed on the government's dime. Prosecutor John Dewey wanted to make his stooges comfortable when they ratted out their former business partners.

Left: Part of an advertisement for the roof's Skyline Café.

Right: The John Barrymore logo.

Children line up for school. Note the electric "Quiet Please" sign at the top of the awning.

Along with hosting film stars, the hotel itself was a theater. In August 1935, the management set up a screen and movie projector on the roof. One of the films shown (with sound) was *The Blue Light*, codirected by and starring Leni Riefenstahl. The hotel's magazine recorded that the film was "greatly enjoyed by the assemblage." Two years earlier, this same picture had inspired Hitler to commission Riefenstahl to make a series of Nazi propaganda films. The hotel's magazine made no note of the connection.

Around the same time, in 1935, Ernest Hemingway came to attend the annual meeting of the Saltwater Anglers of America, an organization founded at the hotel devoted to fishing. During the ceremony, the *For Whom the Bell Tolls* writer was elected vice president. It's unclear what he did at this event or for the organization afterward, but the bar was open.

While it may seem like the Gramercy Park Hotel was just a place to party, it *did* do something to help the millions of unemployed during the Depression. In the 1930s, the Skyline Café on the Gramercy Park Hotel's top floor became the premier meeting ground for charity organizations. The café resembled the deck of a sea cruiser, with lounge chairs and tables only large enough to hold an ashtray and a drink. Waiters in smart pine-green coats with matching trousers took orders for "cocktails, high-balls, and Planter's Punches" starting at thirty cents each. Facing the bar was a ping-pong room and, on the other side, a bright solarium filled with wicker furniture and cylindrical lamps.

The café's advertisements showed men in bowties flashing whimsical smiles alongside short-haired flapper girls in lace dresses. The menu offered dishes like "brook trout sauté meunière" and "filet of beef provençale." There was even a cigar section. If a guest was bored, they could read Robert Ingersoll's original manuscripts and perhaps find an excuse to order another drink.

In June 1937, the Debutante Committee held a benefit on the hotel's rooftop to raise money for a vacation fund. Accompanying the *New York Times* article about the event were soft-focus pictures of the seventeen-year-old female hosts: one in pearls with her hair braided à la Princess Leia and the other in a puffy-shouldered prom dress. Along with participating in a ping-pong tournament, guests watched a fashion show of summer "country clothes."

The names of the participating organizations, like the Department of Welfare, State Charities Aid, and the American Association of Social Workers, remind us how much public assistance was really needed at the time. One luncheon of the National Social Work Council in 1933 featured a speaker who predicted a higher living standard and less disease "after these dark years have passed." On top of New York in a first-class hotel, with views of the Chrysler Building on one side and a private park on the other, the moneyed guests came up with ways to solve poverty while eating a $1.25 meal (when the average salary was $5 a day).

The Committee on Trust Funds hosted a few luncheons, as did the National Recreation Society, which awarded fellowships to college graduates to study recreation. Enjoying cool air before the advent of air conditioners, the guests learned about the inadequacy of the country's public playgrounds, swimming pools, baseball diamonds, and tennis courts. Everywhere, people wanted food, but the hotel's clients wanted more space to play.

Charles Schwefel Takes Over

On the eve of World War II, the hotel saw a major management shift. The leaseholder, Gramercy Park Hotel Corporation, had $1.6 million worth of debt it couldn't pay. The hotel went bankrupt, and in the auction,

the insurance company purchased it for $560,000. New York Life then brought in hotel operator Charles Schwefel, who was already a figure in the neighborhood, to manage the place. He soon moved, with his wife, Elsie, and two sons, William and Charles R., onto the twelfth floor of the hotel, facing the park.

Charles W. Schwefel was born in 1895 in Brooklyn, New York, and was "the grand old man of hotels," as the bellhop Pinky once put it. He was hearty and robust, with a prominent belly and chest, premature gray hair, and a taste for bowties. He also had "a lively interest in politics," according to a *Sports Illustrated* profile. Schwefel had served bravely as a corporal in France during the Meuse-Argonne offensive of World War I. Oddly enough, in 1925, when the Gramercy Park Hotel opened, Charles W. Schwefel was an employee of Bing & Bing and was put in charge of the company's 1925 holiday party at the St. George Hotel. As a young man, he must have formed a strong impression of the Gramercy's owners at that time, who were involved with projects throughout the city.

Later, Schwefel became the manager of the Hotel Jermyn in Scranton, Pennsylvania. One evening in 1929, he was called in to quell a party that was being held by the New York Yankees in one of the hotel's rooms. Schwefel responded to the Yankee legends without being intimidated. There, Babe Ruth and Charles Schwefel became fast friends. Later that year, Schwefel

Charles Schwefel (*center*) with Roy Battersby (*left*) and Brigadier General Frank Wirsig (*right*) at the annual Combat Correspondents reunion held in the Gramercy. *Photo by Lou Lowry.*

found himself working as the night desk manager at the George Washington Hotel (three blocks away from the Gramercy).

Now that Schwefel was closer to the Babe's favorite watering hole, the two men saw more of each other. Throughout Ruth's life, the two often went fishing together, and Schwefel regularly served as Ruth's golfing partner at charity events.

At the time, Schwefel lived in Brooklyn with his younger sister-in-law, Marian Hunt, an angelic-looking model considered a "flapper girl." Schwefel and his wife disapproved of Marian's partying, but this was the Roaring Twenties. One night, an argument between Marian and Schwefel boiled over, just as Marian was about to leave for a party. Schwefel shouted at Marian that if she left, she shouldn't return home. The young woman went out anyway.

Later that evening, she returned to the Schwefel home and drunkenly knocked on the door. Schwefel and his wife refused to open. Perhaps in revenge, Marian Hunt swallowed a vial of poison. To make sure she finished the job, she pulled out a pistol and shot herself in the temple, dying on their doorstep. The effect on Charles Schwefel must have been immense. Years later, it would affect how he ran the Gramercy Park Hotel.

Despite this grisly tale, Schwefel rose to become the manager of the George Washington Hotel and became head of the 23rd Street Association, which hired additional street cleaners for the neighborhood. He also ran the Circus Saints & Sinners, a nonsectarian charity organization.

When Schwefel became manager of the Gramercy in 1941, he immediately hired his relatives to work in the hotel. Schwefel's management style was strict, however, perhaps because he'd seen the negative effects of partying firsthand. "He had us like soldiers," remembered Victor, the hotel's eventual maître d'. For the time being, the hotel's pendulum swung in the direction of order and discipline.

World War II

Though, in retrospect, World War II seemed inevitable, it didn't feel that way to many Americans in early 1941. In the late 1930s and into 1941, the hotel published advertisements on the back of its magazines addressed to "Mr. Average Citizen." It advised him to "stand firm so that the folly of 1914–1918 shall not occur again." Charles Lindbergh, the famous aviator and leader of the antiwar movement, was even known to frequent the hotel. Alas, Pearl Harbor changed everything.

Once the war began, the Gramercy Park Hotel itself became a front. On March 27, 1942, around 8:20 p.m., an alarm buzzed at the armory on Park Avenue and 34th Street; 226 guardsmen grabbed their stacked rifles and marched in double time down Lexington Avenue. The traffic was diverted until the khaki-clad men, their guns and bayonets ready, reached Gramercy Park. There, Major Robert J. Geis set up temporary headquarters in the hotel as his men moved into their assigned positions around the "strategic area."

While the commanders drew up battle plans in the bar, a guest bought up all the whiskey, fearing a siege by German seamen. Another guest ran upstairs to hoard food and ordered everything from room service. Outside, soldiers circled the hotel, on guard for bombings and sabotage. Another part of the regiment went into the park, and men were stationed at the entrances. Everything, of course, had been a drill.

Many of the hotel's staff members soon enlisted, including Pinky, and their names were displayed on a stand in the lobby. Also in the lobby was a cardboard train, each car representing $15,000 that the hotel had raised in its ongoing bond drive. By the end of the war, the hotel had raised millions of dollars, its lobby filled with a long, cardboard train.

Not only did the hotel raise money, but it also offered space to war-related charity organizations. In room 204, the United States Committee for the Care of European Children operated rent-free. It received two thousand letters from people who offered to take French and English refugee children into their homes. In room 302, the Red Cross opened a chapter. Down the hall, in room 308, Bundles of America worked in its rent-free office, creating care packages for the troops. In addition to providing these offices, the hotel regularly hosted drives seeking donated supplies to be sent abroad.

When the army needed metal for its factories, the hotel hosted a "treasure hunt" that yielded three tons of scrap metal from old bed springs, refrigerator coils and units, ranges, kitchen cabinets, old lamps, copper wire, and brass fixtures. Some hotel guests who stayed after this event had their furniture collapse underneath them. But that was a small price to pay to protect the world from Hitler.

The Creative Class During the War

The hotel still served as a beacon for the creative class, though much of its life at the time revolved around the war. In 1943, the hotel was home to Mary McCarthy (author of *A Charmed Life* and *The Oasis*) and her husband, the writer and critic Edmund Wilson (author of the early Soviet history *To the Finland Station*). Their home soon became a salon, attracting the who's who of the era's literary scene. Among their many guests was the Russian writer Vladimir Nabokov, who met his future editor at the *New Yorker*, Katharine White, at the Gramercy.

On New Year's Eve 1943, the literary couple hosted a party in their apartment. Among their friends present that evening was art critic Clement Greenberg and an old flame of McCarthy's, the literary critic Philip Rahv. As the New Year finally approached, Rahv lay seductively in McCarthy's lap as she sat on the floor with her back against the wall. Within months, McCarthy and Wilson would split, and Rahv would reappear romantically in McCarthy's world. Though McCarthy and Wilson stayed only a short time, the hotel left its mark on the writers and their relationships.

Shortly after, author E.B. White penned the children's book *Stuart Little* in one of the Gramercy's rooms. In a letter to his editor, written on Gramercy Park Hotel stationery, White wrote that he expected him to be "shocked and grieved to discover that the principal character of the story has the attributes and appearance of a mouse." White was afraid of the comparison to Mickey Mouse, a celebrity in 1944. Yet because the mouse Stuart Little had appeared in his dreams, complete with "his hat, his cane, and his brisk manner," White felt obligated to keep the character as is. Children everywhere would soon be thankful. At the end of his letter, White advised the editor to stop by, since "we are enjoying room service and would like to see you." Underneath our many layers, we are all the same it seems.

The end of the war was met with celebrations at the hotel. When the troops returned from Europe, the hotel's rooms were so overcrowded that a bishop was forced to sleep in the women's restroom in the lobby.

Schwefel Buys the Gramercy

In May 1949, Charlie Schwefel purchased the Gramercy Park Hotel from the New York Life Insurance Company. Now, as the hotel's owner, Schwefel turned his sights toward charity work. This included the P.S. 600s, a school system set up for helpless, troubled children. Through this program, at P.S. 614, Schwefel met Floyd Patterson, the future heavyweight boxer. Schwefel was so impressed by Patterson's boxing record in the school that he became his self-appointed guardian angel. Schwefel also introduced Patterson to Cus D'Amato of the Gramercy Gym, which was six blocks from the hotel. According to Schwefel, "I investigated Cus D'Amato up one side and down the other when Floyd started fighting." Despite his public desire to keep the mafia out of boxing, Cus D'Amato was mobbed up and connected to the Genovese crime family. Most likely, Schwefel never found this detail out about Patterson's legendary trainer, who, years later, went on to coach Mike Tyson.

After Patterson won his very first professional fight, Schwefel invited the young boxer into the hotel's executive office. Schwefel delicately placed three $100 bills on the table, the total of Patterson's winnings from the fight.

"Floyd," Schwefel said, "This looks like a lot of money, but it isn't. I want you to work here at the hotel in between fights." Patterson agreed. He soon took a job assisting housekeeping and the hotel's decorator. During his work breaks, Patterson jogged around Gramercy Park. Schwefel also employed

Patterson's brothers to work in the hotel, so he'd always have someone to spar with. The hotel's proximity to Cus D'Amato's Gramercy Gym became a major benefit as well.

In 1952, at age seventeen, Patterson won the Olympic gold medal in boxing in Helsinki. He returned to America and went back to work at the hotel. Though he was now a contender for the world championship, he still needed to be given a championship fight by boxing promoters. Schwefel had a plan for his employee.

For Patterson's twenty-first birthday, Schwefel hosted a party on the second floor of the Gramercy Park Hotel. He invited telecasters, sportswriters, boxing promoters, and the borough presidents of Brooklyn and Manhattan, among other politicians. Schwefel put it bluntly: "There is going to be another heavyweight champion from New York pretty soon if I have anything to do with it." *Sports Illustrated* then interviewed Patterson and Schwefel in one of the hotel's rooms.

The scheme worked. Overnight, the hotel birthday party made Patterson a celebrity. Within a year, Patterson got his shot at the title and defeated Archie Moore by knockout in five rounds. He was the youngest heavyweight boxing champion in history at the age of twenty-one. Once again, the hotel had worked its magic. This time it changed the course of boxing history.

THE END OF SCHWEFEL'S REIGN

In the postwar years, the hotel lost none of its charm from the 1920s and continued to be a hangout for Yankee players, including Mickey Mantle, Joe DiMaggio, and, of course, Babe Ruth. When Babe Ruth was stricken with cancer, Schwefel remained by his side.

As a token of gratitude, Babe Ruth gave his 1923 World Series watch to Schwefel. Ruth engraved it with the words "To my pal Charles Schwefel." The watch was later auctioned for $717,000 in 2014. When Ruth died, Charlie Schwefel arranged the funeral. Later, Schwefel hung an autographed picture of Babe Ruth in the bar as a memorial.

Perhaps in honor of the Babe, many Yankee icons continued to visit the bar. On November 23, 1955, Schwefel hosted a dinner for the Circus Saints and Sinners to honor Joe DiMaggio on the second floor of the hotel. DiMaggio had just split with Marilyn Monroe weeks earlier, and the hotel was mobbed with members of the press. After a round of speeches, the slugger was awarded a silver dish engraved to the "Yankee Clipper." There, in the same rooms that had made Floyd Patterson a household name, Schwefel reached his summit. Not only had he befriended some of the greatest athletes of his generation, but he had also become their mentor.

Then tragedy struck. Schwefel's son Charles R. Schwefel, aged twenty-four, died from Hodgkin's disease a few weeks after he was married in the hotel. Schwefel himself died in his hotel room in August 1956. His coffin, like that of a fallen hero, was escorted through the streets of New York by Mayor Wagner. His second son, William G. Schwefel, a USMC captain who fought in the Jamestown trenches in Korea, then took over the management of the hotel for a year or so. He was soon followed by Herbert R. Weissberg.

Not long after the hotel was sold, however, William Schwefel hanged himself. Mrs. Schwefel died soon after. One wonders what role, if any, the hotel played in these tragedies.

Did the family become cursed while living in the hotel, as *New York* magazine once suggested about my own family? The truth is, even if I thought there was a curse, I would never admit it. All I can do is narrate the facts. Who believes in curses anyway?

What follows is the story I know best—that of my own family.

4

H.R. WEISSBERG CORPORATION

1958–1968

New York City in 1958 was in great shape. It was then under the leadership of Mayor Robert Wagner Jr., who grew up in the Gramercy Park Hotel and still got his hair trimmed there. The city's economy outperformed the rest of the nation. And though the city lost the Brooklyn Dodgers to Los Angeles, the Yankees still won the World Series. The skyline had just added the new Seagram Building. The Puerto Rican community got the Puerto Rican Day Parade, which made *them* happy. And for the first time, homes across the nation tuned in to watch Leonard Bernstein conduct the New York Philharmonic for a series of *Young People Concerts*. There was so much money and opportunity that New Yorkers didn't seem to mind that the mafia and unions took a piece of the action.

In the heart of Manhattan, Gramercy Park's iron gates, its oak and cedar trees, its gravel paths, and forest-green benches remained as they had a century prior. With the closure of the Third Avenue elevated train, along with the prohibition on buses (including school buses), Gramercy Park was once again as quiet as it was at its founding. But things were about to get much louder.

In April 1958, Herbert R. Weissberg became the hotel's new owner for $3 million in cash. By then, Herbert was a rising hotelier and the owner of a small chain of hotels. One journalist asked at the time: What did the "R." in his name stand for?

"I don't know," Herbert replied, a smile accentuating his dimples. "I added a middle initial years ago because it kind of rolls out the name. When I was a kid in the New York slums forty years ago, I was called everything but my name."

Herbert R. Weissberg

The blue-eyed Herbert was the second oldest of five children, born to a poor tailor, Max (my namesake), and his wife, Rose Weissberg, in the Lower East Side. He started out as a paperboy in Brooklyn before he graduated to checking coats on Broadway for a production of *Green Pastures*, and then he went on to become a delivery boy for the *Wall Street Journal*. The Weissberg family, led by the luftmensch Max, then left a trail of landlords from Manhattan all the way to Yonkers. Early in the Depression, they acquired a candy business in Yonkers near Sherwood Park called the Sugar Bowl. But the business was so bad the family ended up eating all their merchandise.

One day, Herbert and his brothers watched in awe as a man in a fine tailored suit exited a brand-new silver Cadillac. The man entered the office next door. The boys observed the sign hanging above the door, which read, "Real Estate." Yet none of the boys knew what the words meant.

That night, Herbert and his brothers asked Max what *real estate* meant. He didn't know either. But all three of the Weissberg brothers, Herbert, Larry, and Marvin, decided that they would go into real estate because they wanted to wear Italian suits and drive Cadillacs. Eventually, all three became multimillionaires in the land business.

Herbert R. Weissberg (*left*) and Ruth (Danny) Weissberg (*right*).

Herbert's first experience in hotel life was working as a clerk at the Bradley Beach, New Jersey Inn one summer in the 1930s. There, he learned how to manage the switchboard and check customers in and out. But this lasted only a summer. At the height of the Depression, he still needed a job. So his mother, Rose Weissberg, waited outside Mayor LaGuardia's door and *demanded* one for him. Apparently, the Jewish mother overpowered the mayor, and Herbert became a welfare investigator for the city. Later, he also taught English, where he met my grandmother Frances, a Polish immigrant who fled Europe in 1938.

When World War II began, Herbert got a job at the Wright Aeronautical plant in Patterson, New Jersey, building B-29s. He started working for $0.60 an hour. Three years later, when he was laid off, he was earning $150 a week as a supervisor.

By then, Herbert had two children with his wife, Frances. The eldest was Robert (my father), born in 1941. Martin "Marty" was born in 1945. Since these two will come back later in the story, let me mention that Robert, as a kid, was always reading books and eventually became a professor. Tasked with collecting the rent, Robert once took the wad of cash and passed it out to strangers on the street. Marty was different, however. Whenever the family ate in a restaurant, Marty would circle the tables and pocket any tips the waiters hadn't picked up yet. These stark differences would play out years later in the Gramercy's drama.

Immediately after being laid off in 1945, Herbert used his savings to acquire rooming houses. Early on, the story goes, he lost all his money. Undeterred, he saved up and invested again. In a few years, Herbert and his wife went from being the owners of a single furnished apartment to owning several major hotels in the Upper West Side, including the Franconia, the Bolivar, and the Taft. As if to make a point, Herbert bought the building he was born in on East Fifth Street in the Lower East Side.

In his early forties, Herbert was a premature gray, handsome, and often physically compared to the Hollywood actor Joseph Cotten. Herbert was jovial and frequently had a boozy grin on his face. As he himself explained, "If I should drink three or four martinis, I should buy half of New York." The first major hotel he acquired was the Shelton on 49th Street and Lexington Avenue (now a Marriott), which he bought from his mentor Louis Schleifer, whom he had met at the automats. Their relationship began when Herbert asked him to change a quarter and Schleifer unapologetically asked for a commission. *This is a man I can talk to*, Herbert realized.

Day after day, inside the mechanical café, Herbert eagerly listened as Schleifer told tales of noisy pets, messy children, unruly plumbing, mice, cockroaches, and late or nonexistent rent payments. Whatever Herbert wanted to know, he got an answer, whether it was keeping a customer without electricity happy or learning the ins and outs of stealing deposits. Interestingly, Schleifer always hired a rabbi to bless his contracts, which impressed Herbert.

Eventually, Herbert sought to purchase the Shelton Hotel from his mentor, almost as if to show him that the student had surpassed the teacher. Their negotiations lasted twenty-six hours. Near the end of the bargaining, Louis ordered sandwiches and coffee from room service. The cheese was rancid and the coffee cold. Herbert said, "He had lousy food sent up because he figured it might weaken me physically. What a rough trader he was. He would look in my eyes all the time. If I flickered an eyelash, he changed his tactics immediately." In the end, Herbert made a deal.

As far as maintenance and operations were concerned, Herbert was so tight-fisted, he could squeeze a nickel into a dime. He would grease the palms of unscrupulous warehouse managers, who would find him unclaimed furniture in exchange for wads of cash. Much of the furniture in his locations also came from bankruptcy auctions in old hotels. As the auctioneers went room to room, auctioning off items, Herbert would skip ahead a few rooms to pour water on the carpets and furniture. Later, when the bidding commenced, the other bidders would mistakenly think that the items were stained.

Perhaps Herbert's favorite pastime was bribing people. Early in his career, he achieved rent increases in his rent-controlled units by paying off a bureaucrat in the Operation Prices Administration (OPA). In his typical showy way, he brought his son Robert along for the occasion. Another time, when a building inspector refused to take a bribe and sign a form, he scribbled a signature on the form himself. It landed him in court, but he lived to see another day. Often, Herbert would solve his legal problems by asking, in a way that suggested a payoff was imminent, "Who do I need to see?"

When his hands no longer needed to do all the dirty work, Herbert quickly relished in playing the part of a businessman. He liked to chew cigars and wear expensive suits, his initials monogrammed on his cuff links and shirt pockets. Naturally, his car was a Cadillac, driven by a chauffeur, and he had two phones installed, one for each ear. He drank fine whiskey and could accurately discern, by taste, the number of years belonging to a rare malt. He called women "broads," though he enjoyed their company. Cynical at times, he was always witty. His laugh roared like that of a circus ringleader trying to be heard by those in the back of the tent.

Dangling cash was another one of his preferred pastimes. When Herbert wanted a table in a restaurant, he would remove a wad of twenty-dollar bills he kept in his pocket. Even if the room was half empty, Herbert would bribe the maître d' for the best table in the house. His favorite was the corner table. With the confidence only money can bring, he would inevitably draw the attention of the entire room. His favorite thing wasn't the money, of course, but the dependency other people had on him. He was like the lord of a medieval castle.

When Herbert took Robert and Marty to Yankees games, he never arrived early to the park and never bought tickets. Out came the roll of twenty-dollar bills. When Herbert decided that Robert should have some sex education at the age of twelve, he pressed an Andrew Jackson into the palm of a strip club bouncer, and Robert was given a front-row seat for the lesson.

It was as if Herbert read about the life of a businessman in a comic book and worked overtime to make sure every detail, from his Cuban cigars to his platinum money clip, matched perfectly. Now, Herbert was just like the man he had once seen as a kid, exiting a Cadillac and entering a building with "Real Estate" written atop it.

Herbert liked to make his deals on napkins in crowded bars. A handshake was enough for him to send millions of dollars flowing one way or another. Any objections from family members or business partners were met with a "Whaddya talkin' about? *You're crazy*." And this was always accompanied by a dramatic shrug of the shoulders. Herbert was proof that one could become a successful businessman without being a bean counter or a legal nitpick.

Herbert and Frances's messy public divorce in 1951 divided his hotel empire, however. Herbert then married Frances Daniels, who changed her official name to Ruth to avoid confusion. Herbert called her "Danny" instead, and that became the name everyone used. Growing up, I always heard that Ruth, when she met Herbert, was a nursing student in the Red House, one of Herbert's properties, and had trouble paying her rent. The *Daily News* told another story. By bugging the household phones, Herbert's own private investigators discovered his wife, Frances, was having an affair. Their code word for sex was *coffee*, and Frances was caught on tape making repeated innuendos about her coffee being hot. Herbert made sure the *Daily News* printed the story. The investigators also accused Frances of trying to poison Herbert by sneaking pills into his soup, something that was probably true. There's no doubt both were cheating, but Frances had taken the animosity to another level. For Frances, the divorce was a public disaster. But she ended up with weekday custody of the kids in any case.

After marrying Ruth, Herbert had another son, Steven, born in 1954. Ruth quickly got pregnant again. For the second child, the couple had problems coming up with a name. "Maybe we'll name him Yonkel!" Herbert would joke. And Ruth would say, "No we're not! We're gonna give him a good name!" Herbert would joke back, "What are ya talkin' about? Yonkel is a good name." Back and forth they would go. They finally settled on David by the time the child was born on December 30, 1955.

Though he had young children at home, Herbert was always busy with important business matters. As the new owner of the Gramercy, Herbert's first act was to abolish the human resources department. Simply by having each department hire its own people, he would save tremendously on staffing costs. He also made himself personally available to staff. Immediately, the employees were transformed by his laid-back style. With the employees more relaxed, the guests felt less hustled for tips. The place lightened up. The lobby was now regularly filled with laughter. Just to make sure things didn't fall apart, however, Herbert hired a young German, Klaus Mangold, to be the resident manager.

Around this time, Herbert doubled the size of the bar. He did this by installing vertical wooden blinds around the adjacent area of the lobby. The couches that had previously occupied the space were replaced by chairs and drink tables, on top of which Herbert placed candles inside cherry-colored glasses. In the far corner of what became the lounge, Herbert added a baby grand piano.

In the hotel and bar business, music was needed even when a musician could not be found. The radio wouldn't work either, as advertisements and the announcer's voice were disturbing to guests. So Herbert made a contract with General Electric's RCA to provide soft Muzak in the lobby and elevators, replacing a service that had fallen by the wayside during the hotel's last budget crisis.

Aside from modifying the atmosphere a little, Herbert changed the hotel's official name from Hotel Gramercy Park to the Gramercy Park Hotel. He also changed its address from 52 Gramercy Park North to 2 Lexington Avenue, which he thought would add to the hotel's cachet by emphasizing its location at the head of a major avenue.

As for staff changes, Herbert's taciturn brother-in-law Nat (married to his sister Gurdie) became a desk clerk. When Herbert's kid sister Belle got married, her lanky husband, Harold Weiss, was "put on the payroll" at the Gramercy to become the auditor. Herbert's chauffeur, selected from among his many cab drivers, was a beefy thirty-one-year-old named Frank, or

"Frankie" X. Guma. He had greasy black hair, combed straight back, and a toothpick that perpetually dangled from his mouth. Though quiet, the World War II veteran clearly had the potential to be lethal. "I'll take care of it," he would promise in his thick Long Island accent.

Herbert quickly learned, to his satisfaction, that Frank was the nephew of Joseph "Socks" Lanza, the head of the United Seafood Workers Union and a capo in the Genovese crime family. Not long after learning of Frank Guma's connection to the mafia, Herbert promoted Frank to "secretary" of the H.R. Weissberg Corporation. He also did this so he wouldn't have to hire someone to sign documents in his absence. Frank continued his duties as a chauffeur, however.

Like Curtis Judson, the Gramercy Park Hotel's legendary owner a century prior, Herbert was unsatisfied to own merely a small chain of hotels. He wanted an *empire*. In the late 1950s, the leisure capital of the world was Havana, Cuba. Herbert made enormous efforts to acquire the Havana Capri, which gangster Meyer Lansky was looking to unload while retaining the casino. (This was the hotel made famous in the Soviet film *Soy Cuba*.) Santo Trafficante was also a partner in the hotel and was looking to raise money for a much larger deal elsewhere in Cuba.

Herbert made a series of visits to kick the tires of the property. Coincidentally, he was at the Presidential Palace the night of the revolution on New Year's Eve 1958. (This is the same party where Michael Corleone gives Fredo the kiss of death in *The Godfather Part II*.) After the Cuban Revolution began, however, Herbert was *still* determined to get a Cuban hotel. In his typical showy manner, he sought to negotiate directly with Castro to gain control of the Capri. In April 1959, using the help of legendary actor Errol Flynn (a friend of Castro's), Herbert actually got to meet the Cuban dictator. According to Herbert, in the meeting Castro was very full of himself and unappreciative of the role a businessman plays in running a hotel. Alas, Herbert walked away from Cuba unable "to make a deal."

When I asked him about this years later, Herbert insisted that he backed out of the deal after a candid observation: everywhere in Cuba, the pay phones no longer worked because Castro had forced the telephone companies to charge five cents for a pay phone call instead of ten cents. Herbert felt it was a symbol that the government's price regulations would destroy whatever business he or anyone else could build there.

There is another explanation, however. During Herbert's last trip in Cuba, a photographer caught him with Errol Flynn; his girlfriend, Woodsie; Ruth; his "man in Havana" Frank Sinatra (no relation to the singer); and

Herbert Weissberg in Cuba with actor Errol Flynn and some of Castro's men after the revolution in April 1959.

some of Castro's men having dinner at the Havana Capri. The photo soon appeared in the local *Gramercy Graphic*, and Herbert became the most talked-about man in Gramercy Park.

After the photo was taken that evening in April 1959, some of the men present at the dinner asked Ruth to dance. She obliged, and the men started getting handsy with her. Sitting at the table, Herbert went into a fury. Alas, machine guns were everywhere, and he could not object. After a few dances, a Cuban teenager tried to put his tongue down Ruth's throat. At that moment, I think, the Cuban deal was finally toast in Herbert's eyes—not because of the pay phones. Despite this bitter disappointment, however, Herbert still dreamed of owning a mob-backed casino and hotel somewhere south.

Back in New York, the first Weissberg to move into the Gramercy was my father, then-eighteen-year-old Robert. He checked in for an "extended stay" in 1960. Robert had recently enrolled in Syracuse University, but he'd grown bushy sideburns and become unhappy with the school's "too strict" environment. So he dropped out and caught a bus to New York City. On this occasion, Pinky, by now in his forties and still possessing most of his teeth, wheeled Robert's luggage to the hotel's seventh floor. Inside his room, knowing that his father would pay for it all, Robert had hardly any motivation to return to Syracuse.

The next morning, Herbert met Robert for lunch. Herbert demanded Robert promptly check out of the hotel and return to Syracuse.

"They're not sophisticated up there," Robert explained, sounding like an Upper East Sider in between tennis matches. "I couldn't take it."

"Sophisticated? *Whaddya talkin' about?* You think Syracuse isn't sophisticated? You haven't been to the jungle." For Herbert, the "jungle" was no more than a subway ride to a distant part of the city.

The two took their menus from the maître d', the mustachioed diminutive Frenchman Alan Petite, who wore a jacket with sleeves that were too long for his arms.

Herbert called the Latino busboy Pedro to the table and summarized the situation.

"Oh yes, Mr. Viseberk," Pedro said, nodding. "*Your son should go back to school.*"

"You see? I told ya so!" Herbert roared, no doubt making a mental note to leave Pedro a fat tip.

"Listen to yer fader. He's a very smart man," Pedro repeated, pointing to his head.

"Ya see?" Herbert crowed. "Ya see?"

By the end of the meal, the entire staff of Le Parc had lined up next to the table. All nodded their heads and repeated, "Yes, Mr. Viseberk," and "Listen to yer fader." Often, this was how discussions ended in our family.

Robert hid in his hotel room. When the bill came, he just signed. Living off a diet of shrimp cocktails, he listened to Thelonious Monk at the Blue Note and the Half Note in the Village. Every night, he searched for himself in Bleecker Street bars and late-night cafés on Cornelia Street. Every morning,

Robert (*left*), Herbert (*center*), and Marty (*right*).

he woke up late to the city sirens on a king-size mattress. Then he ordered room service.

Like many others of his generation, he read Jack Kerouac's *On the Road*. When he talked, he ended every other sentence with "man." This was the beginning of a decade that would bring more drugs, miniskirts, and rock 'n' roll to America. Herbert wanted Robert out!

Pinky described Robert's life in the Gramercy: "Your fader used ta come bring in gals—broads, redheads, he liked 'em all. I remember all da time dese gals. Then if it worked out, ya see, then ya'd see them the next day having strawberries and cream for breakfast. Strawberries and cream for breakfast." He repeated this while leaning in, as if it meant something salacious.

After four months, Herbert came up with a solution. He offered Robert an apartment on Cornelia Street and suggested he study at New York University for the summer. Then Herbert hired two plainclothes detectives, who visited Robert in his new place and made a bunch of vague threats about what would happen if he stayed in the city.

After softening up his target, Herbert offered to send his son to San Francisco to live with his brother Larry and attend San Francisco State College. Robert reluctantly agreed. With Robert out of the hotel and far away, Herbert got back to business.

H.R. Weissberg Corporation: A Teamster-Backed, Mafia-Friendly Company

At the end of 1960 in the Gramercy Room, Herbert called together his first meeting for his corporation, H.R. Weissberg Corporation, newly incorporated in Delaware. Through an intricate mortgage finance system, he controlled over six hotels: the Winslow, Paramount, Brittany, and Gramercy Park Hotel in New York; the Montmartre in Miami Beach; and the Lord Baltimore. Present at the meeting were Herbert, his brother Marvin, Donald Gallagher, Frank Guma, Louis Primo, Robert Bennot, Phillip Jamre, and three investors who knew Marvin from Washington D.C..

Some words about these goons. Marvin Weissberg had his own real estate firm in Washington. Donald Gallagher was the general manager of the Gramercy and kept his job by saying "yes" to anything Herbert said. Louis Primo acted as the insurance agent for the company (and was supposedly mobbed up). Bennot and Jamre (always referred to collectively) were Herbert's interior designers. Both were also called "Herbert's gay decorators." Bennot was effeminate, impeccably dressed, and small in stature. Jamre was stout, about five feet, six inches tall, with an ample nose and a permanent five o'clock shadow, and he was of Lebanese heritage, which affected his impeccable taste. Though Herbert's board members had corruption written all over them, they were tolerant folk.

As the meeting came to order, the room was filled with clouds of cigar smoke and the sound of ice rattling in whiskey glasses. Then Herbert stood and gave a speech: "This business is a family business. All of you to me are like family. I brought you all here to the Gramercy to show how far we have come. President Kennedy stayed in this hotel, and now we own the place. Our best customers are artists, creative people. Now I'm asking you to be creative. All of America could be like this hotel. Reasonably priced. Big. And with the kind of friendly staff that makes people want to come back." For a moment, things got awkwardly quiet as the room seemed to lack Herbert's sentimentality. He came to the main part: "Listen, what I need you all to do is to *sell* this vision. Sell our stock like your lives depend on it." He leaned back in his chair and took a puff from his Cohiba for emphasis. "And then we'll die like a bunch of rich bastards." The room laughed. Though the speech was somewhat crude, it energized the room.

Bennot and Jamre designed the stock certificate. The letters "HRW" were joined in a cursive seal between two lithographs of the Lord Baltimore and Gramercy Park Hotel. In the corner was a depiction of the Edwin Booth statue in Gramercy Park, his back to the hotel's Neo-Renaissance façade. (If the name "Booth" sounds familiar, it's because Edwin was the brother of John Wilkes Booth, who assassinated President Lincoln.)

All of Herbert's siblings bought stock in the new corporation, except for Belle, who couldn't afford it. Herbert gave her stock anyway. Herbert's parents, Max and Rose, got shares, along with Rose's siblings and their children. Even Herbert's ex-wife, Frances, bought $25,000 of H.R. Weissberg Corporation. According to Marvin, Herbert's brother, the rest were mainly "inexperienced investors." Those who bought it remember they got in because the Weissbergs liked to brag. Also, it paid dividends. According to family lore, many investors were landlords or other suppliers who had made bundles of cash during the war, charging fees off the books (not allowed by the OPA), and were now looking to wash their money through real estate. Herbert didn't care—he would take money from anywhere.

Shortly after H.R. Weissberg Corporation's launch on the Nasdaq exchange, it was flush with cash. With this income added to the lump sum payments from the mortgages on his hotels, Herbert rapidly financed an

NUMBER AU13622

SHARES -12-

H. R. WEISSBERG CORPORATION

INCORPORATED UNDER THE LAWS OF THE STATE OF DELAWARE

CLASS A STOCK

SEE REVERSE FOR CERTAIN DEFINITIONS

This certifies that MRS FRANCES WEISSBERG
1285 HASTINGS ST
TEANECK N J
is the owner of

-TWELVE-

FULLY PAID AND NON-ASSESSABLE SHARES OF THE CLASS A STOCK OF THE PAR VALUE OF ONE DOLLAR ($1.00) EACH OF H. R. WEISSBERG CORPORATION transferable on the books of the Corporation by the holder hereof, in person or by duly authorized attorney upon surrender of the Certificate properly endorsed. The Corporation will furnish without charge to each stockholder who so requests, the designations, preferences, and relative, participating, optional or other special rights of the Class A Stock and Class B Stock of the Company.

This Certificate is not valid unless countersigned by the Transfer Agent and registered by the Registrar.

Witness the facsimile seal of the Corporation and the facsimile signatures of its duly authorized officers.

Dated: OCT 15 1963

SECRETARY

H. R. WEISSBERG CORPORATION CORPORATE SEAL 1960 DELAWARE

PRESIDENT

REGISTERED: IRVING TRUST COMPANY (NEW YORK) REGISTRAR BY ASSISTANT SECRETARY

COUNTERSIGNED: THE CHASE MANHATTAN BANK (NEW YORK) TRANSFER AGENT BY AUTHORIZED SIGNATURE

Twelve shares of Herbert's stock, issued to his ex-wife, Frances.

acquisitions spree. To fuel the company's rise, he bought advertisements in financial newspapers across America. Every week, the image of the Gramercy's façade reached all corners of the country alongside the message that H.R. Weissberg Corporation had paid a consistent dividend over the last few quarters and counting.

With his financial worries over, Herbert still had to deal with the IRS. He discovered that if he depreciated the value of his hotels, he could eliminate the profit on paper. This worked because each year, theoretically, a building loses value because of its age; in some cases, it loses up to one-third of its value. At the time, the capital gains tax was 25 percent (compared to 15 percent today), so this delayed the day of tax reckoning until he sold the hotel. For now, at least, Herbert wanted to take his chances.

As his company grew, Herbert attracted the attention of the mafia. The first hotel the mafia suggested H.R. Weissberg Corporation buy was the famous Flamingo Hotel in Las Vegas. Herbert went to inspect the property himself, and he was eager to get a piece of the rapidly growing strip. Something dark happened, however, and his life was threatened. Unfortunately, I do not have all the details of this story, but it was related to a territory dispute between the Chicago and New York crime families. Herbert backed off his bid, allowing some investors from Miami to take the property instead. I suspect Herbert's caginess was related to the fact that he was beaten up or violently attacked in some way. He would never say—and he would never go back to Vegas. Even decades later, he was still afraid to set foot in the city.

The Black Hand in New York then suggested he purchase a troubled hotel in New Orleans. Not wanting to leave the corner table of the Gramercy, Herbert sent his younger brother Marvin, the "southerner of the family," to make a deal. So, in 1961, Marvin traveled to see the Fontainebleau Hotel in New Orleans.

At that time, New Orleans was run by Carlos Marcello, a mafia boss who would soon allegedly organize the Kennedy assassination. Marcello's control of the city's underworld played a major role in its lax ways. Bourbon Street was filled with bars and strip clubs that doubled as brothels and casinos. With its swampy atmosphere and voodoo beliefs, New Orleans exemplified the old way of doing things, a system that descended from Sicilian and Napoleonic law.

The Fontainebleau wasn't located in the city's popular French Quarter. But it was the largest hotel in the city at the time, perfect for conventions and budget-minded travelers. It had two hundred rooms, most with balconies

Herbert (*left*) and his younger brother Marvin Weissberg (*right*) at the Fontainebleau Hotel in New Orleans, Louisiana.

that faced a semicircular pool. The hotel also had multiple dining rooms, formal and informal lounges, evening entertainment, and dancing areas. As one would expect in a mob-run town, all of the hotel's vending machines, including the cigarette, candy, and pinball machines, were owned by Carlos Marcello's organization.

The hotel's owner was Zachary A. Strate Jr. Known as "Red," Strate was then in his early forties, a powerful construction executive and a Louisianna State University graduate. Red's nickname came from the color of his hair on his melon-shaped head. He spoke in a thick Louisiana drawl. He liked linen suits and was a "nephew" of Carlos Marcello—that is, he was a mafia associate, one step away from being a made man. But Red was half Italian and half Greek, so he couldn't be "put on the books" for that reason. Nevertheless, Red often did favors for his mob friends. Marcello's own hotel, the Town & Country Motel, was right down the street from the Fontainebleau, and the two men often consulted with each other.

Though he was "easygoing," as Marvin described him, Red could lose his temper and fly into a rage. When Marvin met him, however, Red was living off room service in the Fontainebleau. For him, it was mornings at the pool, afternoons in the massage parlor.

Red Strate had borrowed $2.3 million from the Teamsters pension fund (controlled by Jimmy Hoffa) to build the Fontainebleau Hotel. For a while, the name of the hotel was spelled "Fontainbleau" after Strate got a threatening letter from the lawyer of the famous Fontainebleau Hotel in Miami. When Red needed more money to build an extension, the Teamsters generously gave him another loan. According to court testimony, however, Red used only $1.3 million from the first loan. The remaining $1 million was "cut up" and taken by Red for "unauthorized uses," as the FBI would later explain it. At this time, the FBI was actively investigating what happened to the money after it "disappeared." But for the time being, everything seemed fine for Red.

After Red Strate took his million-dollar kickback, he was uninterested in the day-to-day operations of the Fontainebleau Hotel. One day, his partner William Sherman (who invested $100,000) asked Red why $90,000 in bills hadn't been paid.

"To hell with the bills—burn up the bills!" Strate shouted back.

Chaos quickly took over. Bill collectors were loudly knocking. Investigators were tiptoeing around the premises. It was time to call in Herbert R. Weissberg. If anything could be said about him, it was that he always paid his bills.

Top: Teamster President James R. Hoffa (*left*) and codefendant Zachary Strate (*right*), August 17, 1964.

Bottom: A postcard view of the Fontainebleau Hotel in New Orleans, Louisiana.

The first evening, Marvin and Red had dinner in the hotel's rose-colored dining room. There, Marvin peppered Red with questions—the number of rooms, the amenities, the kitchen, the various seasons, the revenue, the local taxes, *the payoffs*. Everything seemed to be in order—except that the hotel practiced racial segregation. That was something the Weissbergs were advised not to touch, only because it would upset the locals. The hotel's manager, Vincent J. Rizzo, a former player and manager for the Pelicans, New Orleans's minor league baseball team, was quite popular around town, though he was known to be a racist.

Back in New York, Marvin reported to the board. Herbert was pleased. So the H.R. Weissberg Corporation made an offer for $7.5 million to buy the Fontainebleau. Red quickly accepted. Herbert's two decorators, Bennot and Jamre, caught the next plane to New Orleans to freshen up the place. But they left the celebrity manager in place.

Red remained a resident of the Fontainebleau while the IRS went after him with a claim of $1,192,981.63. They argued Red Strate "liquidated and diverted known assets in a concerted act tending to hinder collection of income taxes," according to the *Los Angeles Times*. The feds still hadn't found out what happened to the money, but the IRS could fine him for hiding it.

Aside from his scheme to build the Fontainebleau, Red Strate received a loan from the Teamsters pension fund in a ruse to personally help Jimmy Hoffa, head of the Teamsters, settle a failed real estate scheme. Some background: Hoffa had previously invested Teamster pension money in the Sun Valley Village, a plot of land in Florida, but the land was never developed because the developer died. When Sun Valley Village filed for bankruptcy in 1958, Hoffa was in danger of losing a $400,000 deposit he had made to build roads and bring utilities to the land that was being held by the bank. Because Hoffa had made the loan from his own local Teamster chapter in Detroit, he had to pay the $400,000 to the developer who owed the bank to make everything look legit and not lose the union money. To raise this money, Hoffa decided to issue loans from the Central States Pension Fund, worth over $200 million at the time, and charge kickbacks for the loans. Anyone who got a loan had to pay the "vig," i.e., a percentage off the top for Hoffa. According to court testimony, Red Strate got in on the action and personally delivered a kickback of $165,000 to Hoffa, stuffed inside his shirt.

In other words, these were men Herbert "could do business with." We'll come back to this.

At the next board meeting, Herbert revealed the company had been offered a one-year management contract for the Balmoral Hotel in Costa Rica to conduct a renovation. Herbert ordered Marvin to San José to reorganize the staff and import carpet and other materials from their wholesalers in New York (collecting a nice commission). When the work was completed, Herbert sent Bennot and Jamre to redecorate and create a menu for the new restaurant on the hotel's top floor. Introducing the first Caesar salad to Costa Rica, they forever changed the local cuisine.

Herbert then bought the Emerson in Baltimore and the Western Hills Hotel in Fort Worth, Texas. By the end of 1961, he'd bought his twelfth hotel, the Rio Motor Hotel in Fort Worth, Texas. Through these transactions in Texas, Herbert was introduced to Jack Ruby at his dingy strip club called the Carousel Club. As a fellow Jewish Yankee businessman, Ruby had much in common with Herbert. Unlike most strip club owners, Ruby gave cops and newspapermen free drinks and kept the hooking under control. After Herbert encountered a dispute over the local bank that refused to continue the mortgage on his hotel, he sought Ruby's advice on who to pay off locally for some support. Jack Ruby would later shoot Kennedy assassin Lee Harvey Oswald in the basement of the Dallas Police Department. According to Herbert, Ruby gained access only because he had the police "on the payroll," a necessary aspect of doing business in the nightclub world. Ruby was also backed and bankrolled by Carlos Marcello, which explains Ruby's eventual role in Oswald's assassination.

As Herbert traveled more frequently between his hotels, his trips assumed a routine: employees would circle in and out of his room while Herbert, still in pajamas, gave instructions. Later, Herbert called this his "pajama management" style. Despite his stature as a businessman, Herbert was filled with experience on plumbing and electrical matters and could locate the best place to buy cheap furniture in any town. But he liked to do things casually.

As his momentum increased, Herbert wanted a second mortgage on the Lord Baltimore. But this time, he didn't go to a bank. Instead, he went to the Teamsters, a major trucking union run by James Riddle Hoffa, whom Herbert affectionately called "Jimmy."

Serendipitously, Hoffa was in New York to meet Joseph "Socks" Lanza about the Teamsters and the International Longshoremen's Association (ILA) unions working together in Puerto Rico. Herbert sent an invitation to Hoffa for dinner at the Gramercy. The two already had cordial business relations, as the Edgewater Beach Hotel provided the 5:00 a.m. breakfasts Hoffa had requested for the union's early morning strategy sessions. Though this breakfast service inconvenienced the hotel, it endeared Herbert to Hoffa. A business relationship spawned.

At the reserved table in the bar of the Gramercy, Herbert sat with Hoffa, who wore a heavily starched white shirt and a plain black tie. Hoffa ordered a soda, mentioning that he never drank.

"What I'm trying to do for da union," Hoffa began, "is to build 'em up. Make 'em grow. I can't do that by pinching the freight too hard. I do it by getting more workers. That's how I make the pension grow—more workers."

Used to being shaken down by union officials, Herbert was impressed with Hoffa. The union leader was five and a half feet tall but had the same presence as Napoleon. Like Herbert's wife, Ruth, Hoffa was the son of a poor coal miner in Michigan. Though he was a dropout in grade school, Hoffa had become the president of one of the most powerful labor unions in the country. Most importantly, he did not make assumptions about how easy it was to manage a hotel. Later, the two men transferred the conversation to the dining room, and Hoffa insisted on being called "Jimmy."

After the food arrived, the conversation drifted to Puerto Rico. Both men felt it was going to be the next Cuba (minus the revolution). The Teamsters, Hoffa explained to Herbert, had been organizing Puerto Rico since the late 1950s. Herbert told Hoffa of his Cuban adventures and expressed his enthusiasm to build something in Puerto Rico. Hoffa was likewise ecstatic, mentioning that he had one of his best organizers in Puerto Rico, Frank Chavez.

As the waiters cleared away the dishes, none could entice Hoffa to have dessert. By the time Hoffa got up to leave, Herbert had secured a second mortgage for the Lord Baltimore Hotel from the Teamsters' Central States Pension Fund. Herbert agreed, of course, to kick back 2 percent of the loan to Hoffa.

Herbert and the Teamsters Get into Bed with Each Other

You may ask: Why was Herbert so eager to get into business with Hoffa and his mafia associates? He himself explained it to a journalist:

> *When you're dealing with banks or insurance companies, or out of town businessmen, they always bring up the fact that you are a Jew. Out-of-towners feel all New Yorkers are sharp and so they put up a brutal defense mechanism to drive a hard bargain. But then if it's a New York Jew, they become unreasonable. All this would have no meaning if it weren't*

for the fact that in big business—I mean in deals involving millions—New York businessmen are objective because everyone makes money. Am I going to argue about $100,000 when millions are involved? Also, it's very expensive to make a deal because of the lawyers' and accountants' fees. Those birds love an ignorant client—somebody who didn't go to college, say—because it makes them feel important.

The Teamsters and the mafia were used to dealing with not only Jewish businessmen but also Italians, as they were frequent business partners. It was said in the old days that New York was controlled by the three Is: Italy, Ireland, and Israel. Something about Jewish and Italian people endeared them to each other. Nowhere was that truer than in the mafia. An old joke was that the mafia was ten guys named "Guido" and one guy named "Murray" who could count and pay the bills. The relationship went beyond convenience. At the turn of the century in the Lower East Side's red-light district, Italian women lined up on one side of Allen Street, and the Jewish women lined up on the other. Both Italian and Jewish men were known to visit the services of the opposite ethnicity when visiting the area. By the 1950s, when the Italian mafia controlled many small businesses and unions in America, those in the Jewish community were once again natural partners. Call it corruption if you like. But the combined entities, both inside and outside the "syndicate," built many important hotels, apartment buildings, restaurants, shopping malls, garages, casinos, and other edifices.

By 1962, Herbert had Teamster mortgages on the Lord Biltmore, the Palm Beach Biltmore, the Montmartre, and the Edgewater Beach. Built in 1924, the Palm Beach Biltmore was an elegant twin-tower, ivory-brick building that held over one thousand rooms. The Edgewater Beach Hotel in Chicago, like the Palm Beach Biltmore, was a massive complex of several large Art Deco buildings. Facing Lake Michigan, the hotel had five dining rooms, multiple cocktail lounges, a swimming pool, a putting green, and tennis and shuffleboard courts. Its popular

HOTELS OWNED AND OPERATED
BY THE H. R. WEISSBERG
CORPORATION
CHICAGO
Edgewater Beach
LOng Beach 1-6000
NEW ORLEANS
The Fontainebleau
HUnter 6-6111
NEW YORK
Gramercy Park Hotel
GRamercy 5-4320
WASHINGTON
Gramercy Inn
DIstrict 7-9550
BALTIMORE
Lord Baltimore
LExington 9-8400
The Emerson
MUlberry 5-4400
PALM BEACH
Palm Beach Biltmore
TEmple 2-1781
FORT WORTH
The Western Hills
PErshing 7-6644
The Rio
PErshing 2-1611
SAN JUAN
The Ponce De Leon

nightclub, the Open Air Walk, was a haven for the wealthy Chicago elite, including former guests Frank Sinatra, Judy Garland, Charlie Chaplin, Franklin D. Roosevelt, and Dwight Eisenhower. One of Herbert's first acts was to launch a burlesque show à la Minsky's, which was very popular.

On the eighteenth floor of the Edgewater, the Teamsters kept a spacious $1,000-a-night two-bedroom suite. Chicago was an important shipping hub in the United States, and the Teamsters usually kept the beds full. In 1963, when Hoffa negotiated the first nationwide Master Freight Agreement at the Edgewater, Herbert let him know that the FBI had rented a couple of rooms. The next day, Hoffa publicly denounced the FBI's spying. As a result, Herbert's reputation as a "friend of labor" spread quickly. The label helped boost business throughout Herbert's kingdom, especially in the Gramercy.

Remembering Hoffa's sage advice, Herbert called up Marvin and sent him to Puerto Rico to buy a plot of land for a future hotel. Marvin inspected and purchased a chunk of beachfront property adjacent to the Hilton. They had big plans, but they weren't sure what they were going to do or how they would do it.

"Everything was expanding rapidly. The stock started at $10 and later it went up to $19. I thought he was on his way," Robert remembered. By 1962, Herbert's company had a revenue of $17,044,158, up from $7.3 million the previous year. It seemed the sky was the limit.

With so much going on, the Gramercy Park Hotel remained the crown jewel of Herbert's empire and the location of his board meetings. In the lobby, Herbert placed a dozen bronze stands, designed by his son Marty, each with a picture and description of a hotel: the Paramount, the Winslow, the Brittany, the Lord Baltimore, the Emerson, the Palm Beach Biltmore, the Balmoral, the Everglades, the Fontainebleau, the Rio Motor Hotel, the Western Mills, and, by the elevator, the Edgewater Beach Hotel. The addition of a new hotel was a reason for the staff to celebrate. It wasn't just to kiss Herbert's ass either. Many of the employees owned nonvoting shares of stock, so they were in on it, too.

In 1963, Herbert added two more properties in Washington, D.C.: the Diplomat Motor Hotel on New York Avenue and an apartment building on Scott Circle. Sending Marvin to oversee the job, Herbert renovated the apartment building into a 350-room hotel with a swimming pool and renamed it the Gramercy Inn. "Just you wait," Hebert said. "Soon, I'll have a Gramercy in every major city in the world."

The First Cracks

In 1963, the federal government issued indictments to Hoffa and his business partners over loans made from the Teamsters' pension fund. The feds then interviewed Herbert about his connection to Red Strate and the Teamsters. This development would dog him for years to come.

Herbert explained his discomfort to a *Los Angeles Times* journalist: "Due to the fact that the government is creating such a furor over anyone using Teamsters pension fund money, we wouldn't want a Teamster mortgage today. I hear of so many being called to testify before the grand jury in Chicago that it's not worth it." It would seem that Herbert had made the conscious decision to stay away from his mob-connected friends. In truth, he was actually running straight into their arms. Everyone involved in the federal indictment targeting Hoffa was either giving or receiving kickbacks from the Teamsters pension fund, yet somehow, Herbert remained squeaky clean. Perhaps as a favor to his benefactors, he promoted Frank Guma to chief financial officer of the H.R. Weissberg Corporation.

In the spring of 1963, the entire Weissberg family gathered for Marvin's wedding in the Gramercy Room on the hotel's second floor. During his trip to Puerto Rico, Marvin had fallen in love with a woman, Gloria Marshak, whose family owned the island's largest used car business. Marvin proposed marriage. The young couple chose the Gramercy for their reception.

Alongside a picture window view of Gramercy Park, a Cuban band played salsa and cha-cha-cha tunes while the hotel served plates of fresh tropical fruit, caviar, and chopped liver.

Max took generous helpings of the liver until Rose cut him off sometime around the eighth cracker. Harold Weiss and Belle sat quietly by the window (Belle liked to smoke), while Gurdie, at the same table in a pink dress, talked about *everything* under the sun. Larry and Herbert sat at opposite ends of the room, still in a fight over whether the wine had to be kosher. Herbert's sons sat at the kiddy table with their cousins, and after receiving his seating arrangement, Marty felt humiliated. Steven and David ignored their seating arrangements altogether and ran around the table while Ruth screamed at her two children. Frank Guma, celebrating his promotion perhaps, ate three prime ribs and drank a bottle of Chianti all by himself. Pinky inhaled a glass of whiskey and then another before being asked if he was with the bride or the groom. It was hard to tell who was and who wasn't a Weissberg.

The family at Marvin Weissberg's wedding in 1963. Herbert (*left*) is standing behind a young Steven (*front left*) and David (*front right*).

The first dance of the newlyweds began after the cake-cutting ceremony. The two, both good dancers, formed a silhouette against the emerald-colored trees of Gramercy Park, visible through the glass windows. Turning around, Gloria stumbled distractedly.

"Who are these people?" She asked Marvin, regaining her rhythm quickly.

She pointed to several tables filled with strangers, some of whom were wearing wide-brimmed hats and licking their fingers while the waiters replaced their linen napkins. Marvin marched over to Herbert and demanded an explanation.

Herbert answered, "Dat's da guy I got managing the Western Hills and his wife." Herbert pointed, "And dat's da guy I got managing the Lord Baltimore, along with his wife."

"Why the hell did you invite the managers of the hotels? And what's Frank doing here?"

"Whaddya crazy? Dis here is a *corporate affair*."

In other words, Herbert had invited his employees for the tax write-off and charged the whole thing to H.R. Weissberg Corporation. Marvin was furious. He had dealt with a pushy older brother, but this was the final straw. His wife was equally furious. She would never forgive Herbert for this.

In Herbert's defense, he made little distinction between his family and the staff. As a result of Herbert's changes to Marvin's guest list, Marvin resigned at the next board meeting. But Herbert knew he would be back.

Herbert's Children

Unlike Marvin, Herbert's children were far more amenable to his lifestyle. As young children, Marty and Robert often spent as much as an hour waiting in the lobby of Herbert's hotels for their father to appear. Though Herbert was assigned the responsibility of looking after his older two children on the weekends, he often passed this responsibility off to his staff or his wife while he took care of "business matters" elsewhere. Robert remembers Ruth in the dining room of the Shelton—and later the Gramercy—drunk as a skunk, firing staff that Herbert would have to rehire the next day. But he made up for his absence in other ways.

For their vacations, Robert and Marty visited Herbert's many hotels, running up bills while they explored the city. Steven and David spent their winters in the Palm Beach Biltmore, drinking coconut juice and taking yacht cruises. The Gramercy alone bled thousands in operating expenses due to family consumption. To be a prince in Herbert's kingdom had many perks.

One afternoon in the Gramercy's main dining room, the Rolling Stones ate lunch. An eleven-year-old Steven, oblivious to who they were but aware that the band was attracting attention, asked Mick Jagger if he could sit in his lap. After no one said a word, the rock star agreed. Later, Steven asked Keith Richards if he could strum his guitar. At some point, Mick Jagger wanted a beer, but the drinking age was twenty-one in New York. So Herbert was summoned to personally approve the order from the bar.

When the Baltimore Orioles played the New York Yankees, Steven and David were allowed to visit the dugouts of Yankee Stadium for autographs. This was thanks to the Emerson Hotel, which Herbert owned and which had a tiny share in the Baltimore Orioles. The hotel owned the stake because it generated business from visiting baseball teams.

Marty's taste for the hotel industry differed from that of his brother, however. Marty initially wanted to go to hotel school, but his father forbade him. Herbert hated hotel schools and spoke dismissively of their graduates. At age seventeen, Marty spent a summer working as a bellhop at the Western Hills Hotel in Fort Worth, Texas. What better way to learn the hotel business than by starting at the bottom?

Marty's job led to a dispute with the manager, however. The details are hazy. Steven claims Marty was fooling around with the boss's daughter. What's certain is that the experience turned him away from working in a hotel. By the end of the summer, a journalist asked him what he thought of the experience. "I think I'll become a lawyer," was his response. Marty didn't want to be his father.

Marty then traveled back to New Jersey and lived at his mother, Frances's, house until he was married. Forever after his bellhop experience, Marty dismissed hotels as corrupt places, anathema to a "true" family life. Suburban life—the life of barbecues, Frisbee games, and PTA meetings—was morally superior to urban life. And in the suburbs, Marty wanted to stay.

This resentment of hotel life would have a profound impact on the Gramercy Park Hotel decades later.

Puerto Rico

Just after his wedding in 1963, Marvin got a life-changing letter from the Puerto Rican government. "This was a letter out of the clear blue. So then I called Herb and said, 'Guess what? We got a casino license in Puerto Rico.' It was a legitimate casino license if we built a hotel. Herb knew nothing about building. So he says to Red, 'Why don't you go down to Puerto Rico and build this hotel? You'll own one-third of it.'"

A few phone calls later, the H.R. Weissberg Corporation and Red Strate had entered the gaming industry. For Herbert, Red's participation was to not only help build the place but also to get approval from mafia sources. A casino like this needed to make payoffs to keep employees from getting killed. It's unclear what the level of mafia involvement was. Danny Guma, Frank Guma's son, told me that Joe Socks and the Longshoremen were silent partners. An old man from eBay who sold me some casino dice from the hotel insisted that Meyer Lansky was the silent partner. The FBI, thanks to one of its informants based inside the Teamsters in Puerto Rico, claimed Tampa gangster Santo Trafficante was a major stakeholder. Perhaps they all had a piece.

From the start, Herbert was intimately involved in the new hotel's rapid design process. He insisted to architect Morris Lapidus (who had designed the legendary Fontainebleau Hotel in Miami) that *every* room should have an ocean view. The Russian immigrant, himself a stern man, did not take the demand lightly. But in the end, the hotel rooms all had a seaside vista (the hotel was located on a peninsula).

When it was finished, the Ponce de Leon had 350 rooms on seven oceanfront acres in Condado Beach, directly across from the Caribe Hilton. It had a health club, tennis courts, restaurants, four nightclubs, countless meeting rooms, and five swimming pools. Its ballroom sat 1,500 people. Its garage held 450 cars. Alongside every seating area, Herbert added a scruffy teenager and a row of liquor bottles.

Because Red Strate and Herbert were "friends" of the Teamsters, it was understood that the union would represent their employees. Frank Chavez, the head of the local Teamster chapter and a close Hoffa ally, personally organized the six hundred employees into a union via a card count recognized by Herbert. This was done instead of holding the more typical National Labor Relations Board election. In fact, outside of this instance, I have never heard of an employer anywhere voluntarily recognizing a union without requesting an election. Since the 1947 Taft-Hartley Act, the Supreme Court has ruled that card counts by themselves do not guarantee union representation, as employers may always request a secret election.

Herbert's recognition of the union through a card count quickly caught the government's attention. FBI investigators began to suspect that some of the money to build the hotel had come from the Teamsters but was off the books. By my math, roughly $4 million came from somewhere besides Chase Manhattan Bank. Herbert himself put $1 million of his own money into the project (outside the corporation). Hoffa was most likely providing the rest. The feds also suspected that Red had paid for his share of the Ponce de Leon with the "cut up" $1 million from the Fontainebleau Hotel in New Orleans.

By October 1963, the casino was ready to open, and Herbert flew to San Juan for the occasion. On October 3, 1963, all of Puerto Rico, it seemed, was watching Herbert in anticipation for the opening night of his casino. Steven threw out the first dice to officially commence all the gaming. But immediately, there were problems. Herbert and Strate had varying hotel management philosophies. According to newspaper reports, Strate was telling everyone, including Herbert's employees, what to do. He was also there full time.

Marvin visited a few weeks after the opening. Some of his friends were unable to get rooms at the Ponce, despite having reservations. Marvin angrily confronted Herbert, but he didn't care. For Herbert, the money was flowing and nothing could stop it. The H.R. Weissberg Corporation had just added some shopping centers and a garage complex and was going to build new hotels with the help of Teamster loans. The future was bright, Herbert yapped. He talked about properties in San Francisco and Los Angeles and how he was working on a deal with Holland America to bring mob-backed casinos to its cruise line. What did a few fucked-up hotel reservations matter

This page: Ponce de Leon Hotel in San Juan, Puerto Rico. *Image taken from a hotel brochure.*

in the face of such glistening plans? Herbert explained, pausing only to take a few puffs of his cigar. Marvin was livid.

Days later, President John F. Kennedy was assassinated. Because of this, Herbert's plans soon came to a halt.

War in Puerto Rico

In the 1990s, I asked Herbert if he knew anything about the mafia and the Kennedy assassination. According to mob lawyer Frank Ragano and the FBI, the conspiracy was organized by Herbert's business partners. He was initially reluctant to say anything. Then finally, he said, "They were drunk with power." As if that summed it all up. When I asked who organized the whole thing, his response (after I posed the question many times) was one word: "Marcello."

John F. Kennedy's assassination suddenly put more eyes on Herbert. A 1963 FBI file that was part of the Kennedy assassination investigation linked the Ponce de Leon Hotel to the mobster Santo Trafficante, Jimmy Hoffa, and the president of the Puerto Rican chapter of the Teamsters, Frank Chavez. The information came from "Ace," an informant within the Teamsters' San Juan office. The document also pointed out that Red, Hoffa, and Trafficante all shared the same mob lawyer, Frank Ragano, as if to erase any doubt the men were connected. This file was shared with the leadership of the Puerto Rican government, who were already eager to counter Hoffa's growing influence in Puerto Rico.

If things couldn't get any worse for Herbert, Frank Chavez sent a mocking letter to Bobby Kennedy just after John F. Kennedy was shot. (This was the same Frank Chavez who organized Herbert's employees in the Ponce de Leon.) Chavez wrote that his Puerto Rican Teamsters chapter was going to make sure that Oswald's grave always had fresh flowers. The FBI immediately began investigating. They quickly discovered that Red Strate was signing all the checks and acting like the boss at the Ponce de Leon. To them—and ultimately, many others—the business was a mafia front.

The fact that Red was close with Marcello was a major problem. Hoffa, Trafficante, and Marcello all had good reasons to kill Kennedy, according to Frank Ragano. All three were being prosecuted by the Kennedy administration. Marcello was perhaps the most furious after he was kidnapped and deposited in Guatemala by Bobby Kennedy's minions in 1961 because he lacked the appropriate citizenship papers. (Marcello was born in Tunisia and never became a U.S. citizen.) Bobby Kennedy had always disliked the Teamsters and even mocked their physical traits in his book *The Enemy Within*. To Bobby Kennedy, the national power of the Teamsters union was a huge threat, as it had the ability to cripple shipping in the United States in a strike. Bobby Kennedy took them head-on and also sought to end the mafia's control of gambling and other enterprises.

In 1963, inside his room at the Edgewater Beach Hotel, Hoffa said during a game of gin rummy, "Suppose something happened to the president instead of Booby." (Hoffa called Bobby Kennedy "Booby.")

"I can give you an answer to that," answered Bill Bufalino, one of Hoffa's lawyers. "Lyndon Johnson would get rid of Bobby."

"Damn right he would," Jimmy said. "He hates him as much as I do. Don't forget, I've given a hell of a lot of money to Lyndon in the past." The card game continued, and the lawyers thought nothing of it at the time. Hoffa later asked Ragano to relay a message to his clients Marcello and Trafficante to kill the president as they had planned. Ragano passed along the information (thinking that Hoffa was joking), and he was met with stone-faced looks. The two gangsters weren't surprised and didn't want to speak about it further. After the assassination, Marcello later told Ragano, "When you see Jimmy [Hoffa], you tell him he owes me and he owes me big."

The shared gripes of Marcello, Trafficante, and Hoffa led to Marcello organizing the assassination with the expectation he would be repaid with

The Edgewater Beach Hotel in Chicago.

Teamster loans. As part of the conspiracy, Marcello used Jack Ruby to rub out Oswald, as Ruby was deeply in debt to Marcello. Trafficante also played a role assisting Marcello, but exactly what role he took on is unclear. In the eyes of mob lawyer Frank Ragano, Hoffa's role in the conspiracy was perhaps related to financing the operation.

After John F. Kennedy's assassination, however, Bobby Kennedy seemed surprisingly tame toward those who were behind his brother's murder. At the time, he said to one of his aids, "I knew they would get one of us. I always thought it would be me," a clear reference to the mafia he was battling. Following the change in the presidential administration, federal cases against Marcello and Trafficante faded away. But the "Get-Hoffa Squad" remained resilient, and Hoffa's cases that had already been started continued toward their ends.

In 1964, Hoffa, Red Strate, and a dozen others went on trial for fraud in connection with loans from the Teamsters pension. Governor Muñoz Marín, to whom John F. Kennedy had awarded the Presidential Medal of Freedom, saw this as an opportunity to strike a blow against Hoffa. When the Ponce de Leon's casino license expired in May 1964, the Puerto Rican government refused to renew it.

This meant war. The Teamsters fought back with picket lines in front of other major Puerto Rican hotels and the San Juan docks. Across the United States, Teamsters picketed in front of ships loading merchandise bound for Puerto Rico. Using their workers in the airline industry, the Teamsters announced their plan to shut down all air routes to Puerto Rico. Then Hoffa demanded that both he and Governor Marín take lie detector tests to determine who had "the best interests at heart" of the Ponce de Leon's employees. Clearly, this was a disaster for the island commonwealth. The government forecast that up to $20 million worth of goods would be prevented from reaching the island.

Through his control of the island's labor and transportation routes, Hoffa threatened an embargo. That he was willing to do all this during a federal trial in Chicago demonstrates the importance of the Ponce de Leon to Hoffa. Officially, he had no stake. But clearly, he did. Marvin didn't seem to know whether Hoffa had a stake in the hotel or its casino—and perhaps he didn't want to know.

The solution to the Ponce De Leon's problem, Herbert believed, was for Red to sell him his share of the hotel. Based on Red's contributions to the hotel's construction, this was only $250,000, an amount Herbert could afford. This way, Governor Marín would also lose his argument to withhold the license. Herbert sent word to Chicago (where Red's trial was being held) that he was going to send Red a check for $250,000. No response.

One day in late July 1964, Herbert sat in the bar of the Gramercy Park Hotel. Horace Jr., the son of the late Horace Sr. (who started in the hotel circa 1928), kept Herbert's glass of whiskey full while he sat on a stool in the corner. Herbert motioned for the telephone, which Horace Jr. brought from underneath the bar. Herbert dialed. There was no answer.

An hour passed. Red still didn't answer.

After lunch, Herbert marched to his office. He picked up the phone and dialed the manager of the Ponce de Leon. "Close the hotel." The manager was confused. Herbert replied, "They'll come begging to us. You'll see!" So, the Ponce De Leon Hotel, the largest hotel in Puerto Rico, was suddenly closed and the employees laid off. The guests were told to leave. Reservations were canceled. In short, Herbert created a mess. Overcome by a feeling of self-satisfaction, Herbert relaxed in his chair and waited for the phone call from the government announcing their capitulation.

The next day, Hoffa aborted his plan to continue the strikes and quarantine of Puerto Rico. Officially, he did this due to a promise from Adam Clayton Powell, chairman of the House Labor and Education Committee, that a hearing would be held. The truth was that Hoffa could not win a war given his ongoing legal trouble. Despite all the huffing and puffing, Hoffa suddenly got cold feet. Perhaps he was also worried that the Ponce de Leon's fate would impact his trial. Meanwhile, the government still refused to reissue the license.

Herbert had completely misjudged the Puerto Rican government's reaction. They didn't budge an inch after the hotel's employees lost their jobs, which Herbert thought would matter.

A day later, Herbert was back in the bar of the Gramercy Park Hotel. The phone rang. Horace answered. It was Chase Manhattan Bank. They wanted to know how Herbert was going to pay back the $7 million loan.

"Tell 'em I'm out," Herbert responded, chewing on the end of a cigar.

Horace dutifully followed his boss's orders. "I only answer the phone if they owe *me* money," Herbert joked. The bar was again in good spirits.

Sometime later, Marvin called. That was a call Herbert could not ignore. The two agreed that Marvin would go to Chicago to negotiate with Red. Herbert didn't disclose, however, that he had already gone to his old friend, mobster Frank Costello, to help "sort it all out." Herbert was realistically examining all his options, including having Red Strate rubbed out for a price.

Marvin took a room at the Edgewater. After Red was finished meeting with his lawyers, at ten o'clock in the evening, the two met in a coffee shop. For a moment, the two sat quietly. Then, "I'm not gonna let him get a license," Red said. If Red was going down with the ship, he wanted Herbert to go down with him.

"I hear Herb's been talking to Frank Costello," Strate continued.

"How the fuck did you know that?" Marvin said, his mouth dropping in disbelief.

"That's what I found out," Red said, leaning his stocky shoulder against the booth cushion. Red took deep breaths through his nostrils. "What do you want to do? Cause a mafia war? He's naive. He doesn't know what the hell's going on."

Marvin assured Red he knew nothing. His hands were shaking. By now, hours had passed. "Suppose I get Hilton to buy the Ponce de Leon? Then will you sell?" Marvin asked. (The Ponce de Leon was next door to the Caribe Hilton.)

"OK," Red finally said. At 2:30 a.m., they made a deal. Though he hated Herbert, Red needed a way out for himself, too, and money to stay out of prison.

Marvin returned to New York and found Herbert in the corner of the Gramercy's dining room. Herbert was pale and looked as if he hadn't slept. On his forehead, small liver spots were forming, a sign of his stress and the alcohol he used to treat it. Marvin had some good news, but it wouldn't sound that way to Herbert. He persuaded Herbert to meet with the head of Hilton, who had expressed interest in taking over the Ponce de Leon. Without any other options, the broken Herbert bowed to his younger brother's request.

At the meeting, Hilton offered $13.3 million for the Ponce de Leon, much of which would be used to pay off debt. Like a zombie, Herbert accepted. He knew the deal would have ripple effects for his business, but he had no choice.

A week later, a jury found James R. Hoffa, Zachary A. "Red" Strate, and five others guilty of conspiracy, as well as mail and wire fraud, in their use of the union's pension funds. Red was sentenced to three years in jail and a $5,000 fine. Three of Herbert's hotels, the Palm Beach Biltmore, the Everglades, and the Fontainebleau, were cited by the prosecution as having irregularities in their Teamster loans. Herbert narrowly escaped indictment, however. Others were found guilty for paying kickbacks to Hoffa, something Herbert had done himself. His luck was astonishing.

Yet Hoffa's guilty verdict ended Herbert's chances for more Teamster loans, at least for the time being. Chase Manhattan Bank lost money in the Puerto Rican deal, and along with every other bank, it wasn't going to give Herbert another line of credit. To make matters worse, the overall economy had slowed. In order to raise some cash, Herbert sold off the titles to the Gramercy Park Hotel and the Fontainebleau Hotel in November 1964 but leased them back immediately (keeping control but losing the actual deeds). The Montmartre in Miami and the hotels in Texas were also sold to raise money. Everywhere, there were cuts. As if things couldn't get any worse, eighteen employees at the Fontainebleau went on a wildcat strike after the manager, Vincent Rizzo, told them, "N——s don't need civil rights! They need to go back to Africa!"

At the next board meeting, Marvin was nowhere to be found. The accountant revealed that major taxes were due, and Herbert made a mental note to fire the accountant for his insubordination (but he never got around to it). Nothing could fix the crisis, Herbert reasoned. Business had to pick up by itself. His only plan was to keep costs down using the same skills he had learned in the Depression.

New York Collapses

In Herbert's own version of events, the election of Mayor John Lindsay in 1965 was officially the "beginning of the end" for his business. Mayor Lindsay was strikingly handsome, WASPy, and famous for being the first "limousine liberal." He had bright ideas, but ironically, the city had a blackout just after his election. During the power outage, Herbert, Ruth, and their two children stayed at the Gramercy (their 2 5th Avenue apartment was on the sixteenth floor). For the occasion, management set up candles on the stairways. In the bar, guests took turns singing songs, all accompanied by the piano, while kids played with the candle wax. Inspired by the camaraderie, Herbert opened the kitchen and bar and let people have whatever they wanted for free. Of course, it was all going to spoil anyway.

Just after Lindsay's inauguration, the transit workers went on strike. Twelve days later, Lindsay gave in to their demands. Then other public sector unions, including the teachers, sewer workers, bridge operators, and trash collectors, went on strike.

The trash in New York suddenly became a noticeable problem. Everywhere, people scraped their shoes on curbs to clean off what they had just stepped in. Police cars broke down on the streets. Junkies shot heroin in Tompkins Square Park. While Steven and David stayed up late to watch Mayor Lindsay on *Johnny Carson*, Herbert lay awake worrying about the future.

Herbert's brilliant deals, it turned out, had been for hotels near the end of their lifecycles. Maintenance and heavy mortgages ate up the profits of the corporation, and soon the money began to run out. The H.R. Weissberg Corporation responded by issuing more stock in lieu of the usual dividend, printing up paper like a South American dictatorship. Stockbrokers and analysts called around the clock with questions. One day, Herbert handed Robert the phone in his office.

"You explain it, Bobby," Herbert instructed.

The future professor explained everything as best he could. By the time Robert hung up the phone, he actually felt impressed with himself.

The next day, however, the share price of H.R. Weissberg Corporation dropped 2 points.

By December 1967, Herbert's company had gone from owning fourteen hotels to filing for chapter 11. The Edgewater Beach, where so many wealthy Chicago families leisurely spent their summers, was gutted and torn down. The other buildings were seized by creditors and corporate raiders. Hoffa, Herbert's friend and financier, finally went to jail. Red Strate also went to jail for attempting to bribe Edward Partin, an anti-Hoffa witness, in the Fontainebleau's restaurant (an attempt to spring Hoffa from prison). Even the socialist Norman Thomas, Herbert's loyal tenant, had a stroke and died soon after.

Since Herbert's siblings, in-laws, and even his ex-wife, Frances, were investors, the collapse of his company affected everyone around him. As the stock dropped, people started asking Herbert for their money back. Besides Herbert, Marvin had been the largest shareholder and lost hundreds of thousands of dollars. The two agreed to meet for a cup of coffee in the Gramercy Park Hotel. Marvin explained, "He was down. He was really down. Really a broken person. He looked at me, and I swear, tears were about to come down his eyes. 'Don't tell me I made a lot of mistakes. I know it. You don't have to tell me.' I had never seen it before. I really had not. He was not the person to admit to a mistake." The clock was ticking. Herbert would soon have to give up the Gramercy.

As Herbert's empire crumbled, his son Robert and his new girlfriend, Georgeanne Hume (my mother), paid a visit to the Gramercy Park Hotel. They had explicitly made the trip so they could announce their nuptial plans to Herbert. At King Herbert's throne in the corner of the hotel's dining room, my grandfather was pleasant and got along well with Georgeanne. It seemed Robert had nothing to worry about, including the check.

A few days later, Robert went to the hospital for a hernia operation. When he came out, Georgeanne was gone. Herbert had ordered her to fly back to Wisconsin. He then invited his eldest son for lunch at the hotel.

"You can't marry her, Bobby," Herbert began, unfolding a napkin onto his lap.

"Why not?" Robert asked.

"She's not Jewish."

"But Danny—"

"What?"

"Why do you care about that? I'm going to marry her."

Herbert then called over the Gramercy's busboy to ask his opinion. Despite the busboy's convincing argument, Robert would not yield.

"Bobby, I'll take away your inheritance."

Robert ignored his father and returned to his future wife in Madison, Wisconsin, where he was studying political science at the university. Soon after he married Georgeanne in a courtroom, Robert received an official notice from Herbert's lawyer. He was disowned for the second time. (The first time had been over another girl.)

Marty

In 1967, Herbert's second-oldest son, Marty, was now the physically largest person in the family, with sideburns, fuzzy hair, thick glasses, and one eye that was bigger than the other. Marty was also funny and knew how to make a woman laugh. But his wit made him many enemies, especially when he felt a challenge to his dominant persona. Though he had spent the least amount of time in New York, Marty sounded the most like an aggressive New York Jewish man. In 1967, Marty returned home from college and, having no place to go, moved in with the family of his middle school girlfriend, Laura Wexler. Within a short period, Marty decided to marry Laura.

Though Laura was Jewish, Herbert didn't approve of her either. Herbert thought she was *too* Jewish. He called her "JAPy." The day before the wedding, in the Gramercy's elevator, Herbert turned to his son and said, "I'll give you fifty grand if you don't marry her tomorrow." No doubt, Herbert had just seen the television show *Let's Make a Deal*, a hit on NBC. "Fifty grand if you cancel it right now," Herbert repeated, loud enough so the other three people in the elevator could hear.

"Dad, are you serious?" Marty asked.

Herbert increased his offer. "Take the money and the trip you planned to Italy—only without Laura. You'll meet someone and have a good time. And there'll be fifty grand to help ya," he said, and he added a smile to help sell his offer.

How Herbert had that much money in his darkest financial days remains a mystery.

Marty called Herbert an asshole and many other words. The next day, Marty married Laura. The chip on his shoulder would never heal. Eventually, it would impact life at the Gramercy.

By 1968, Herbert had lost half his sons. He was then forced to sell the Gramercy in a bankruptcy proceeding and was finally out. Left with a bunch of worthless stock, Herbert's cousins and aunts on Rose's side were angry. One cousin called up Max and Rose and said, "You owe us the money." Years later, Herbert's accountant, Charles Augsburger, would be held *personally* liable for inaccurate tax filings related to the Lord Baltimore and the Paramount Hotel. The assessment found he owed $210,092 in fines and back taxes.

Herbert's life as a hotelman appeared to be over.

5

INTERREGNUM

1968–1975

Not since King Croesus lost the Lydian Empire had a ruler taken a harder fall than King Herbert. Who would think that building the largest hotel and casino in Puerto Rico would set in motion a chain of events that would lead to the loss of the Gramercy? Like the great Alcibiades, he had done everything right but failed because of the jealousy of others, namely the Federal Bureau of Investigation. When it came down to it, Herbert was the victim of forces larger than himself. The Kennedy assassination. The Hoffa investigation. The downward trend in the hotel business. All had conspired against him.

In 1969, Herbert was a bitter and short-tempered man. Much of Herbert's days were spent seething at the bankers and bureaucrats who had betrayed him. What friends did he have who could loan him a dime? They had either disappeared or been put behind bars. Herbert felt like a country deep in the throes of a losing war. Surrender came as a last resort. But it came nonetheless. For him, retirement meant humiliation.

Herbert's financial collapse meant he could no longer afford his 2 5th Avenue apartment, so he moved to Lawrence, Long Island, where he found a pleasant house with space for himself, Ruth, and his two younger sons, Steven and David. Far away from the concrete playground of Manhattan that had always been his home, Herbert planted a garden filled with rose bushes and tomatoes. Like an ordinary person, he bought groceries. He waited in line. When he walked down the street, no one shuffled into their places or stood at attention. And when he arrived home, Pinky was not there to carry his things.

Slowly, Herbert began to lose his dream of Gramercy Park. Now that Herbert was no longer an important hotel man, his younger children, fifteen-year-old Steven and thirteen-year-old David, were under his care. In the past, he had pawned off his fatherhood responsibilities to the hotel staff. But no more. To make matters worse, Steven was an aspiring guitarist, and David dabbled in the drums. When their playing got loud, Herbert often found himself promising things in exchange for peace and quiet. Soon he was paying them to stop playing.

One of the items in Herbert's possession was a small stamp collection, which had fallen into his hands after a guest at the Gramercy didn't pay his bill. In such scenarios, the guest's luggage was confiscated and often never reclaimed. (Our household microwave came from an unpaid bill.) After many years, Herbert took the stamps to a dealer and discovered they were worth something. A lightbulb went off. At that time, stamps were popular among a select crowd of individuals. Jewish people in New York especially would often buy stamps and say things like, "If I have to flee the country in a hurry, I can always grab these stamps and live comfortably." While the goyim built bunkers, Jewish people relied on rotting pieces of paper.

Soon Herbert found a reliable way to make money. His secret was to acquire large collections that happened to contain some Japanese art stamps, which many Americans didn't realize were valuable in certain markets. Herbert's stamp trading allowed him to flex his deal-making muscles on a regular basis. Within a year or so of visiting trade shows and studying stamp magazines, he had made himself wealthy again. After a few years, Herbert became one of the largest stamp collectors in the world, specializing in Japanese art stamps.

Herbert's Children

By late 1969, the bar mitzvah of Herbert's youngest son, David, was approaching. For Herbert, who had once lorded over dense ballrooms and sent teams of waiters in motion with a flick of the wrist, the upcoming event was somewhat terrifying. What would the family pictures look like with his elder sons missing? What would the other relatives say? Having failed in business, he did not now wish to fail with his family. Eventually, it dawned on him that he needed to cultivate relationships with his elder children.

Right: Robert and Georgeanne in 1968.

Below: *From left to right*: Marty, Steven, Herbert, Ruth, David, and Robert in 1968.

It had been eighteen months since Herbert had cut off his oldest son, Robert. So he picked up the phone and called. "All is forgiven. Let me buy you a car," he said. Robert agreed and was officially back in the family. Herbert sold a small part of his collection to pay for a Chevrolet Impala.

While Robert had been disowned and cut off from the family funds, he coauthored a book that was to be published by McGraw-Hill. It was probably the first book ever written by a Weissberg, and Herbert was delighted. He also attributed it entirely to his influence; in his typical showy way, he spent the next few months telling people, "I wrote a book."

Marty would cost more than his easygoing older brother, however. After marrying Laura and refusing Herbert's offer of $50,000, Marty seldom spoke to his father.

Laura described Marty at this time: "He loved to paint. He fashioned himself a painter. An artist. He would paint portraits, scenes. He was more of a traditionalist. He never really developed his own style. He was very talented, actually. He had a very successful [advertising] business, started in 1968."

Of those I have seen, Marty's paintings were drab-colored cityscapes, fruit scenes, and the occasional abstract, artfully painted inkblot.

Laura later described their life in suburban New Jersey as newlyweds: "I was standing out in front of the house, and my neighbor from across the street came over. And this is all a new community, you know, new housing, real suburbs. 'What's your name?' she said. 'Oh, are you related to Herbert Weissberg?' I said, 'He's my father-in-law.' 'I hate that son of a bitch. That son of a bitch he sold me down the river! He cost us a fortune.'"

In other words, Marty and Laura's new neighbors had been investors in the H.R. Weissberg Corporation. Even when Marty tried to get away from his father, his shadow remained.

Marty soon started his own advertising business called Weissberg Associates, which was run by Marty and his partner Robert Weissberg. (This Robert Weissberg wasn't related to the family but coincidentally had the same name.) Perhaps to make up for disowning Marty, Herbert made a $50,000 investment in his business, the same amount he had planned to give Marty to leave Laura.

For the time being, this improved their relationship. Marty attended David's bar mitzvah, and peace reigned.

Two years later, Marty and his partner got into a dispute. Marty needed out. So Herbert "bailed him out," as Herbert himself put it with a grin and shrug of the shoulders. There were no more bar mitzvahs that Herbert needed Marty to attend. For the next few years, Herbert enjoyed hanging this bailout over Marty's head.

From then on, their relationship seldom showed signs of improvement. Later, Herbert hired Marty's advertising firm, though he openly complained that Marty was overcharging him.

With his familial relationships in order, Herbert felt it was fair to reward himself with a six-month cruise around the world. Thirteen-year-old David was sent to live with Herbert's elder sister, Gurdie, in Canarsie, Brooklyn. Fifteen-year-old Steven was left at the Lawrence house in the care of the maid and her boyfriend, Herbert's chauffeur.

Herbert and Ruth then traveled the world. Their trip ended in England, where Robert had gotten a prestigious one-year fellowship at the University of Essex in Colchester. Together, they went to pubs, bought tweed outfits, and walked the grounds of the university.

Back home, however, Steven was growing anxious. He wanted to become a famous guitar player in Hollywood. So he convinced the maid's boyfriend, a heroin addict, to take Herbert's Cadillac and drive west.

Initially, the pair lived off Steven's bar mitzvah money. But when that money ran out, they had to sell their instruments. One by one, Steven's collection got smaller. Eventually, the trip ended in the Grand Canyon, where they were almost broke. There, Steven and the maid's boyfriend were arrested for selling marijuana to an undercover park ranger. By the time Herbert returned to America, he had to fly to Tucson, Arizona, to bail out Steven. In the end, Steven (then still a minor) got off. But the maid's boyfriend did hard time.

David (*left*) and Steven (*right*) Weissberg.

While all of this was happening, David was living with his aunt Gurdie (Herbert's older sister) in Canarsie, Brooklyn. Gurdie, who was then in her late sixties, remembered, "He had terrible friends. They came to visit me, and I was shocked. I don't know how they got the address. He used to go begging for money, you know."

Every day, David skipped school and took the train into Manhattan. There, he would panhandle on St. Marks Place in the East Village until he had enough money to score. At age thirteen, David tried heroin for the first time in Tompkins Square Park. He quickly became an addict.

It was obvious to Herbert that a tremendous price had been paid for his six-month cruise. But still, he did not feel he was the person to fix the problem. So he sent his children to Robert and Georgeanne, who were now based in Ithaca, New York. (Following the England fellowship, Robert landed a job in the Government Department at Cornell.)

Robert described the situation: "Herbert thought the country had miraculous cures. It's the Catskills mentality. Ship people to the country. I think my father honestly assumed that cows were walking down the street in Ithaca. People with overalls and straw hats. He had no idea that Ithaca is, in many cases, a miniature of the big city."

In Ithaca, Steven didn't appreciate having Robert, who was just fourteen years older than him, for a parent. Soon he found the same type of friends he had back in Lawrence. In his free time, he played Led Zeppelin on his guitar. Other times, he made clay sculptures and painted pictures. David eventually joined him.

In Ithaca, the two brothers went hiking through the gorges and played guitars on Eddie Street. Taking drugs was a favorite pastime of theirs. Robert and Georgeanne didn't come home until evening most days, and Steven and David were free after school until dinner. Though they were not David's parents, Robert and Georgeanne started to feel there was something seriously wrong with him. He was smart but very distant, like a young Rasputin.

Robert remembered:

> *One day, I walk back—and they must have heard or seen me coming—and suddenly, the window, it was a second-floor window, opened and suddenly a huge cloud of blue smoke blew out. I heard all this noise in there, "He's coming! Quick, get that outta here."*
>
> *Then we took David down to a school, the Canyon School, a private school for basically rich kids with problems to keep them out of jail. David then moved into that house. When we took David to the special school, all the kids were in their pajamas, and they all looked like they were stoned. They probably were on medication.*

All Herbert wanted to do was write a check. But this was one problem money couldn't solve.

Herbert Almost Retakes the Ponce De Leon

In 1971, the Ponce de Leon Hotel, now renamed the San Geronimo Hilton, was up for sale. The Hilton complex in San Juan was enormous and wasn't selling enough rooms, so Hilton planned to close it. In the auction, Herbert bid $7 million against Chase Bank's $6.8 million and won. The deal required $1.5 million up front, with the rest to be paid in installments.

Despite his impressive stamp collection, Herbert didn't have enough money. But an offer this good, he thought, would have no trouble finding investors. So he phoned one of his old New York acquaintances, Abe Wolfe, a short Jewish businessman with hairy nostrils, who promised him $1 million. As for the rest, Herbert managed to secure commitments. For a moment, it seemed like Herbert was going to quickly bounce back to his summit.

In November 1971, the *Wall Street Journal* printed an article announcing Herbert's plans to "protect [his] original investment" and to give the hotel yet another rebranding as the "*Gramercy* San Juan," a telling indication of where Herbert's sentiments lay.

But then Abe Wolfe got cold feet at the last minute and backed out. The result was that Herbert lost the deposit. It was practically all the money he had: $1 million. Once again, he was nearly broke. For weeks, he went into a deep depression.

The Sam Peck Hotel

In 1973, Herbert got a phone call from a woman in Little Rock, Arkansas. Many years prior, she had stayed in the Gramercy Park Hotel and remembered it fondly. Now that she was a widow, she needed someone to take over her deceased husband's hotel, the Sam Peck. Herbert paid a visit.

Located in Little Rock, the Sam Peck Hotel was a modest-sized Art Deco hotel with an ivory façade and blue cloth awnings over its windows. Perhaps it was better suited for Miami Beach than Arkansas, but its unique design put eyes on it. And it was in an ideal location on Capitol Avenue, within walking distance of the state capitol.

Herbert liked the terms and quickly made an agreement. All he needed to do, more or less, was continue making the payments. As part of the deal with Herbert, Peck's widow remained in the hotel for free. Other than modest renovations, Herbert's big improvement was that he allowed women to wear pants in the dining room. Other than that, he left things more or less how they had been.

Though only around 240,000 people lived in Little Rock at the time, it was the largest city in Arkansas and the center of the state's political life. Consequently, the hotel relied heavily on business generated by the state and city governments. To keep the money flowing, Herbert made sure he kicked part of the hotel's business back to the politicians who authorized the contracts. Also, he created a back room reserved for only politicians, where they could have lunch for free. Perhaps unsurprisingly, Herbert's new club became the prime location to brag about local corruption. To be clear, Herbert had no interest in government policy. He merely wanted to ensure that business continued to flow to the hotel.

Robert later explained, "Herbert always said he never hired the politicians in Arkansas. He inherited them. When you bought an estate in Russia, it came with serfs. When you bought a hotel in Arkansas, it came with politicians."

Herbert saw the corruption up close, according to Robert: "Herbert had gone there and actually encountered the police chief convention. And they had naked women, hookers, all over the place. What struck my father was that they were doing this in front of the employees. He attributed this to power. Later on, this became very influential in his analysis with the

A postcard from the Sam Peck Hotel, circa 1975.

Clintons. Nobody can touch you. My father always said if you've ever been in Arkansas, you realize that it's a feudal country."

Herbert quickly put Senator William Fulbright and Congressman Wilbur Mills "on the payroll." Other politicians were granted unlimited free food and drink at the hotel, which they were not shy about consuming. During Herbert's visits, he and Fulbright drank heavily in the bar. Once, Herbert encouraged Fulbright to call his son Robert, the political science professor.

Herbert explained to Robert through the phone, "Hey, Bobby! I'm here with Billy Fulbright. Why don't you two talk politics?" Robert could hear a loud bar in the background. Moments later, Senator Fulbright came on the phone. But according to Robert, he was too drunk to speak intelligibly.

In early 1979, Bill Clinton became the governor of Arkansas. Not long after the election, Clinton made Herbert one of his "Arkansas Travelers," a title awarded to outsiders who helped Clinton gain office—that is, those who gave him money. Twenty years later, Hillary Clinton added her name to the document over lunch at the dining room of the Gramercy Park Hotel. Despite his affections, Herbert maintained that Arkansas was the most corrupt place he had ever done business. What he observed in Arkansas could easily fill another book, and we all know what it would include.

Hoffa Gets Out of Jail

Hoffa's release from jail sparked another opportunity for Herbert.

Hoffa, along with Herbert's former business partner Zachary A. "Red" Strate Jr., had gone to prison in 1967 for jury tampering and wire fraud. The prison term for Hoffa was set at thirteen years. Strate eventually served a little over a year from 1971 to 1972 for his role in the Teamsters loan scandal and witness tampering. In December 1971, Hoffa got out after paying a $750,000 bribe to the Nixon administration, according to Hoffa's lawyer Frank Ragano.

As a condition of Hoffa's release, however, he was not allowed to serve as president of the Teamsters union until 1980. This part of the deal was disclosed to Hoffa only after he was released, which made him furious. His lawyers were figuring out a way for him to return, however, and he had tremendous support within the rank-and-file members of the Teamsters.

Hoffa and Herbert were soon reunited. In 1973, Herbert began spending part of his year at Seacoast Towers in Miami Beach, where his parents also owned an apartment. For a while, Steven lived in Miami with Rose Weissberg and attended the University of Miami along with David. Hoffa's Florida home was around the corner from Steven's apartment, and Herbert often met up with his old friend to discuss business around the pool. Many of Hoffa's cronies joined them. But when lunchtime came, Herbert would crow, "Steven, go take Jimmy to eat some grass."

Then the group would separate. Herbert and Hoffa's cronies would go eat regular food while Hoffa and Steven consumed health-conscious things like wheatgrass drinks and salads. Hoffa was still in great shape with prison muscles. He began his day with pushups and pullups, drank only tea and water, and never dropped his routine, not even for a day. At one point, Hoffa advised Steven, "Steve, get plenty of rest. Sleep. Don't stay up late. Don't drink. Don't smoke. Eat right. Exercise every day. Make sure you eat right. Always be in good shape. You never know when you're going to have to take a beating." Steven kept quiet, but the last line stayed with him.

HERBERT MAKES A DEAL IN DETROIT, INCLUDES JIMMY HOFFA

In July 1975, Herbert got a phone call from Detroit. The Sheraton-Cadillac Hotel, the largest hotel in Detroit, was up for sale. Initially, Herbert wasn't interested. But the seller was absolutely desperate. So he boarded a plane to see the old hotel for himself.

The Sheraton-Cadillac, originally the Book-Cadillac Hotel, was built in 1924. At the time it was built, the thirty-three-story hotel was the tallest in the world. With over 750 rooms, its façade resembled that of the Plaza Hotel in New York City: Corinthian columns, ash-colored plaster, copper balconies, and a moss-colored shingle roof. On the balustrade were life-size figures from Michigan's history, including French explorer Antoine Laumet de La Mothe, sieur de Cadillac, the founder of Detroit. Its public rooms included an ornate tearoom, a Venetian dining room, and a grand ballroom, which, year after year, hosted the high-society balls of the Motor City. Often, the hotel's second-floor showroom held the unveiling of Detroit's new car designs, and the room was equipped with a special freight elevator to bring in the vehicles.

By 1975, however, the hotel had fallen on hard times and was mostly empty. Local vagrants had taken over the lobby. Robert explained, "Sheraton hired a bunch of rent-a-cops. Irish guys in their seventies, frail, and for $4.20 [an

A postcard from the Cadillac Hotel in Detroit, circa 1925.

hour], they would sit and would not defend the hotel from these guys coming into the hotel and robbing the guests. The hotel was completely defenseless."

Surrounding the hotel was a city that was in worse shape than New York. The decline in the auto industry had led to skyrocketing unemployment in the Motor City. With unemployment came increased crime and, ultimately, white flight to the suburbs. Without economic support, those who remained in the city became divided along racial lines. The problem came to a head in 1967, when police raided an unlicensed bar, the Blind Pig, kickstarting a five-day riot that destroyed more than two thousand buildings and killed forty-three people. After this, many residents gave up on the city and left for the suburbs.

The closure of the Sheraton-Cadillac not only endangered the city's convention business, but Sheraton's owner, the massive conglomerate ITT, was worried it could also threaten its many defense contracts with the federal government. Sheraton was also contracted to house all Michigan-based army recruits at the Cadillac before they were shipped off to basic training. If Sheraton closed the hotel and wrote it off as a loss, this would mean ITT was *giving up* on Detroit. The political fallout could be immense. So everything was done to keep the hotel open, despite its failing nature.

Herbert sensed an opportunity. Beaming with chutzpah, he asked Sheraton to hand him the lease, along with $900,000 to make the first year's payments. The idea that the hotel would *pay him* to take the lease instead of closing it and collecting a tax write-off was absurd. Perhaps never before in the history of hotels had something like this been proposed. But somehow, Herbert got Sheraton to agree.

In disbelief, the newspapers announced the deal, noting how unusual it was that neither Sheraton nor Herbert divulged the purchase price. The *Detroit Free Press* asked Herbert what his plans for the hotel were. Sharply dressed in black, wearing trendy, tinted glasses, he replied, "I want to liven the place up. I want to pep up the help and the services. Open the place up. Bring some life back downtown. I want to bring back music and entertainment." In other words, Herbert had zero plans.

Following the purchase, Herbert decided to move into the hotel and run it himself. Steven and David soon joined him. For his resident manager, Herbert kept a holdover from the Sheraton, James Tuttle. Tuttle was polite, said "yes" to everything Herbert asked, and knew how to work with a small budget. To the staff, he was like a drill sergeant. Tuttle also liked to brag every time he caught an employee stealing, which endeared himself to Herbert.

As for Herbert's recent business failures, he managed to brush them off in an interview. "I'm a compulsive person once I get into something. But about two years ago, I finally was having a health problem, and after a thorough checkup, my doctor told me the best cure would be to take a few hotels off my back," he said, adding a smile to help sell the lie. "This is a challenge. A great challenge," he continued, getting back to the subject of the hotel. Then he shot out, "Look, I'm crazy."

Though his story didn't add up, the whole city seemed to be cheering him on. Everyone wanted the hotel to succeed.

Herbert's first act was to change the name to the Detroit-Cadillac Hotel. He then tasked Steven and David with inspecting the rooms, inventorying the furniture, and bringing the rooms up to speed. Cleverly, Herbert acquired the chandeliers from the closing Heritage Hotel. But of course, Herbert was more concerned with the security than the decorations.

"Herbert hired five sociopaths," Robert explained. "He gave them a deal they couldn't refuse. They had to wear suits and ties. As long as they stayed in the hotel, they could eat and drink for free. And they got a chance to harass the waitresses. They would be looking for these 'characters' [street people who wandered into the hotel]. They would beat them up, take them down in the basement. And if you listened real carefully, you could hear the moans and the groans from the basement."

Word quickly spread among the local vagrants that the Cadillac was off-limits.

Steven and David were mostly bored with their new positions—there wasn't much business in the hotel. But they encountered some of the visiting rock bands that came to the hotel, including Aerosmith and Kiss. When the New York Dolls visited, Steven and David stayed up until 4:30 a.m. (when the group returned from their gig) to eat breakfast with David Johansen and the band. David also met Leslie West from Mountain during his stay at the Cadillac, and the two got high together.

Every week, Steven and David visited the Pontchartrain Hotel's Sunday jazz brunches. That hotel was connected to the convention center and mall that faced the Detroit River. There, David met Debbie Levine, his first serious girlfriend. Debbie had short black hair, pale skin, dark eyebrows, and "generally Russian Jewish features," according to Steven. She carried an expensive pocketbook and wore fancy heels. She had spent her youth as a champion horse rider, which her father, a successful lawyer in the Southfield suburb of Detroit, no doubt paid for in the hopes she would avoid people like David. Within weeks of meeting him, however, she moved into the brothers' four-bedroom Cadillac apartment, bringing her riding trophies and blue and gold ribbons along with her. As time went on, David left his room less and less. He and Debbie lived off the drugs and room service delivered to their door.

Because the Teamsters held mortgages on several properties in downtown Detroit, they were a key part of all negotiations over the city's future. Herbert felt the only salvation for the Cadillac and Detroit itself was to get a gaming license. As part of his scheme, Herbert easily convinced Hoffa to become a silent business partner. Using Teamster money, Herbert explained, he could renovate the hotel into a first-class destination, with showgirls and fine dining. The employees would be unionized by the Teamsters, of course.

Mayor Coleman Young also supported the idea of bringing a casino to Detroit. Perhaps Herbert offered him something, too. In any case, only two weeks after taking over the hotel *for free*, Herbert was once again on top of the world. Finally, he was going to get his casino with the government as a partner.

On July 29, Herbert, Steven, David, Jimmy Hoffa, and Mayor Young met in Herbert's dining room inside the hotel's presidential suite. They ate sandwiches and discussed the plan for the casino in detail. Who would need to be paid off. Who would need to be made quiet. How it would help the city.

The short, thickset Hoffa projected confidence. Coleman Young mostly nodded in agreement, calling out various committees and local boards that would need to be thrown a bone. Herbert kept pushing the food, as if it was a metaphor for how much everyone was going to make in the deal.

During the meeting, Hoffa got on the topic of how he was going to retake the Teamsters. He cursed Frank Fitzsimmons, the current Teamster president, for betraying him. Herbert offered to throw Hoffa a party at the Cadillac to celebrate the day he became Teamsters president again, which delighted him. From Herbert's perspective, now that John and Bobby Kennedy were both dead, nothing could stop his friend Jimmy. For his business, that meant a river of money and influence.

The next day, July 30, 1975, Jimmy Hoffa waited at the Machus Red Fox restaurant in Bloomfield Hills, Michigan, for a meeting that never happened. After an hour of waiting, a car pulled up, driven by his adopted son, Chuckie. Hoffa got inside. He was never seen again.

Days later, the FBI interviewed Herbert, Steven, and David. They had little to say. Herbert was devastated. Hoffa had been one of his few friends—one of the few who understood his way of doing things.

After that, Herbert lost his optimism for the Detroit Cadillac. Without Hoffa's support, the casino could never happen. The idea immediately became bogged down by local community organizations, and without the Teamsters and Hoffa, there were no golden carrots to be handed out. Soon, Herbert was looking elsewhere—to Gramercy Park. He gave up living at the Cadillac Hotel within a few months of taking over, choosing instead to run the property via his pajama management method while the money slowly ran out. When the $900,000 for the lease payments was finally gone in September 1976, he handed the key back to Sheraton.

In the 1990s, I sat at the corner table of the Gramercy Park Hotel with Herbert and Ruth wanting to know who killed Jimmy Hoffa. At first, Herbert ignored my question. I (age thirteen) repeated it—again and again. He said it didn't matter. Clearly, it was a touchy subject. But I would not go quiet until he answered. Finally, after waiting for the waiters to disappear, he told me: "Tony Pro." I had no idea who that was. Some years later, I looked into it, and his answer sounded correct. Of course, Tony Pro was only the person who ordered the hit, not the person who carried out the job.

The Hotel Interregnum

In the years that followed Herbert's departure, New York fell into a state of further decline. Generally speaking, the Gramercy Park Hotel's business was bad after 1968. As crime reached epic proportions, New York City became a less-popular tourist destination and white flight accelerated. By 1972, the annual murder rate hit two thousand, a shocking figure. The streets, like the subways, were now covered in colorful graffiti. Hot dog vendors carried loaded .22s in their aprons. The unhoused were so numerous, they had their own political representatives. Budget deficits were soaring. And even though the Twin Towers opened for business in 1973, it felt like the city was sinking into the ground.

Despite these disastrous headlines, over at the Gramercy Park Hotel, things weren't *so* bad. In October 1972, a group called the Association for a Better New York dined on baked salmon as they listened to real estate heir Lewis

Rudin explain that New York "is 105 percent better than what you have read." The negativity wasn't a result of crime, the businessman explained; rather, it was the result of an "inferiority complex" held by New Yorkers that causes them to complain. "All that talk of a business exodus from New York was just a lot of wishful thinking by other cities and our neighbors in the suburbs," Rudin said proudly. To prove he was a man of the people and not just a rich, out-of-touch developer, the Cadillac-driving Rudin took out a thirty-five-cent subway token and held it high for the audience to see. They were unimpressed. But the food was good.

The speaker got one thing right: instead of feeling proud, New Yorkers now complained about *everything*. About the subways. About the smell. And especially about New York's political leadership. The Lindsay administration had failed New York, causing the city's debt to skyrocket. By the end of his term, default seemed inevitable. Alas, the "living problem" had overwhelmed city residents. For many, living in the suburbs and commuting seemed like the only way to live quietly and enjoy city life.

In November 1973, Abe Beame, the former comptroller, was elected mayor in a split contest with 34 percent of the vote. The first fully Jewish mayor in New York, Beame was five feet, two inches tall with dopey glasses and appeared to be the opposite of the six-foot-four-inch-tall Lindsay, who oozed charm and sophistication.

Beame's timing was not great either. Once the banks stopped lending money in 1974, it finally seemed like New York's financial house of cards would collapse. Beame's only hope was a federal bailout. So he went to Washington and begged for money. Like a father trying to teach his son a lesson, Gerald Ford responded with a public speech suggesting that a default might actually benefit the city. The next day, the *New York Daily News* printed the headline "Ford to City: Drop Dead." Just as New York was about to go bankrupt, however, Ford had a change of heart. New York was too important to flush down the drain. With the stroke of a pen, the city was saved with a new round of federal financing.

Responding to the budget shortfalls, Beame slashed the city's workforce by sixty-five thousand, an astounding number. Among those he threatened was the teachers' union, which held its strategy sessions inside the Gramercy Park Hotel. Al Shanker, president of the teachers' union, authorized a crippling strike from his luxurious conference room at the Gramercy. Five days of labor turmoil followed. Finally, the mayor and labor leader met in the hotel. Bonding over a round of shrimp cocktails, they eked out a deal. By dessert, Shanker had agreed that the union would purchase $150 million in city bonds in exchange for the city's terms. New York was once again saved. If the food had been bad, who knows what would have happened. In any case, for the next few decades, the Gramercy became the bargaining headquarters of the United Federation of Teachers.

More crises followed. When a lunatic lit fires to several phone routing hubs in Manhattan, phone service was cut off for the entire East Side, including the hotel. The telex machine, the 1970s version of the internet, failed completely, causing reservations to plummet. But the guests at the Gramercy Park Hotel still had room-to-room service (and room service), thanks to an old hand crank behind the front desk that generated electricity. Once in a while, it paid to be behind the times.

Famous Musicians During the In-Between Years

During the interregnum, there were several visits from famous musicians. Once, I asked Pinky if the rock band The Doors (my favorite group) had stayed in the hotel. I had reason to believe this had occurred in 1968. Smelling of gin, Pinky said to me, "Oh yeah. They came here and they drank up a storm, and in da middle a da night, da manager calls up and says some fan got a key and we gotta change da locks. So in da middle a da night dey came and changed all da locks. I was dere. Dey all stayed here."

It's possible Pinky got confused and told a story involving "doors" that happened to another rock band. I really don't know. The Doors keyboardist Ray Manzarek returned to the hotel to drop acid not long after Morrison's death, however, so there was at least some connection to the hotel.

Also in 1968, Broadway playwright and author of *The Life*, Ira Gasman, moved in temporarily. He finally checked out in 2018, when he passed.

Along with the "Glamercy" moniker, the hotel was often called the "Gram Parsons Hotel," thanks to The Byrds' bandleader's frequent visits. During one visit to the hotel, The Byrds found inspiration for their song "Gunga Din," which was later used in the 1969 film *Easy Rider*. It came to them when the band visited the dining room. Band member John York remembered, "I wanted to take my mother to dinner, but they wouldn't let us in the dining room. In those days, it was real silverware and cloth napkins and very snooty. They sure liked our money, but they didn't like the boots and leather jacket I was wearing at the time. Normally, I would have let it roll off my back, but because my mom was there, I really went off and started screaming at the maître d'."

John York offered to take his jacket off, but the dining room didn't allow men in without a jacket. How much had changed since Herbert was in charge. But the experience led to song lyrics for the band.

In January 1970, Paul McCartney came to the Gramercy with his new wife, Linda. The couple checked in as "Mr. and Mrs. Paul Martin" and sent the hotel's bill to McCartney's father-in-law's law firm, Eastman & Eastman. At this time, rumors of McCartney's death were at a fever pitch, just as *Abbey Road* reached number 1 in the charts. Two weeks earlier, McCartney had just finished recording his final tracks for The Beatles on the *Let It Be* album, and he was about to announce his departure from the band. A lot must have been on his mind during his stay.

No doubt, Paul McCartney chose the hotel because of its famous high-level discretion. But an employee in the hotel leaked the visit to the press—something Herbert would have frowned on. For many, however, McCartney's stay at the Gramercy provided proof that he was alive and allowed them to breathe a sigh of relief. During his stay, McCartney also hung out in the bar and mingled with guests, just like John Lennon would almost a decade later.

In 1973, David Bowie came in February and November, hosting legendary champagne and lobster parties in the Wedgewood Room that were attended by David Johansen, Cyrinda Foxe, and Wayne County. As I've mentioned before, Bowie and his crew turned the hotel into a dormitory. Never using the elevators because of his claustrophobia, Bowie took the stairs between floors. In room 612, he tried on a fan-created kimono lined with press-studs for easy removal. In room 305, he slept with a who's who list of women, and he stuck his wife, Angie, in room 602. In what's now called the "Park Room," facing Gramercy Park on the second floor, he spoke fondly of Japan to the Japanese media during a press conference (he was about to head to Japan). There, Bowie made a subtle dig at Mick Jagger, who wasn't allowed into Japan because of a drug bust.

Between Bowie's two visits, Kris Kristofferson moved into the hotel in 1973, and there, he wrote several songs, including "I've Got to Have You." During his time at the hotel, he also had a steamy affair with the legendary singer and songwriter Carole King. Kristofferson introduced King to Bob Dylan and others, and the songs "Anticipation" and "Three Days" came out of this brief relationship. Though things burned hot at the Gramercy, the couple's touring schedule soon caused their relationship to dissipate.

As for the hotel's owners at this time, the first after Herbert was Wellington Associates, an insurance company. Then real estate operators

Sol Goldman and Alex DiLorenzo bought the hotel through their company, Avon Associates, and leased it to Mrs. Kranson (her first name is unknown), also known as the Tip Tree Corporation. Kranson's major renovation was painting the lobby a hideous dandelion color, which matched the color of her Porsche that she parked outside. The hotel key tags were also made the same shade of yellow, accented with a scarlet-colored font. Later, when the hotel failed to generate a profit, the Tip Tree Corporation attempted to convert the building into condos (that also failed). Finally, after several years, the hotel's ownership reverted back to Sol Goldman. In 1975, Goldman needed an operator to lease the operation, so his company made a list of its former owners. At the top of that list was Herbert R. Weissberg.

Herbert Retakes the Gramercy

As Herbert himself explained it, he went for lunch in the Gramercy Park Hotel's dining room. By the time the bill came, he had determined the only way he could afford the meal was if he owned the place.

Sol Goldman's offer was generous: $300,000 a year for a twenty-two-year triple net lease, which meant Herbert would need to assume all liabilities for the hotel (including taxes, insurance, and maintenance). The first year's lease was free, but by taking over, Herbert was immediately liable for the taxes and other costs. Herbert was intrigued but didn't have the money for the investment. It was also risky. If he failed to make a profit and the hotel could not afford its taxes, he could go into personal debt. Plus, there was the hotel's crippling maintenance to think about. It all came down to whether he thought New York was going to improve or not. In 1975, Gramercy Park was encircled by low-class bars and methadone clinics. Every evening, working girls lined up on nearby Park Avenue, and the junkies lined up on 3rd Avenue. If that wasn't enough, a large section of the West Side Highway collapsed just after Mayor Abe Beame was elected to office. Everywhere, there were signs that things were not going to work out.

Herbert's deal was a risky bet on New York City's future. If New York failed, he would fail, too. As a sweetener, Goldman provided a $400,000 loan to Herbert under the stipulation that it be used solely for the hotel's upkeep.

Herbert thumbed through his contact list to find a partner, and he hoped a name would pop out at him. The first was his brother Marvin, who immediately refused the offer. Next, Herbert called a bunch of "good friends," all of whom said no. Finally, he called his former decorator Robert

Bennot, who was now living with his lover and business partner, Philip Jamre, in their six-room hotel in the Virgin Islands. Their conversation began bitterly. Herbert smoothed things over by reminiscing about all the wonderful decorating and design work the two had done. Though New York was in shambles, Bennot's mouth watered at the deal's terms, as Herbert explained it. Robert Bennot would be the general manager, Philip Jamre the resident manager. Best of all, Herbert added, they were going to be partners, to the tune of 50 percent apiece. Then, as quickly as possible, Herbert glossed over the details of the triple net "all yours" lease. Oddly enough, Herbert, at this time, was operating as a DBA instead of an LLC or C corporation, meaning he was personally invested in the outcome of his business operations.

Herbert's former decorators were skeptical. But Herbert won them over with the $400,000 "decorating budget," as he put it. Consequently, the deal allowed Herbert to price his rooms at a discount. He immediately lowered the prices from an average daily rate of thirty-eight dollars to twenty-four dollars, causing guidebooks to spread a favorable word to budget travelers. Herbert's deal not only benefited him, but it also enabled up-and-coming acts to find their muse in the heart of New York City.

Within the walls of the Gramercy, several problems needed fixing by Herbert. He discovered, for instance, that the price of scotch and gin had unnecessarily doubled in the bar, scaring away routine customers. The hotel's bellhops, Pinky and Charlie, wore glum expressions, the result of a low occupancy rate. The desk clerks also weren't handing the keys directly to the bellhops, which resulted in them receiving fewer tips. The bulbs in the elevators needed to be replaced. The chandeliers were causing the ceilings to slope. Occasionally, a cockroach would jump out from a crack in the bar, as if to make its presence known.

The maître d' Petite was no longer so petite. By now, his uniform was a group of linen rags held together by a string. Worst of all, the hideous yellow paint in the lobby made the atmosphere unwelcoming.

Herbert hired an experienced painter to assess the damage to the lobby. After a weeklong chemical process, the mustard paint vanished. As if a miracle had occurred, the hotel returned to its 1925 look. Herbert then obtained new beds, carpeting, drapery, lamps, and a new set of silverware for the dining room, all chosen by his decorators. Bennot and Jamre also designed some new logos for the hotel, including the legendary (for me, at least) broccoli tree logo, in forest green, with "Gramercy Park Hotel" written underneath. This logo soon appeared on the menus, brochures, and linens.

Giving the hotel a modern 1970s look, albeit in a small way, was the least Herbert could do to stimulate business.

Herbert also abolished Le Parc's rule requiring a dinner jacket, which had previously kept The Byrds out of the dining room. The rock trend accelerated, thanks to the hotel's low prices and its proximity to Tramps, Irving Plaza, Max's Kansas City, and several recording studios around the corner on 21st Street. In the grim environment of New York, Herbert would take whoever he could get. David Bowie had something to do with it. But in my mind, it was mostly Herbert.

Leaving Detroit, Herbert moved onto the eighth floor of the hotel with Ruth, joining Steven and David, who moved in closer to the sale. Herbert then invited his former resident manager from the Cadillac, James Tuttle, to come live and work at the Gramercy—something that would turn out to be a huge mistake.

Crime at the Gramercy

As the murder rate in New York City held above two thousand, crime did occasionally poke its head into Gramercy Park. At 1:30 a.m. on September 1, 1975, a well-dressed man in his early thirties and a "very attractive brunette" in her late twenties casually strolled into the hotel with suitcases under their arms.

"I'd like a room please," the man said. By the time the night manager, John Purtz, turned around, there were revolvers in his face. The thieves ordered the workers to the floor and tied them up with duct tape and handcuffs. Two more men showed up. Using a chisel and a hammer, they looted the safe deposit boxes. At one point, a bellhop showed up and was also held captive. By the time the gang left fifty minutes later, they had opened ninety boxes and scored more than $60,000 in cash.

Outside the hotel, the thieves littered the street with jewels, traveler's checks, personal checks, and passports as they scurried to their getaway car. No fingerprints or evidence was left behind. It seemed like they would get away with their crime. But then they got greedy. Two weeks later, the gang was arrested in the middle of another robbery.

A few years later, another robbery occurred inside the Gramercy's elevator. A dance instructor, Barbara Pensar Brezzler, was mugged, and the robber exited out the front door. As the robber looked behind himself suspiciously, the doorman Phil Younger heard the woman's screams and chased him.

Amazingly, a few blocks away, Younger caught the robber and held him for the police. The *Daily News* awarded Younger $1,000 for being the crime fighter of the week.

The Gramercy doorman's heroics also caught the attention of Brian Setzer and the Stray Cats, who were staying in the hotel at the time. One day, as the band was leaving to film scenes for their new music video "(She's) Sexy & 17," they invited Younger along to join them. In the video, the skinny mustachioed doorman plays a teacher who roughs up a student, appearing around the one-minute mark. Now that Younger was "famous" within the walls of the Gramercy, he soon became Pinky's son-in-law via a marriage ceremony at the hotel.

6

TELEGRAM AT THE GRAM

1975–1985

The German philosopher Arthur Schopenhauer once wrote, "Imagine this race transported to a Utopia where everything grows of its own accord and turkeys fly around ready-roasted. Where lovers find one another without any delay and keep one another without any difficulty. In such a place, some men would die of boredom or hang themselves. Some would fight and kill one another. And thus they would create for themselves more suffering than nature inflicts on them as it is."

Just as our body would burst without the pressure of the atmosphere, Schopenhauer argued, so too would the arrogance of man expand if toil, calamity, and frustration were removed from our lives. In other words, the philosopher believed we *require* a certain amount of suffering, as a ship requires a ballast in order to keep a steady course.

When I read Schopenhauer's ideas for the first time, I wondered if he would have written them if he was getting comped room and board at the Gramercy Park Hotel. Surely, life at the Gramercy must have been an exception to Schopenhauer's bleak formula.

In the fall of 1975, Herbert's younger sons Steven and David moved into the Gramercy. David's girlfriend Debbie Levine also joined them. They took the best apartment in the hotel, room 721. Nestled between the two towers of the hotel, the three-bedroom 721 had a spacious outdoor patio that overlooked Gramercy Park.

Steven and David's space allowed them to have two large dogs: a Newfoundland Labrador and a white German Shepherd named Max. One day, Max the German Shephard jumped off the terrace while chasing a pigeon, horrifying the pedestrians below. So Steven and David replaced the dog with a male Doberman Pinscher, which mated with the Newfoundland Labrador. Like magic, there were suddenly nine dogs. David named them "doberdors."

The dogs soon destroyed their rooms, eating everything. The frequent barking likewise disturbed hotel guests whose windows faced the patio. To deal with the dog poop, the brothers flushed it down the toilet. Then the pipes clogged. So they called a plumber to fix the pipes. While he was there, the plumber stole Herbert's $20,000 Patek Philippe watch, which, for some reason, was in his sons' possession.

Furious, Herbert forced Steven and David to remove the dogs. The doorman took two puppies. The kitchen staff took a few. A clerk took one. The two dogs that didn't find a home were flown to Robert, who by now had moved to central Illinois to teach at the University of Illinois.

Between the two younger sons, Steven was by far the more social. While Steven served drinks to Bob Dylan and hung out with the first cast of *Saturday Night Live*, David spent his time taking pictures of graffiti and punks in mohawks and chains. He also hung out with some of the bands who came to the hotel. His camera became a way for him to meet people, and he had a knack for putting people at ease as he snapped away. David's interest in street art took him to all parts of the city. In a Jesus-like beard, wearing tinted glasses, the lanky Jewish kid found his artistic calling in the streets of Harlem and the Bronx.

With his girlfriend Debbie's help, David set up a small photo studio in his apartment and advertised that he'd take actors' headshots. This brought in some money. But the couple's drug expenses exceeded what they earned. One day, David desperately sold off his camera equipment to buy heroin. Later, he told Herbert that his equipment had been stolen, and he got some money to buy new gear. Suddenly, David found a new way to make money.

After Herbert paid to replace David's equipment multiple times, he asked his moonlighting NYPD security staff to get the rap sheets on David's friends. Herbert was disturbed to learn that his candy-colored Eldorado Cadillac, sometimes driven by David, was known to all the drug dealers and police officers in the East Village. Herbert seemed powerless to do anything. Ironically, he seemed more concerned with a methadone clinic that had popped up around the corner on 22nd Street and started a political letter-writing campaign to have it closed. The most Herbert did for David was pay for the rehab clinics he checked into.

Despite his heroin problems, David regularly joined Steven in the nightclub scene. In the mid-1970s, one of the city's top clubs aside from Studio 54 was Max's Kansas City, which faced Union Square. Along with CBGBs, the club had a reputation as the main hangout for the burgeoning glam rock movement. Aerosmith played their first gig there. Sid Vicious played his last. A symbiotic relationship developed between the club and the hotel, as many guests either performed at the venue or were taken there by Steven and David. There, in the VIP room, the brothers reconnected with David Johansen and were introduced to major figures in the rock and art worlds. The parties that began in Max's often ended in room 721. Through Steven and David's influence, the Glamercy became a regular meeting place for eccentrics and iconoclasts, many of whom became residents of the hotel.

For some groups, arriving in the hotel became a rite of passage, a way to define themselves. If they came to the Gramercy, they belonged. One afternoon, the band Journey sat on one of the hotel couches to speak with journalist Martha Hume, who tactlessly brought up a reviewer's comparison of the band to Led Zeppelin. "This band can be compared to no one!" Steve Perry screamed. "We're unique. How can you categorize a band that can play a rock and roll song—heavy metal, if you wanna call it that—like 'Light a Fire' on this album, and then turns around and does 'Good Morning Girl' or 'Walks Like a Lady'? There's just not one category for that kind of band."

For the Weissbergs, there was one category for this kind of band: customer.

Not long after Journey's impassioned speech, Squeeze frontman Chris Difford sat in the hotel's dining room, picking at a plate of seafood. "America seems to be a place that thrives on heavy-duty promotion. It's like hamburgers. You've really got to get out there and sell it," he explained to journalist James Henke. Ironically, Herbert liked to price the hamburger in the dining room obscenely high, just to keep out the riffraff.

Many were proud to come to the Gramercy, as Tom Gray of the band The Brains once explained, "The Gramercy Park Hotel is a middle-class rock 'n' roll hotel of New York, and for us, it's a big step up from the cheap rooms off Time Square." The Gramercy, he described, had "rock stars galore haunting the bar and lobby." But the band could afford only two rooms for themselves and their crew, causing them to draw the high card to determine who slept on the bed.

Though drugs were so often the topic of conversation, it was easy to get laid in the hotel, too. Beyond the groupies and rock stars were ordinary New Yorkers who liked to drop by the bar, since it was cheap and always attracting cosmopolitan individuals. In the early 1980s, a poster appeared in the lobby

Squeeze in the gift shop on February 3, 1981. The gift shop paid no rent to Herbert, and its operator purchased the spot from the previous gift shop manager when he retired. *Photo by Ebet Roberts.*

advertising a new meetup: "More and more women are sharing their men. Now a workshop teaches women how to cope with sharing a man." The workshop, run by divorcée Audrey Chapman, was immensely popular.

"Cum stains on the chair. Cum stains on the desk. Cum stains on the sheets. Cum stains on the floor," was how a record company executive once described the hotel to me. In truth, I never noticed anything other than the occasional newspaper guide to sexual favors left in the closet. More about that later.

Few stopped to think how many people passed through the hotel. In the span of a single year, a hotel room would house hundreds of different guests. The bed was just as likely to have been occupied by a smiling tourist from Italy as it was to host a rock star on a world tour. Everywhere, there was inspiration. While David Mamet waited for the reviews to come in on his play *American Buffalo* on the fourteenth floor, on the seventeenth, S.J. Perelman penned his last book beneath the Oscar Award he had won for the film *Around the World in Eighty Days*. Happiness, Perelman wrote, is a brown paper bag of possessions and a room in a hotel. While Ira Gasman penned lyrics in the lobby as a sea of people flowed by, Carlos Santana was on the rooftop practicing for his next album. For most, the hotel was the place to be

The Cars on July 17, 1978. *Photo by Ebet Roberts.*

to think creatively, but there were also those like Tina Turner and Marianne Faithfull, for whom the hotel was a refuge. Yoko Ono also put her faith in the hotel, hosting both her lawyer and her psychic John Green there. Often, Yoko called him with such mundane questions as, "What color dress should I wear?" When needed most, however, the Gramercy psychic did not deliver.

Important meetings that forged new collaborations occurred in the hotel's dining room and bar on a daily basis. If nothing else, the lounge's free Goldfish crackers and fried chicken wings fed many skeletal punk rockers who snuck in to eat without paying for anything. Quite literally, the hotel was keeping much of the creative spirit alive in 1970s New York, all while earning money that would one day allow me to have a college education.

In an environment that was never without people who, like the old hotel ad had promised, were "immortal," it was hard for Steven and David to focus on the things that make life a success and not just a wild ride. Were they working during this time? Who knows. But they experienced the swift passage of desire and gratification—or what Schopenhauer defined as "happiness."

Top: A room inside the hotel, circa 1990. *Photo by Max Weissberg.*

Bottom: *Photo by Max Weissberg.*

Pax Herberto

After one year back, in 1976, the hotel lost money. This freaked out Bennot and Jamre. Even though they had gotten a good deal, they now personally owed money to the state tax authorities. So they fled. Bennot and Jamre had done important work for the hotel to give it a more modern feel, but they did not have the stomach for running a triple net lease operation in turbulent times. Most likely, there were also major disagreements over the hotel operations. With Bennot as general manager and as a partner, the hotel effectively had two kings. Though two kings may have worked for Sparta, it did not suit the Gramercy Park Hotel.

To oversee the day-to-day business, Herbert hired the stocky Irishman Tom O'Brien, formerly an assistant manager at the Ramada Inn, as general manager. At his first meeting with Herbert, O'Brien bonded with him over their aversion to the corporate hotel system, or "bean counting," as Herbert liked to call it. O'Brien had grown up in a large Catholic family in South Boston, a somber background made worse by the endless rivalries among the local children. His foray into hotel life began when his cousin couldn't make a job interview for a bellhop position and asked O'Brien to fill in. Later, he became a clerk and eventually a lackey in the middle management of Sheraton. Herbert trusted Tom so much that he gave him a large room and eventually let his children occupy several rooms at the hotel for free.

Working alongside O'Brien was the resident manager, James Tuttle from the Detroit-Cadillac, who was in charge of all the furnishing and keeping the rooms up to speed. Oddly, there was no banquet manager, like at most hotels. The underpaid O'Brien took over the position to earn the banquet manager's commissions. According to family members, this contributed heavily to his drinking and to the general sloppiness of the hotel. For whatever reason (and even I do not understand it), this suited Herbert. I should point out that, technically speaking, embezzlement not only cheats the business, but it also cheats the IRS out of payroll and income taxes. Often, my family members speculated that this was the real reason Herbert liked to underpay people and let corruption slide.

Photo by Max Weissberg.

Thanks in part to New York's slow recovery, the hotel began to turn a profit in the late 1970s.

Photo by Max Weissberg.

By now, Herbert had "learned his lessons" in the hotel business. In other words, his ambition no longer took him beyond the confines of the hotel. Everything he needed was there. If he felt hungry, he could pick up the phone and order room service. If he was thirsty, he could go to the bar and sit in Babe Ruth's old spot. If he wanted his clothes cleaned or his apartment tidied up, there was the phone. If he felt ill, he could simply go to the hotel's annex, and Dr. Brown was there to hear his complaint. Every week, he got his haircut in the barbershop by his trusty Luxembourgian barber, William, occupying the same seat that had hosted Eleanor Roosevelt and James Cagney.

In the lounge, Herbert hired a nightly pianist, Roy Bailey, to sing jazz standards. Every night, he sat among his guests and munched on Goldfish crackers, a kind of ritual. Later, at his corner table in the dining room, Herbert was greeted by maître d' Petite and, eventually, by the Ecuadorian waiter Victor Palma. Victor's son-in-law, Juan "Juanito" Correa, also a waiter in the Gramercy, talked about his experience:

> *Juanito: Every time we used to celebrate his birthday in August, he would bring all his employees together and have a nice time. He used to point and make people give speeches.*
>
> *Me: Did people get nervous?*
>
> *Juanito: Yes, and some people were shy 'cause, you know, they were like, "What am I gonna say?" And you got to say something, somebody's gotta say something, and it was very interesting, you know. I remember General Manager O'Brien, he was picked to say a speech. He delivered a very nice speech about Mr. Weissberg and thank-you for the way it's going.*

Herbert's title, used by both his sons and employees, became "King Herbert." His favorite dishes and their particular sides were named by the dining room staff "à la King." The hotel did indeed feel like a little medieval castle. As long as the employees were dependent on him, Herbert let sloppiness slide. It was typical for someone to work thirty or even forty years for Herbert. Often, children and the grandchildren of employees took jobs in the hotel.

Faced with payroll additions who turned out to be late or lazy, unable to remember instructions or incapable of following them, Herbert would only grin. Sooner or later, they would learn. And when they did, loyalty would follow. Once, in the 1990s, Herbert was offered $20 million in cash to hand over the lease to the Gramercy. Listening to the offer in the dining room, Herbert waved his arms around and asked, "Where else are these people gonna get a job?" To him, the employees were family.

Herbert Buys Steven and David a Hotel

With so much partying going on in the hotel—and with rehab not doing much good—Herbert believed he could turn his younger children into hotel owners by giving them a hotel to own. Why start at the bottom when you can start at the top? To accomplish this, Herbert teamed up with an Israeli businessman, David Kogel, to whom he had sold the Brittany Hotel (now a New York University dorm) many years earlier. Together, they took over the Lancaster Hotel in Murray Hill on Madison Avenue and 38th Street (it later became the Jolly Roger but is now called the Hotel Roger Williams). Herbert set up the deal so Kogel owned half the lease, while Herbert and Steven each owned a quarter. Debbie Levine moved much of her stuff into the Lancaster, so it appeared to her parents that she lived there.

Herbert didn't particularly like Kogel but figured his military-like discipline could have a positive effect on his two younger sons. Kogel had been a Polish refugee after World War II and later served in the Israeli army. Kogel was tough as nails, to put it mildly.

Robert described Kogel: "Kogel was wearing this suit that somehow didn't fit him, but I had the impression that nothing fit Kogel. He was about five-foot-seven, five-foot-eight. His pants were falling down and his shirt had a split so you could see his belly, and he was very animated. He had 'untrustworthy dealmaker' written all over him."

When the Lancaster failed to show a profit, Herbert suspected that Kogel was dishonest with the books. According to Steven, Kogel was dishonorable with the staff as well: "Kogel slept with the maid and fired half the maids and made the maid that he was sleeping with make up all the rooms and do four maids' work."

After a while, David stopped showing up for work. Herbert confronted him. "Dad," David said, "I just don't want to waste my time." Despite Herbert's best efforts, David simply lacked ambition. He wanted to live off room service in the hotel and take photos. He also mused about becoming a rabbi.

Without any confidence that he could fix the situation, Herbert dissolved his agreement with Kogel and quit the Lancaster. But he hadn't quite given up on his sons yet.

Herbert then bought the Lakewood Motor Inn in New Jersey for his sons to run. Steven and David were soon drinking with the employees after hours. Business slumped, and the outcome was the same as it had been at the Lancaster. To collect a tax deduction, Herbert *donated* the Lakewood hotel to the Yeshiva, and it was transformed into a rabbinical school.

Meanwhile, David and Debbie planned to get married. But they never made it to their wedding. One night in the middle of a fight, David punched Debbie in the face. She left soon after. Debbie called the police, and David was arrested. With the help of his lawyers, David made a deal for rehab in Florida.

Steven described David at this time: "He kept leaving rehab. Other rock stars in the hotel that were living there were using drugs with David. Finally, [Herbert] moved him out of the hotel and moved him back to Florida."

Who were these rockstars? Guitarist Leslie West of Mountain, musician Buddy Miles from Hendrix's Band of Gypsies, and bass player Jaco Pastorius of the Weather Report were the stars most frequently cited. Of course, David got high with many others—basically anyone in the bar who wanted to. Steven first met Jaco Pastorious in the bar, dressed in rags and looking like he hadn't showered in weeks. Pastorious was strumming on a bass while enjoying a cocktail. Steven turned and said, "You sound just like Jaco Pastorious." He replied, "I *am* Jaco Pastorious." Through this meeting in the bar, David and Jaco eventually became close friends for the wrong reasons.

"Herbert sent [David] to rehab," Steven continued. "Sent him to doctors. David went to Westchester. To Connecticut. Then he was finally down to Florida. He would stay in rehab and then move back into the hotel. Eventually, he moved down to Florida. David lived there all winter, and in the summer, he went to the hotel. They looked at it like he was sick. They didn't look at it that he was sick in one specific area. They looked at it that he was *sick*. And he was. He got colds. He was in bed. Skinny, not eating. He wouldn't even eat the room service. A mess."

David soon found out that Debbie had gotten AIDS and died from it. He was devastated. The grief would shape him for years to come.

Steven was having better luck, however. One night, he met his future wife, Madalyn, while hanging out at The Roxy NYC over in Chelsea. The roller-skating nightclub was labeled the "Studio 54 of roller rinks," because it had a disco ball and was hard to get into. In the practice ring, Steven offered to help Madalyn Weiskopf, a novice, learn to skate. Steven had skated all the way from the hotel to the club. Their chemistry was instant. Madalyn was an uptown, petite Jewish girl, the daughter of a wealthy businessman in the shmata business. With money and Manhattan accents, the two seemed like a perfect match.

Through Madalyn and her sister, Margaret, Steven met the club's owner, Steven Greenberg, that evening. Greenberg wore a dark suit. "I wouldn't go out with a guy you meet here," Greenberg joked. Steven Greenberg will come back later in this story as the brief owner of the Gramercy Park Hotel, partly as a result of this meeting.

With time, Madalyn and Steven fell in love. The two spent most of their time in the Gramercy. But the hotel was not to their standards, according to Steven. "The hotel was embarrassing. I would show her around and there would be all these employees sitting around not doing anything and looking disheveled. The hotel wasn't as nice as where she lived. Her parents lived on 59th Street, Central Park South. She lived in a pink and white apartment in the Upper East Side. She did her best with David. She tried to get along with him. She was afraid of him. David and I were very close before Madalyn."

While it's true that rock stars were frequenting the hotel and overdosing in the rooms, on most days, the lobby was just a bunch of drab furniture and ringing bells. In other words, life in paradise became humdrum.

In mid-1980, six months after their first meeting, Madalyn and Steven married. Their reception was held in the hotel. There was a huge custom cake, lobster flown in from Maine, and plenty of Moët & Chandon champagne available for everyone. To make the event tax-deductible, Herbert invited his accountant, lawyers, business associates, and a lot of

Opposite: Madalyn Weissberg. *Photo by Steven Weissberg.*

Right: A postcard of the Gramercy, illustrated by Helen Louise Woerner. *Gramercy Park Hotel.*

employees. After toasts were made to the new couple, Herbert visited his employees' tables and made sure they had enough to eat.

Following the wedding, Steven and David moved out of the hotel's terrace apartment. David moved to the back of the hotel, hidden away in the annex. Steven likewise got a new room, but he and Madalyn didn't stay long. As Steven described it, "Some of my wife's clothes were stolen out of the hotel, and I left the hotel to have privacy. The maid stole some of her clothes. We got so upset we decided to go back into [Madalyn's] apartment."

Tom O'Brien then moved into room 721, the only apartment with a patio.

Steven Takes Over the Gramercy

Despite two misses, Herbert still had faith that Steven would prove himself as a businessman. Offers from Herbert to purchase hotels for him came in through the mail, so Steven took trips with Tom O'Brien to examine hotels, all with the idea to acquire one. They looked at a Howard Johnson in Puerto Rico and another hotel in New Orleans. But regardless of the terms, deep down, Herbert was not interested. It was too much risk to buy a new hotel. He merely wanted to placate Steven. Meanwhile, the hotel in Little Rock was making a modest profit, but Herbert was thinking of selling it off for tax reasons.

After Steven insisted on being involved in the Gramercy's management, Herbert went to Florida in 1985 and left Steven in charge. According to Steven, he examined the books and found that roughly $1 million a year was being lost in various departments due to theft. He immediately began to clean house. In Steven's words:

> *I threw out the chef. I threw out the steward. They were taking all sorts of kickbacks on the purchasing. Then I threw out the comptroller, and I threw out the credit manager. They were withholding checks that came in from being deposited and then taking them and then putting them in and taking cash out. So they took a check that they didn't report, and then they would exchange it for the cash. They did it right in their office. Everything balanced, but the money was being stolen. The way I caught them was a friend of mine gave them a check and it was never recorded. I went and told the accountant, Stanley Bressman.*
>
> [Herbert] *saw me catch all these people watching closely. All of these nefarious people were brought to the attention of* [Herbert] *under my guidance with the accountant. The accountant said we have to get rid of this one and this one and this one. And that put $1 million on the bottom line. Four people were thrown out, and $1 million was put back on the bottom line. I ran the hotel that year and broke even on the food and beverage. That had been the way the hotel operated in the '60s. The food and beverage broke even, and the rooms made money. After I ran the business for a year,* [Herbert] *decided to come back. He wanted out of retirement and got mad at me.*
>
> *When he came back, he fired the accountant. He was so embarrassed about the stealing, and he didn't want the accountant to run the business anymore. The accountant wanted him to stay in Florida. So he got rid of the accountant because he was embarrassed. He doesn't want anybody to remember the accounting. Gradually, it deteriorated. He hired the wrong people at too low a salary, and the stealing returned more and more. Anything you tried to do to make a suggestion that was different than the way he behaved was an insult.*

Among Herbert's managers, Tuttle had gone the farthest over the line. In addition to his salary, he lived with full board in suite 1202, which faced the park and had a large-screen TV with cable (a luxury in the early 1980s). Tuttle had fallen into the corruption that was common to resident managers in hotels. To make extra money, he took small kickbacks, or "spiffs," from vendors to choose certain products. But even this side business wasn't enough. So Tuttle secretly made a copy of the safe key and was able to steal hundreds of thousands of dollars over several years.

He also dabbled as a pimp for several sex workers in the hotel using eight rooms, including room 1512, a huge suite. He shamelessly located his clients in the bar and gained them through advertisements. He became so flagrant that a nosy journalist from the *New York Post* wrote an article about one of the girls, April, and the amounts he charged: $120 for a half hour. The article then quoted the clueless Tom O'Brien, who claimed to be unaware: "If anything seemed a little odd, we would investigate."

Herbert had no idea things had gone so far. After far too long, Tuttle was finally removed. A few years after his firing, he died in a car crash.

When I was a teenager, I once asked Herbert about all the stealing in the hotel while we sat at the corner table in the dining room. He immediately eyed me suspiciously. "Isn't that how it works?" I asked him in an agreeable tone. "You pay the employees less and they take a little more, and it works out for the taxes," I continued. In truth, I was just repeating what my father had told me. It was difficult for Herbert to speak, but his troubled expression made me immediately regret my words.

He told me that what I had heard was a lie spread by one of his sons, which was a polite way of saying that my own father had misread the situation. Then he explained how he once hired a detective to investigate his staff. "They love you," the detective told him. Herbert repeated the line several times. For him, the detective's report settled everything there was to say about stealing.

The bar in the 1990s. *Photo by David Weissberg.*

Things Go Back to "Normal"

After Steven's brief tenure, the pax Herberto resumed. While the chaos dialed down, the corruption dialed back up. Like clockwork, guests checked in and out. The bar emptied and filled its liquor battles. The elevators went up and down. Pinky wheeled his squeaky luggage cart back and forth from Lexington Avenue to the many rooms inside. Like Copernicus's model of the universe, Herbert believed the cycle would last forever.

But then there were a series of crises. It began with the installation of a computer to take reservations that replaced the Telex machine. A computer at the Gramercy Park Hotel? To many, it sounded like a risky venture. Herbert ordered it to be installed, and the machine began taking reservations. A few weeks later, however, an army of people filled the lobby with reservations in hand. But the hotel was already fully booked. Apparently, the computer reservation system, a precursor to the internet, set no limits to the number of people who could book rooms.

Herbert unplugged the machine, but to no avail. People kept coming. The chief engineer of the computer company came to the hotel to fix the problem. He worked for days. After much tension, the problem was finally solved. Never again would Herbert wish to use a computer. The old-fashioned Telex machine worked perfectly. I should mention that growing up, I never saw a computer in the Gramercy Park Hotel.

Not long after, a citywide strike was called by the Hotel and Motel Trades Council, the same union that represented the hotel's workers. All of the city's largest hotels were threatened, including the Gramercy. Herbert had a plan, however. One of his tenants was the deal broker Carmine DeSapio, who kept his office on the seventeenth floor. DeSapio was a powerful back-room politician in the Democratic Party and the former head of Tammany Hall. Like a mobster, DeSapio perennially wore dark glasses. But instead of just wanting to look like a gangster, he actually had an eye problem. DeSapio also regularly smoked thin cigars and had a deep smoker's voice, which only added to his mystique.

Herbert arranged a meeting with Carmine. He graciously ordered him a round of room service as a prop in the conversation. Herbert told him forcefully in his crow-like voice, "Carmine, you can't let them strike at this hotel! Or they'll see ya cross the picket line." DeSapio claimed he could do nothing until Herbert offered unlimited room service during the strike. The next day, the union announced the forty-four hotels in the city that would lose their employees in the strike. Miraculously, the Gramercy was not on the

Lionel George, the Swiss "Luftmensch" of the Gramercy. Lionel was a master at avoiding his bill. *Photo by Max Weissberg.*

list. With the competition hobbled, business boomed. This was apparently one of the many times DeSapio influenced the Gramercy's business.

Another major problem in the 1980s was Steven's Swiss resident friend Lionel George, who had moved in during the 1970s and was often unable to pay his rent. Over the years, Lionel George had made himself an indispensable part of the bar's atmosphere. Lionel was five feet, six inches tall with white buck teeth and tortoiseshell glasses. He always wore an expensive suit with a rare plaid pattern. Lionel's grandfather, so it was claimed, invented the automobile clutch. This led to the George family holding seats on the board of Lamborghini. Lionel spoke seven languages and was on a first-name basis with every sex worker in a ten-block radius. Sometimes he would even pass their pictures around in the bar.

Aside from his trips home to Switzerland to beg his relatives for money (so the bartender told me), it was unclear how Lionel paid his bills. As a kid growing up, I often saw him having animated conversations in French with foreign businessmen. Like Herbert, Lionel was a man who *made deals*. Once, he brokered a bulletproof Mercedes to the president of Turkmenistan. On another occasion, he personally introduced the prince of Monaco to one of Lionel's fallen angels. As if to inject some hope into Steven and thereby skip out on his rent, Lionel also introduced him to potential business partners who would theoretically help him "make a deal."

When Lionel got far behind on his rent, manager Tom O'Brien would threaten to evict him in the bar, loud enough for everyone to learn of his deadbeat status. Next, Lionel would go straight to Steven, insisting that the hotel could easily find a better manager (in other words: fire Tom). Steven would then complain to Herbert, emphasizing that Lionel brought "a ton" of business to the hotel. Finally, Tom would settle with Lionel for a fraction of the bill. A routine developed.

I remember Lionel attending many of our family dinners (who invited him was never clear), adding some color to our conversation. You might think I wanted him kicked out of the hotel like the management. But who would I practice my German with in the bar? The hotel needed a polyglot luftmensch—so long as it could afford it.

A waiter, Juanito, explained:

> *Lionel George was Steve's mentor, I think. He would always be telling things that Steven would have to do. We used to call him the freeloader. He would get close to Steven to get his things paid. He would say, "You have to do this right, and do this. What kind of food was this?" He'd eat, enjoy, and then he'd criticize the food.*
>
> *We would make the check and give it to him, and he would say, "Have you seen Steven?" And we would say, "Nope, haven't seen him." And he'd have to put out a credit card or charge it to his home. If he saw Steven, he would talk with him and throw the check on him.*

It seemed like the good times would last forever.

David Expands His Drug Business

While in Florida, David met a bunch of Jamaican Rastas, who sold him weed and also sold cocaine. David wasn't a heavy coke user, but these guys had major connections. David's plan was to buy a half pound of coke from the Rastas for $12,000. As that amount of coke was worth almost $40,000 on the street, it was an incredible deal at the time. It's unclear how David got the money for the initial purchase, however.

The plan went smoothly. Riding his motorcycle, David arrived back in the Gramercy with the drugs. For months, he sold coke to buy heroin and reaped the reward. Then one day, three men he didn't know showed up and robbed him. When David resisted, they hit him in the face, bruising his cheek. They also grabbed some gold jewelry. Rather than report it to Herbert's security, David kept the assault quiet.

After this, David vowed not to repeat his mistake. On his next trip out to Florida, David got a gun license and bought a .22-caliber pistol, the same small-sized bullet that had killed John Lennon. Though David didn't have a

David Weissberg and Nicole Weissberg, circa 1982. *Photo by Georgeanne Hume.*

license for the gun in New York, he brought it back and forth on his trips to Florida anyway.

For the next few years, David built his drug business. He sold coke and occasionally doled out ounces of weed as "favors." What he earned, he immediately consumed. But the money provided independence, a way to tell Herbert that he wasn't in charge of him (free room and board aside). Herbert's security warned him that the hotel was threatened by David's activities, especially because the business depended on a liquor license. But Herbert avoided confrontation and failed to do anything that would change the situation. Everyone was aware of what was happening, especially after David's arrest. But no one did a thing.

Marvin recalled the time he intervened:

> *We went down to Gramercy Park and had lunch in the corner table, and we were sitting there and Herb was talking about this and had this kind of deal, doing this with stock and on about the hotel, having a great business going, and all this. We already had our entrées and they're bringing coffee, and finally, I turned around to Herb and I said, "Herb, I don't give a shit*

> *about the hotel. You're not even talking about your son, damnit. Don't you understand this, the dealing and all these kinds of problems? The people from the Drug Enforcement will come and take away your license." He said, "I know people." I said, "You're family and if* [David's] *dealing in drugs here in the hotel, you'll lose everything. You won't have a liquor license. Don't give me any shit that you know people." And he just sat there very quietly and never once said anything back. I never understood why he never did anything or said anything.*

David sometimes threw parties in his room, causing all sorts of "frightening" characters to enter the hotel. One of the desk clerks, Nicole, disapproved of David's lifestyle and would often snicker when he asked for his mail. Their daily skirmishes morphed into open resentment. One day, David punched her in the face across the counter. She promptly sued the hotel. On his lawyers' advice, Herbert settled for $30,000. Once again, it was time for David to go to rehab.

David's life was mirroring the lives of the rock stars around him, albeit without the musical career. At roughly the same time David got into legal trouble for his fight in 1985, Axl Rose got into a fight with the staff at the hotel. That same year, Chuck Berry also beat up his girlfriend, Marilyn O. Boteler, in the hotel while high on PCP. The woman called the police, but before the police arrived and found the bruised girl, Chuck Berry skipped town without settling his bill. The woman, whose teeth were dislocated and who needed five stitches, sued Berry and got an estimated $5 million. Though the story made the papers, it didn't seem to impact Berry's career.

Though David Weissberg escaped punishment for the time being, other guests weren't so lucky. One day, the FBI quietly informed the hotel's management that a major drug ring had taken up residence in the hotel, so the management should collect its bill. A week later, police busted Howard Z. Fuchs, a Yeshiva graduate and the head of the so-called Jewish cocaine connection. The bust yielded forty pounds of cocaine, twenty-five pounds of marijuana, and seventeen ounces of hashish oil—but the guests hardly noticed anything. Ironically, more guests thought the hotel had been busted after the band the Police put their stickers all over the lobby bathrooms.

7

THE PRINCE OF GRAMERCY PARK

1982–1994

In 1982, Robert, Georgeanne, and their two children, Nicole and Max (me), moved into the Gramercy Park Hotel's room 1705. As I was only seven months old, I have no memory of this time. But Georgeanne recorded the events in her journal:

> *May 2, 1982: On Tuesday New York got 9" of snow—record weather for this time of year. It was cold. On Sunday, the weather was beautiful and we had a typical Sunday. Bob went out for provisions. He came back with milk, donuts +* The New York Times. *After breakfast he took Nicole to Gramercy Park to play.*
>
> *May 6: There is a police detective sitting on a chair at the other end of the hall on the 17th floor. The newly recombined Mamas and the Papas are staying in the suites* [rooms 1712, 1714, 1715] *and McKenzie* [Mackenzie Phillips] *of the group has been threatened by a "sick" fan who sent her a letter with a bullet in it. The person who did this also sent a letter with a bullet in it to a priest. It is in the same style as Jodie Foster was receiving from John Hinkly* [sic] *for in a movie she was in.*
>
> *Last night David, HRW, Danny* [Ruth] *+ myself went to New York University hospital to see Madeline* [Madalyn] *+ baby Michael. Madeline* [Madalyn] *was in a private room with w/7 bouquets of flowers. Her mother said she was getting better treatment since the hospital staff found out her uncle donated an operating room.*

A brochure from the 1980s.

Madeline + Steven have a large 2 bedroom apt near 2nd Ave + 62nd St. Before her pregnancy they had a one bedroom apt. Apartments are very tight and she is in a good location. When she asked for a 2 bedroom apt in the same bldg [building] *she was put on a long waiting list. The apt is rent stabilized and costs just under $1100 a month—a real good deal to a knowledgeable New Yorker. Steven was offered $15,000 for his lease.*

Steven + Madeline each maintain themselves on an allowance. They are each given $500 a week by their parents. They complained that this is not

Steven and Madalyn Weissberg. *Photo by David Weissberg.*

enough for them to live on. Madeline goes out and buys $450 boots, has expensive lunches, a recent $500 dry cleaning bill, then pressures Steven who runs to his father for more $.

A # of affluent couples with young children live in this area and have keys to Gramercy Park. They spend their summers in the Hampdens [sic]*—one has a house on Fisher Island. When I asked about babysitting the woman told me of the Salvation Army residence for women on one corner of the Park. Young women who live there will babysit for the going rate of $3 an hr. in the evening. I asked her what she does during the day and she told me there are no day care centers in this area—only in the projects of public housing. She uses her housekeeper.*

Typical day:
5 a.m.—breast feed Max
7:30—feed Max cereal
8:00—get Nicole up + ready for school
9:00—Bob walks Nicole to Gramercy Park School where she is attending kindergarten for $350/mo.
9:30—I go back to sleep, Max takes a nap
12:00—Max eats lunch. I eat peanut butter + cream cheese or wine, apples + cheese from the Cheese Shop or order room service for lox, bagel + cream cheese. Bob usually orders room service
1–5—excursions to different parts of New York City
5—pick up Nicole from school
6—order room service for Nicole, feed Max
7—eat in hotel dining room
have dinner drinks or come back to room to read or watch hotel cable movies.

The hotel takes care of the laundry and of course cleans the room every day. We frequently take Max to the park. Mrs. Reynolds, the 75 yr old wife of the hotel engineer has offered to babysit for free. Zara, Al Blum's 15 yr old stepdaughter also babysits for us for $3/hr. The hotel usually picks up the tab.

Hotel security—very good. The hotel uses off duty policemen from the precinct which is about 2 blocks away. They dress in plain clothes. Any trouble and the police are here in force very quickly. I told Nicole to come + see the guys from Hill Street Blues when one day in a matter of minutes at least 15 cops were here in the lobby. It turned out to be a false alarm. There are a growing # of female cops.

May 6: Just met John Phillips—the organizer of the original Mamas + the Papas when his 2 yr old daughter wandered to our end of the hall. We invited her in. Later McKenzie Phillips came in. She was one of the daughters on One Day at a Time. *This sick fan from Clarendon, Ill* [sic] *has been sending her fan letters at the rate of 100 a mo for the last 5 yr.*

John Phillips has been on hard drugs for a long time and his daughter McKenzie followed him into it. They are both clean. John works in a mental hospital (not for a living) and has been talking to David [Weissberg].

Bob tells me Marty [Weissberg] *went to Astro Gems today to buy a gift for Mother's Day for Laura. He knew the owner. Everything in the store was ½ price. Marty picked out a $300 necklace reduced to $150. He asked for his friend. He then paid $125 cash carefully rolled up, given to the clerk who gave it to the owner. It was done discreetly so the other employees wouldn't know. There was no receipt and the cash register was never used. Last night we heard John Phillips practicing guitar so we went to listen. We met his manager Al Hirsh. We were told that Linda McCartney was a groupie + met Paul at the hotel. Also when Bob Dylan stayed here he took up 2 whole floors.*

Nicole told me "I love New York City."

I was introduced to a famous Irish actress Siobhan McKenna in the hotel dining room. She starred in a play where there was only one person. I think she played 7 different parts. She was eating dinner with Father McFadden. (Her play was on Broadway a few years ago.)

May 17: Today Bob called me down to see the hotel lobby. The lobby is filled w/ photography equipment + crew. Two men in business suits are being photographed in front of the hotel desk for an ad for AT+T.

Last night I met a musician on the Dave Letterman show. He lives here in the hotel. He is black and talked of seeing Sly from Sly + the Family Stone at the studio. In 10 yrs drugs has taken him from a robust male to a broken down shadow of a person.

May 31: Last week a Canadian couple and a guy from England were arrested by undercover cops to whom they had arranged to sell heroin. For the past month they lived here at the Gramercy Park Hotel in a $95 a day room and room service. The police warned Tom O'Brien about the impending bust so the hotel could collect the bill before they were arrested. This supposedly was the largest drug bust since the French Connection. The police checked the contents of their room after the bust. They found two steamer trunks filled with hotel paraphernalia—linens, ashtrays, china.

June 5: Last night we heard a crash, then screaming + swearing. Ten minutes later we hear loud sirens. He screamed, "you fucking asshole." A musician here on a week's stay jumped out of his 3rd floor window without opening the window (he went through the window). While under the influence of angel dust or something. He landed on a second floor roof over the kitchen. He was taken to Bellevue. Then he came to the hotel and he asked for the 9th floor, but there weren't any rooms available.

The Russians are here making a movie about Anna Pavlova. They took 23 rooms. The government is paying. The British are also in the movie. I met an actor James Fox who has been in Isadora + the Sovereign. *He asked me whether I was a newspaper reporter (I was carrying the camera with the zoom lens). We had a short conversation when somebody came up + said "Aren't you James Fox?"*

[Note: *Anna Pavlova* also included a cameo by Martin Scorsese playing an Italian opera manager, filmed in the hotel's lobby.]

McKenzie Phillips had her Blaupunkt radio stolen out of her Mercedes when it was parked overnight in front of the hotel.

Around the corner from the hotel and sharing a common wall is Gramercy East—a plush brothel passing itself off as a spa. When you enter there is a bar on your right and girls swimming nude on your left. The cost is $300 ½ hr according to Victor. You can do any fantasy you want.

The Mamas + Papas managers have been served notice for their unpaid hotel bill. They have been staying at the hotel a few days each week.

At this point, Herbert made a deal to the musicians: if they could get David off of heroin, they could live in the hotel for free. John Phillips had been convicted for drug trafficking a year prior and was now leading a public

Steven Weissberg (*center*) mingles with staff. *Photo by Georgeanne Hume.*

antidrug campaign to fulfill his plea agreement. So Steven, David, and the remnants of The Mamas & the Papas began playing music together. When the hallways began to smell like marijuana, Herbert booted the musicians.

It's now known that John Phillips, also known as "Papa John," the writer of "California Dreamin'" and other hits, sexually abused his daughter Mackenzie Phillips during this period. She told Oprah decades later that the abuse began in 1979, after her father injected her with cocaine and heroin on the eve of her marriage at the age of nineteen. According to Mackenzie, their incestuous relationship ended when she became pregnant. She wasn't sure who the father was, so she aborted the child.

NEW YORK IN THE 1980s

Shortly after the birth of Michael Weissberg, Steven and Madalyn had another child, Jonathan. Marty Weissberg had also fathered three children by this time, Andrew, Peter, and Lindsay, who were the oldest group out of Herbert's grandchildren.

Growing up, I saw the hotel in week-long snapshots several times a year. When I think about the New York of my youth, the first thing that comes to mind is Michael Jackson's music video for "Bad," directed by Martin Scorsese. If you haven't seen the full video, it begins in a boarding school that Michael, the only Black kid, attends. Surrounded by young intellectuals, Michael attempts to blend in and does it well. Later, he returns to his Brooklyn neighborhood and is challenged by his lower-class friends, who don't think he's *bad*. Cue Michael Jackson in a leather jacket and chains dancing in the Hoyt-Schermerhorn subway.

Left: Max Weissberg on the hotel's roof in 1986. *Photo by Georgeanne Hume.*

Right: *Left to right*: Michael, Max, and Jonathan in Gramercy Park. *Photo by Madalyn Weissberg.*

Very quickly after seeing this video, I had my own outfit similar to Michael's, filled with chains. I regularly imitated his dance moves. Word about how good I was spread quickly in the hotel. Employees wanted me to "do the Michael Jackson." Strangely, I was not shy. I got so popular, I started charging people a dollar to watch me perform. At eight, I went to the Washington Square fountain, a place popular with acrobats, comedians, and other would-be entertainers, to perform with my boombox. Unlike today, New York in the 1980s was filled with street performers. Everyone was out on the streets trying to make a buck. Breakdancers everywhere carried pieces of cardboard with them just so they could start spinning on the ground if they saw an opportunity to earn a quarter. Another essential accessory was the blue and white cup that said, "We Are Happy to Serve You." Any other cup, and you knew they were a newbie.

It seemed like everyone in New York tried to not only look like someone in the "Bad" video but were themselves trying to *be* bad. Long gold chains. Boomboxes blasting rap music. Flashy sneakers. At the other end of the spectrum: Burberry trench coats. Face-covering glasses. Suspenders, sweaters, ties, and $1,000 loafers. New York publishers even had instruction manuals aimed at aspiring yuppies. Slowly, the city was changing, which was expressed in the fashion at the time. It was morphing into a city where people cared less about each other and celebrated the Dow instead. So absurd had the Dow obsession grown, that by the end of the decade, the Gramercy was hosting a $195 annual two-day convention designed to predict the market by using the stars. Originally, the astrologers planned to host their convention at the World Trade Center. But they failed to predict the 1993 terrorist bombing, after which they were forced to move the convention to the Gramercy.

The Genius

By the time I was eight or so, one of my great pleasures was to personally sign the check in the hotel's dining room for our family's bill, which was paid for by Herbert. Often, I added titles alongside my signature, such as "Max the brilliant" or "Max the smartest." One time, I wrote, "Max the genius," or at least that's what I intended to write. Somehow, I wrote "Max the gunius" instead. The mocking began immediately. For years afterward, my mother, Georgeanne, and sister, Nicole, taunted me as "Max the guyness." I never signed the check with a title again.

Growing up, I often thought about being a hotel man like my grandfather Herbert R. Weissberg. That dream ended after one experience.

That day, Herbert's granddaughter, my sister, Nicole—age thirteen, wearing red glasses, a bob haircut, and braces—wanted to go on a shopping spree at Barneys. The Barney of Barneys was, in fact, a friend and neighbor of Herbert's in Miami. Their relationship began after Herbert made a habit of stealing Barney's newspaper every morning and then carefully folding it back up and leaving it on Barney's doorstep like nothing happened.

For my sister's shopping spree, Barney's son, Fred Pressman, was to personally guide Nicole. This was right after the movie *Pretty Woman* had come out. Shopping sprees had become a rite of passage for the well-to-do.

I was nine years old at the time. Spending a whole day at a clothing store was a form of torture, so my parents let me stay in our room on the twelfth floor of the Gramercy Park Hotel.

At one point, I picked up an empty Snapple bottle and threw it out the window. I watched it fall eleven stories before it shattered in the rear courtyard of the hotel. I repeated this with a couple more glasses and then forgot about it.

That evening Nicole, my bratty sister, who had meanwhile spent $2,800 on clothing, noticed some glasses had vanished. Then she saw the broken glass in the courtyard. Like a young Miss Marple in an Agatha Christie novel, she presented her theory to my mother, who—judge and jury—sentenced me to clean up the mess.

My mother yanked me by the arm to the elevator. Thankfully, it was empty. Downstairs in the lobby, like a soldier pushing along a prisoner of war, she marched me to the front desk and slapped her hand on the counter like a guest with a leaky ceiling. But the clerk didn't know how to get inside the courtyard.

My mother then led me to the executive offices in the custody of Hagop "Jack" Vartebedian, an Armenian refugee who had been promoted to resident manager following Tuttle's removal. Sitting in the stuffy, quiet office, surrounded by files and filing cabinets, I began to feel as if I'd already gone through the worst of it. The secretary, Eileen, pretended to work in my presence.

Two maintenance men appeared. They were scruffy teenagers in brown uniforms with thin adolescent mustaches. One held a broom and a concession-style dustbin. Without any words, they led me up the stairwell to the second floor.

The three of us entered a hotel room that was once occupied by the Kennedys. Then we climbed through the window and out to the courtyard.

Suddenly and unexpectedly, the younger one began sweeping up the mess for me. "Don't worry," he said in a Latin accent. "No one will know. I take care of it. Don't worry, Mr. Weissberg," he said, even though I was nine years old. After that, I never wanted to be a "hotel man" like my grandfather. Were it not for the luxuries of bourgeois life, perhaps this incident could have turned me into a young Che Guevera.

The Hotel Corrupts Me

It's easy to look at troubled children and blame it on the parents. But I was my own man. One of my favorite things was enjoying the hotel's services. In the dining room, I had my own dish called the "à la Max": lamb chops and mashed potatoes. Growing up, I had my hair cut for free, ordered shrimp cocktails and chocolate mousse from room service, and could sit in the reserved section in the bar. Often, my sister, Nicole, and I stayed in room 1202, Tuttle's old room, which had a seventy-two-inch screen TV (rare in those days) and cable. I was only seven or eight when Nicole and I discovered that one channel showed naked dancing people at night, and we watched in prepubescent fascination. At some point, the secret got out and it became yet another reminder of Tuttle's corruption, which we, as kids, did not know about.

Some years later, I learned to charge heaps of candy and magazines from the hotel's gift shop to my room. When I was eleven, the gift shop's cashier unscrupulously sold me my first pornographic magazine, and I had my first orgasm in the hotel. Back in Mahomet, Illinois, I shared the magazines with my friends and became a hero.

Two years later, at age thirteen, I lost my virginity at the hotel. Let me explain. Every one of the Gramercy Park Hotel's rooms was equipped with not only a Gideon Bible but also a yellow pages book. This yellow pages book had an escort section as thick as your thumb filled with enticing pictures. Growing up, I also found newspapers that were left behind in the closets filled with women's photos and phone numbers. The eyes in the black and white photos were covered with black boxes. When I first found these guides, I didn't understand what they were. Later, I noticed every newsstand in New York was selling them for a few nickels.

In June 1994, right around the time O.J. Simpson killed Nicole Brown Simpson, I was in room 901 at the Gramercy Park Hotel, preparing for a teen tour across America. The idea was that I would travel on a bus with a group of rich Jewish teenagers and see the sites of the American West, including Hollywood, Seattle, Yellowstone, and some Canadian glaciers. It just so happened that my cousin Michael Weissberg (Steven's son) had also signed up for the tour. He was around the same age as me, and we were both very excited.

The tour suggested that we have $500 in personal cash for the seven-week trip. To get this money, Herbert sent me to the accounting room on the second floor. Inside were an Asian woman and man counting stacks of money at a desk. I handed them a note filled with my grandfather's scribble. Understanding that I was a Weissberg, the clerk handed me $500 in cash.

A day or so later, I was getting my haircut in the beauty salon when in walked Steven. He was wearing a black Armani suit, white shirt, and fancy shoes but no tie.

"Here. Put it in your pocket," he said, handing me a thick envelope. Inside was $500 in cash. I now had $1,000 for my trip. That Steven had done this in front of the barber, William, I did not appreciate.

That night, I sat in my room alone with my pile of cash, wondering when I would get this opportunity again. I started flipping through the yellow pages to the escort section. There were so many to choose from.

The first place I called, I gave a silly fake name, and the person on the other end was certain I was a kid. "Wouldn't take a chance on it," he said, and then he hung up.

After a few more calls, I spoke to an Asian woman with so-so English. She asked about my youthful voice. I lied and said I was seventeen (I was thirteen). It didn't bother her that I was a minor. She offered to send a "real nice girl." The woman who showed up was in her late thirties, maybe early forties, Italian, and not in the best shape. She wore a tight-fitting corset, lots of makeup, and a heavy perfume scent. She had dark, greasy hair. "Tell your friends I was beautiful," she later advised me. It was not what I imagined, but I wasn't a picky child. I was about to explode. $200 later, I did exactly that, and it took about five seconds.

At one point in the hour-long session, I asked if she frequented the hotel that much. "No, this hotel is a family hotel," she said, and the word *family* echoed in my ears.

I mention this story, by the way—even though it's embarrassing—because I'm convinced some version of it has happened many times in the Gramercy to people I know. As I've gotten older, I've made friends with people who were sex workers in some form or another, and I've come to realize it's not such a big deal. The oldest profession is a staple of the hotel business, even at the Gramercy. Herbert's generosity and laissez-faire management style were, as they were for others, the causal agents of my sexual awakening.

As I got older, I heard more stories. How the maître d' had a regular thing with one of the desk clerks. That my grandfather, too, had his lover among the staff whom he took to Gramercy Park while Ruth watched from the window. There were employees who had been conceived somewhere in the hotel during an unpaid break and then obtained a job there decades later through nepotism. In so many ways, the paradise of the Gramercy was an instigator of romance, a well of the unseen and forbidden behind closed doors. Throughout much of the 1980s and 1990s, in fact, the hotel was located next door to a high-class brothel that ran below the Russell Sage Building. Inside were naked girls in fish tanks and various private rooms. Lionel routinely offered tours for the hotel's bar patrons. The place eventually got busted when the owner started selling cocaine to patrons.

In 1994, Mayor Rudy Giuliani, a former prosecutor, took office as New York mayor and immediately began attacking crime and quality-of-life issues. After the effects of Giuliani's reign began to be felt, New York became the cleanest it had been in recent memory. Using the "broken

Max and Michael Weissberg underneath his house in the Hamptons. *Photo by Monique Cressey.*

windows" approach—going after petty crimes along with major ones—violent crime dropped 56 percent and property crime dropped 65 percent, both to historic lows.

For the hotel, the improvement of the city meant a steadier stream of European clientele than had come in the 1990s. For us, Europeans were the best guests because they seldom complained about the hotel's shortcomings. But they liked to smoke, and one chain-smoker could make a room smell for months. But to us, business was growing, and that's what mattered most.

THE WEISSMAN TEEN TOUR

At age thirteen, I was skilled with three-card monte and, along with this, had an ability to scam people. For me, this satisfied my rotten ego. Just as I began to master this trade, my parents put me on the aforementioned seven-week Weissman teen tour, a bus filled with young teenagers out to see the highlights of the West. And like I mentioned previously, my cousin Michael (Steven's older son) had also signed up for this teenage camp-on-a-bus.

Michael was a few months younger than me and perhaps looked a bit like me. Raised in the Upper East Side and attending Horace Mann, an elite private school, he had been instilled with patrician tastes and excellent grooming habits. His tanned skin looked healthy, and his hair was always brushed. Though I hardly paid any attention, his clothes were the finest a kid could have in Manhattan. Personally, I liked Michael, and we got along well. Visiting his house in the Upper East Side, I was always impressed by the number of Nintendo games he owned. Shockingly, his younger brother Jonathan had his *own* Nintendo and his own collection of games, which overlapped with Michael's just so they wouldn't fight with each other.

The tour began with a flight from New York to Seattle (90 percent of the tour's kids were rich kids from the New York City area). Michael and I decided beforehand that we would tell no one on the tour we were cousins. At the airport, he loudly won ten dollars off of me in a game of three-card monte.

Then on the flight, using Michael's help, I won $10 off the naive kid sitting next to us. In two weeks, we had won over $200—no small amount of money for thirteen-year-olds. But then the forty kids on the bus figured out Michael and I were cousins.

The more money we made, the hungrier we got. We hustled during a Giants game in Candlestick Park. We hustled in Reno inside a hotel lobby. We even hustled other kids on different teen tours whose paths we crossed. When we got into trouble, the next day, we would vanish to a different city and a different hotel room. Herbert, I thought, would be proud of us gamblers who acted like "the house."

On Market Street in San Francisco, we got fake IDs that said we were twenty-one and started selling beer to the other kids. When those IDs stopped working, we got better IDs in Los Angeles and started buying hard alcohol. Back in the hotel room, we snuck girls in and plied them with booze.

While in Las Vegas, Michael and I stayed at the Circus Circus Hotel. It's located on the strip and is famous for its kiddy casino, with acrobats performing summersaults above its patrons. Steven flew out to meet us. Steven had a suite in the Imperial Palace, an Asian-themed hotel on the strip. Its floor plan, Steven explained, was shaped like a swastika. As we drove around, Steven pointed to various buildings he was thinking of purchasing—as soon as he could get his "finances lined up," he told us. I couldn't believe what I was hearing. Were we really that rich? Was Steven really that successful of a businessman? At one point, we ate dinner with a supposed business partner, and Steven hoarded stacks of the restaurant's business cards "for future meetings."

Putting things on the Weissberg credit card, we toured the Imperial's car museum, saw Hitler's Mercedes and Mussolini's Alfa Romeo, and later had VIP seats for the *Siegfried & Roy* show at the MGM Grand.

That evening, I confessed to Michael how I had lost my virginity in the Gramercy Park Hotel. He was intrigued. We found a newspaper guide for sex workers and began dialing. The first pair refused us because we were too young. The second girls, who had been notified beforehand that we were minors, were more willing. They quickly took $200 of Michael's money in exchange for a hand job. I thought the experience was disappointing and a little disgusting. The girls had ripped us off, but I had gotten away without paying a thing. *C'est la vie*, I thought. Michael wasn't worried about the money either.

During those seven weeks, a seed was planted in Michael. In exchange for his history lessons about Herbert and the hotel, I told him all I knew about German philosophers. I explained, in confident detail, how God was simply an idea for the weak. Pleasure and our capacity to enjoy it was not something to be ashamed of. Puritan ideals, the kind that Max Weber would advocate, were simply the values of a sucker. So on and so forth. At one point, I even bought a starter pistol revolver just so I could feel like a gangster.

Our trip ended in Grand Junction, Colorado. One of the counselors busted us for having beer. Even though only two days were left in the tour, they sent us back to the Gramercy Park Hotel, where our trip began.

Herbert Weissberg surrounded by staff on his birthday, circa 1988. *Photo by Georgeanne Hume.*

Appetizers

SHRIMP COCKTAIL	5.75	LITTLE NECK OR CHERRYSTONE CLAMS	3.95
FRUIT CUP SUPREME	2.25	HERRING IN CREAM	2.95
COTTAGE CHEESE, CHIVES	2.25	JUICES, ORANGE, V8, CLAM, TOMATO	1.95
HEARTS OF ARTICHOKES	2.95	PATE MAISON	2.95
LOBSTER COCKTAIL	5.65	BLUE POINT OYSTER COCKTAIL	4.50
LUMP CRABMEAT COCKTAIL	5.95	ANCHOVIES ON COLE SLAW	2.75
MELON IN SEASON	2.25	CHOPPED CHICKEN LIVERS	2.75
with Proscuitto	2.95	SMOKED NOVA SCOTIA SALMON	5.95

Appetizer Chaud For Dinner

HOT SHRIMPS GRAMERCY	7.25
ESCARGOTS BOURGUIGNON	7.95

Soups

DU JOUR	1.15	COLD VICHYSOISSE	1.45
CONSOMME DOUBLE	1.15	JELLIED MADRILENE	1.15
FRENCH ONION SOUP CUP	1.15	AU GRATIN	1.75

MAITRE D' RECOMMENDS

CHATEAU BRIAND BOUQETTIERE FOR TWO	29.95
ROAST RACK OF LAMB JARDINIERE FOR TWO	29.95

(SERVED WITH COUNTRY SALAD, POTATO, VEGETABLE)

Cold Buffet Suggestions

CHEF'S SEAFOOD SALAD, KING NEPTUNE	11.50
FRESH SEAFOOD PLATTER, LORRAINE	13.55
CHEF'S SALAD MAISON	8.75
STUFFED TOMATO, SHRIMP OR LOBSTER, GARNI	9.75
LOBSTER SALAD MAISON	9.75
ASSORTED COLD CUTS, GARNI	8.95
ROAST BEEF, JARDINIERE	8.95
CHICKEN SALAD NICOISE	8.95

Cheese

CAMEMBERT	2.25	BRIE	3.75
SWISS	1.95	ROQUEFORT	3.25
CREAM CHEESE AND JELLY	1.95	BEL PAESE	3.25
AMERICAN	1.95		

SERVED WITH CRACKERS

Desserts

FRUIT JELLO	1.50	MELON IN SEASON	2.25
HOMEMADE APPLE PIE	1.95	CARAMEL CUSTARD	1.95
STEWED PRUNES	1.85	GRAMERCY CHEESE CAKE	2.95
ASSORTED ICE CREAM	1.95	TORTONI OR SPUMONI	1.65
CHOCOLATE MOUSSE CHANTILLY	1.95	BERRIES IN SEASON	2.95
FRUIT CUP SUPREME	1.95	PECAN PIE	1.95

Beverages

COFFEE	1.25	MILK	.75
TEA	.95	ICED TEA	1.00
SANKA	.95	ICED COFFEE	1.00
ESPRESSO	1.45		

Try a Carafe
of Our Special Wines
Red
Rose
White
½ Liter Liter
or ask our
Maitre D' for a
complete wine list

Domestic Beer
or
Imported Beer

HOTEL GRAMERCY PARK

APPETIZERS

Cherrystone Clams $2.50 extra — Little Neck Clams $2.50 extra
Marinated Herring — Chopped Chicken Livers
Fruit Cocktail — Cottage Cheese with Chives
Anchovies on Cole Slaw — Melon in Season
Eggs A La Russe — Shrimp Cocktail $3.75 extra
TOMATO, PRUNE, APPLE, GRAPEFRUIT or V-8 JUICE

OR SOUPS

Potage du Jour — Beef Bouillon Double

ENTREES

	[illegible]	A LA CARTE
Brook Trout Saute or Broiled Amandine	10.95	9.95
Broiled Filet of Lemon Sole, Champignon	9.50	8.95
Bay Scallops Saute Meuniere	11.95	10.95
Fresh Crab Flakes a la Dewey	11.95	10.75
Lobster en Casserole Nantua	11.95	10.75
Breaded Veal Cutlet, Parmigiana	11.75	10.75
Escallopine of Veal Marsala	11.75	10.75
Tournedos, Monte Carlo	14.95	13.95

CHARCOAL GRILL

Broiled Spring Chicken, Vert Pre	9.50	8.75
Broiled Pork Chops, Louisiana	10.95	10.00
Broiled Prime Sirloin Steak, Bercy	14.95	13.95
Broiled Spring Lamb Chops	15.95	14.95
Broiled Prime Filet Mignon, Tyrolienne	15.95	14.95
Broiled Chopped Tenderloin Steak, Bercy	9.50	8.50
Fresh Calf's Liver, Broiled or Saute, a l'Oignon	11.95	10.95

POTATO — VEGETABLE DU JOUR
AND
Fresh Country Salad with Tomato (served with Entree Above)

COLD BUFFET

Stuffed Half Alligator Pear with Chicken Salad Mayonnaise, Sliced Tomato	10.95	10.25
Kennebec Salmon, Mayonnaise, Lettuce and Tomato	11.95	10.25
Gramercy Salad, Tuna Fish, Chicken Salad, Cottage Cheese on lettuce, garnished with fruit	9.50	8.75
California Fruit Platter, Cottage Cheese, Assorted Fruit	9.50	8.75

DESSERTS

Green Apple Pie — Cup Custard
Homemade Cheese Cake $1.25 extra — Rice Pudding
Fruit Jello — Layer Cake
Stewed Prunes — Compote of Fruit
Spumoni — Orange or Raspberry Sherbet
Chocolate Mousse Chantilly $1.25 extra — Biscuit Tortoni
French Ice Cream: Rum Raisin, Chocolate, Strawberry, Coffee, Pistachio, Butter Pecan or Vanilla

BEVERAGES

Coffee — Tea — Milk
Iced Tea — Sanka — Iced Coffee

CHILDREN'S DINNERS AVAILABLE

The Roof Garden, Greentree Room, Gramercy Rooms, Park and Bedford Suites are available for private parties and Banquets

The lobby, looking toward Gramercy Park, in 1928. *Photo by Percy Loomis Sperr.*

The second floor, which has been renamed over the years. The room has hosted events for Joe DiMaggio, David Bowie, Floyd Patterson, and the Weissberg family.

Above: The rooftop lounge in 1928, designed to resemble the home of agnostic Robert Ingersoll. *Photo by Percy Loomis Sperr*

Opposite, top: Herbert with Ruth in the dining room during Steven's bar mitzvah in 1967.

Opposite, bottom: *Left to right, back row*: Marty, Steven, Herbert, David, and Robert. *Left to right, front row*: Laura, Ruth (Danny), and Georgeanne in 1968.

Left: Herbert R. Weissberg at the start of his career in the early 1950s.

Below: Fashion designer Stephen Sprouse with Debbie Harry. *Photo by Martyn Goddard.*

Top: Chris Stein, Debbie Harry, Stephen Sprouse, and an unidentified person. *Photo by Martyn Goddard.*

Bottom: Madness in the gift shop on February 25, 1980. *Photo by Ebet Roberts.*

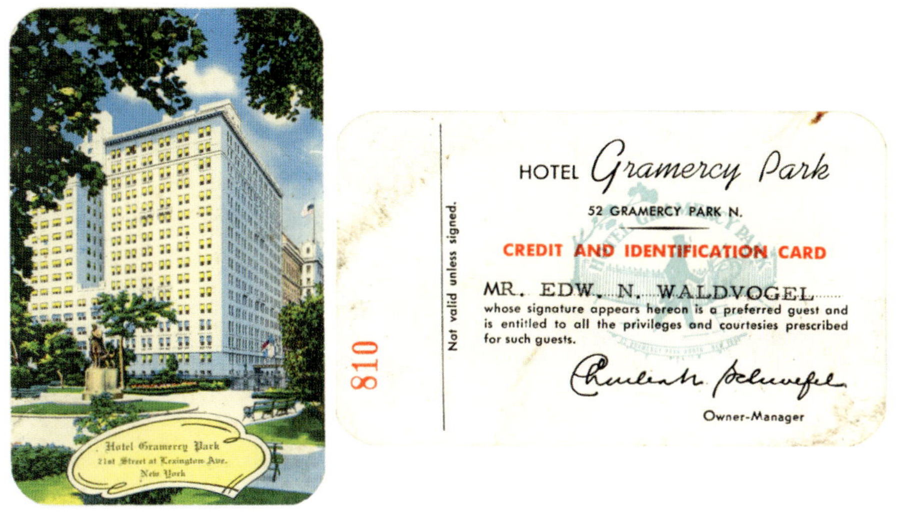

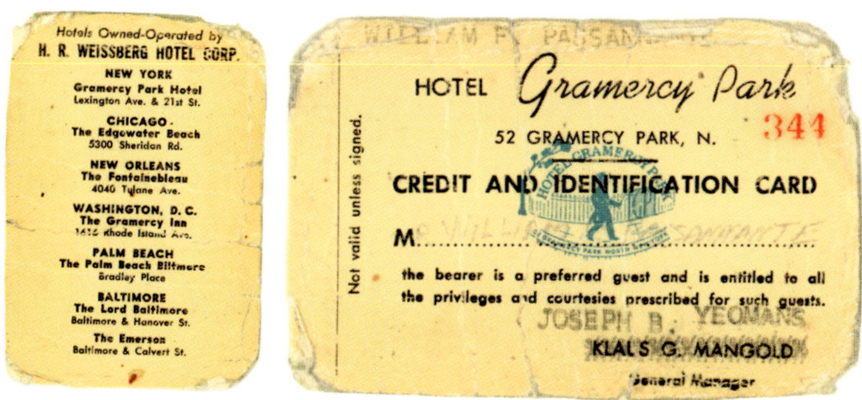

Paper credit cards from the Schwefel and Weissberg eras. Many never paid, and expense accounts were abused by staff and family alike.

A postcard painted by George Ann Gillespie, commissioned by Herbert Weissberg in the early 1990s.

Father's Day 1982. At the time, much of the family lived down the hall from John and Mackenzie Phillips.

The Weissberg clan inside Gramercy Park, the only private park in Manhattan, circa 1983. Eventually, three of the park's benches were dedicated to Weissberg family members.

The awning in the 1990s. The doorman Angel is pictured. *Photo by David Weissberg.*

Father's Day 2001, just after Michael's death. *Left to right*: Marilyn, David, Nicole, Erika, Robert, Ruth, Herbert, Marty, Gayle, and Jonathan (holding Logan). *Photo by Cameron Weissberg.*

From left to right: Ruth, Madalyn, Marty, and Steven on the roof in the 1980s. *Photo by David Weissberg.*

Debbie Harry, also known as Blondie. *Photo by Martyn Goddard.*

Herbert with his maître d' Victor Palma, circa 1982. *Photo by Georgeanne Hume.*

A room in the 1990s. The televisions were terrible because the vendor gave a kickback to the resident manager. *Photo by Max Weissberg.*

Top: The loyal staff along with Marilyn, circa 1996. Succession forecasting was rampant. *Photo by Steven Weissberg.*

Middle: Michael, David, and Jonathan, circa 1988. Michael's overdose and David's death by suicide had major effects on life at the hotel. *Photo by Steven Weissberg.*

Bottom: Cameron, Steven, and Marilyn, circa 1999. Marilyn's presence irked many in the family. *Photo by David Weissberg.*

Top: The Rose Bar in 2006, New York City's premier celebrity destination and performance spot for Lady Gaga and Axl Rose, among others. To the right is Julian Schnabel's *Suddenly Last Summer (Picasso Painting No. 2)*. *© Nikolas Koenig/OTTO.*

Bottom: The lobby of the renovated Gramercy Park Hotel, 2021. *Photo by Sergi Reborado, Alamy Stock Photo.*

Top: *Photo by Sergi Reborado, 2021; Alamy Stock Photo.*

Bottom: The hotel's renovated exterior, 2021. Note the added glass enclosure on the rooftop, added partly to prevent jumps. *Photo by Sergi Reborado, Alamy Stock Photo.*

The Jade Bar in 2006 in the same spot as the hotel's original bar, featuring *Blue Japanese Painting No. 3* by Julian Schnabel. © *Nikolas Koenig/OTTO.*

The Punishment

I remember we sat in the dining room, my father, Robert; my eventual German stepmother, Erika; and I at one table. Michael and Steven at another. Herbert and Ruth in the corner. Except for an older woman and her caretaker near the fireplace, the only customers in the room were Weissbergs. The waiters listened in.

"Max," Robert said, after I had made half a dozen excuses, "I've heard it before. You think you're so smart and then you get in trouble."

Marty came over to our table, fresh from scolding Michael. He didn't bother to sit and waved his arms as he spoke. "They'll break your fucking thumbs. That's what happens to gamblers. You owe them, and then they break your fucking thumbs!" Marty shouted. Robert gave him a look that said, "I got it." Marty grimaced back at him.

"I'm telling him because *you* don't know how to, and your son's gonna end up dead somewhere," Marty continued. He kept repeating that my thumbs would be broken. I wanted to plead with Marty that I'd been thrown off the tour for drinking, *not* gambling, but Marty was full of energy and there was no opportunity to say anything.

Later, I sat at Herbert's corner table and told him my version of the story.

"Bullshit," Herbert mumbled in response, but in a gentle, playful way. It wasn't clear if he was amused or had just given up. After all, this was a man who himself had owned a casino.

Two weeks later, I entered Lake Forest Academy, a boarding school in suburban Chicago. Every day, I wore khaki pants and a tie. I excelled in German and wrestling. Michael and the rest of Steven's family moved into the hotel. That was where our lives split. We had both taken the opportunity to be corrupted by hotel life. Michael, however, remained in it. At a secluded school, I could not get away with the same things the hotel had allowed.

For me, it was the end of the road with my foray into sex workers. I had gotten the experience, and it gave me a sliver of confidence in my relations with women. From then on, I was interested in normal experiences with girls my own age. Never again would I find myself in the Gramercy Park Hotel alone with a stack of cash, free of responsibilities or commitments.

At the Gramercy, however, Michael went off the deep end. Somehow, he got ahold of Ruth's credit card and ordered sex workers on a regular basis. I was fascinated and asked him many questions as he bragged about the details. All the women were older than him. There were regulars, too. But unlike me, he did not have any girlfriends.

I should also mention that after trying pot for the first time (during a college visit to my sister in Madison, Wisconsin), I was eager for Michael to try it, too. Oddly enough, he claimed to have some himself, but it turned out to be fake weed. I gave him the real stuff to try and then went back to boarding school.

By the time I returned to the hotel, Michael was smoking in a week what I would smoke in a semester. He didn't even want to finish high school. When I asked him what he wanted to do with his life, he said that he wanted to be a dictator over the world. Often, he would explain his plan for taking power, but most days, he never left his hotel room. If being a dictator didn't work out for him, he told me, he would live like his father and make deals.

Part of me wanted to cheer him on. It was as if Michael had read Schopenhauer's passage on paradise and was attempting to prove him wrong. But part of me also wondered where the adults were. There would soon be a hole in Michael's life following his mother's death. His father, Steven, was not around, nor was I. But uncle David, the heroin addict, was there.

Father's Day

Because Herbert had only sons and his sons had a disproportionate number of grandsons, Father's Day became the most important holiday in the family. Every year, our family gathered in the hotel, had drinks and Goldfish crackers in the bar, and then ate an enormous meal that always started late. For Herbert, the holiday was not only an occasion to be given presents and read some clumsily written gratitude in a Hallmark card; Father's Day was also the ceremonial recognition of his paternal power.

Father's Day 1998 stands out to me. At the time, I was sixteen years old with muttonchop sideburns. My outfit usually consisted of torn jeans, a grey Calvin Klein sweater, and a Barbour jacket. In June 1998, I was staying in the Gramercy before a two-month-long trip to Germany with my father, his girlfriend Erika, and a fifteen-year-old blond, petite girl whom I'll call Jennifer, who had put me in the friend zone. Since we were traveling together, the entire hotel mistakenly thought the girl was my girlfriend. So everyone was remarkably impressed with me.

I remember Father's Day began as usual, with drinks and Goldfish crackers in the bar. Robert; Erika; my sister, Nicole; her female college friend; my friend Jennifer; my uncle Marty; his wife, Gayle; and his three children, who were older than Nicole and me, were in attendance.

Marty made odds on who would arrive first. "Twenty to one," he said, "that Steven will get here before 4:00 p.m." It was 3:20 p.m. His kids started waving cash. Soon they were betting on when David would arrive—or if he would arrive at all. Not long before, he had punched a desk clerk and provoked a lawsuit, so perhaps he was too ashamed to come at all.

At some point, the conversation focused on me. "I see you've found a nice Jewish girl," Marty said to me, grinning. His wife, Gayle, sitting next to him, also smirked. Obviously, nothing about my blond, beautiful friend was Jewish. Jennifer didn't seem to mind the joke, however. I then thought it a good idea for Jennifer to meet the resident luftmensch, so I introduced her to Lionel on the other side of the bar. He was dressed in his usual tweed suit with tortoiseshell glasses. Halfway through our conversation, Lionel bummed a free drink off of me.

Later, Herbert arrived, then Steven; his new wife, Cameron; and crew. The gathering soon moved to a large banquet table. At the head sat Herbert. Just as we felt comfortable in our seats, Herbert pointed to his cheek. This meant he wanted kisses from all of the children. After I kissed him, Jennifer was also instructed to kiss Herbert's cheek. She complied, amused by the ceremony. I felt practically in horror.

The waiters shuffled in plates of antipasto on vertically stacked trays. We munched on olives and prosciutto until Marty found something to his dissatisfaction and disappeared to the back. When he came back, he told us the waiters had screwed everything up. I could hardly tell.

The conversation shifted to politics. Steven asked Marty if he watched the conservative TV host Rush Limbaugh, who was then very popular. "I have a job, Steven. I *work* during the day," Marty replied. (To Marty, Steven had no job.)

"But don't you have one of those small TVs at the office you can watch?" Steven asked, trying to backpedal. Steven's confidence was unshaken. In his mind, he *was* a top hotel executive. Back and forth they went, Marty trying to make a fool of Steven while Steven listed his accomplishments, like his purchase of a new espresso machine and a set of pens with the hotel's logo on them.

At the other end of the table, my father presented Herbert a framed picture of his parents and told him some Henny Youngman jokes. Herbert chuckled but was near silent. Meanwhile, Marty told our side of the table how he finally stopped Pinky from smoking in the coat check. Then he rambled on about how small Lionel's dick was. While I quietly sipped my ginger ale, Marty continued as if he was the one saving the hotel.

Then Ruth (Danny) got up to make a speech. "I want everyone to stop fighting," she said bitterly. There were people fighting? This was news to me. She repeated this over and over, as if there was some major feud going on behind the scenes.

After the meal was over, then David finally showed. Only my cousin Michael, myself, and Jennifer remained. David was wearing a T-shirt with the image of a tuxedo on it and sounded like he had just come from a *High Times* party. "You know, the Nazis had some of the best submarines," David suddenly said to no one in particular as he nursed a cup of coffee. "They could have perhaps won the war if they had made enough of them." Michael jumped in the conversation, and they were soon speaking about conspiracies. Then David got on the subject of Jesus and how he was the son of a Roman soldier. He told us how one day, when Jesus was a teenager, Mary was leaning over a chest when Jesus jumped on the chest and trapped Mary by her breasts. According to David, Jesus said he wouldn't get up unless Mary told him the real story of his father. Mary then told Jesus the story and revealed the name of Jesus's father: Joseph Pantera. This was all according to ancient Jewish records, David told us.

After he finished his coffee, David disappeared again. So Jennifer, Michael, and I went upstairs to join the others, who were playing pool in room 502 (minus Herbert and Ruth). Marty's wife had left to visit her mother in the hospital, and now, Marty was full-on hitting on my fifteen-year-old friend and Nicole's friend. At one point, Nicole's friend asked for a pool stick from Marty, and he said he wouldn't hand it over unless she kissed him. Later, I disappeared with Michael and Jennifer to smoke pot on the roof.

Over the years, the Father's Day celebrations painted a similar portrait of decline: Herbert talked less and less as Ruth, his docile yet manipulative second wife, began speaking for him. Robert, my father, joked ever louder, trying to turn the attention away from the problems and win the approval of his father. Marty lashed out at the employees and other relatives more frequently and reminded everyone that his marketing was saving the hotel. Steven talked about future deals and was often mocked by Marty. David arrived at the meal later and later until he didn't show up at all. And Nicole, my sister, watched it all and dreamed how she would one day take over. To me and many others, Nicole seemed like the one in the third generation who was capable of following in Herbert's footsteps.

As for the relationships between the brothers, Marty and Robert could not help feeling jealous at the outrageously expensive lifestyle Steven was living at the time. A typical day for Steven included breakfast in the hotel, lunch with a lawyer that might cost him $200 for the hour, and then a shopping trip on Fifth Avenue to buy a belt to match his Armani suit. Then he would go back to the hotel for dinner before getting a nightcap with someone like the singer Joe Cocker. I remember accompanying him while he shopped for a new shotgun from Holland & Holland that cost $20,000. Another time, Steven wanted our side of the family to accompany him to an outrageously expensive sushi restaurant, which Robert claimed he couldn't afford. "Don't you have a credit card?" Steven asked innocently. Unlike Robert, Steven's credit card bill was paid for by the hotel, removing him from reality.

Steven's status as heir came thanks to his mother, Ruth. Like most stepmothers, she was not fond of Herbert's children from his previous wife. The more cocktails she drank in the bar, the clearer this became. Though Steven took the most money, Ruth liked to remind Herbert's children that they were all getting money from their father and were all dependent on him. When I visited the hotel, Ruth always gave me a $100 bill, not Herbert—a reminder that she still had control.

Once, my father was asked by Herbert, "Did you come here or alone?" Robert replied, "Alone." Ruth stormed in from the neighboring room. "A loan?! A loan?!" she groaned. "Bobby needs more money?" Then she listed all the times in the past when Robert had asked for money, going back to the 1960s.

My father, the bookish professor, attempted to ignore the competition for Herbert's cash. Though he would dismiss Steven's lack of a job and dependence on the hotel, how could he not secretly envy such a leisurely life? Robert and Marty's relationship, however, was cold. In the 1980s, Robert and Marty ran into a bitter dispute following their mutual ventures into the clothing industry. Excited by an encouraging speech from Barney Pressman (of Barneys fame), Georgeanne and Robert set up a big and tall shop in Champaign, Illinois, in the mid-1980s. At that time, Marty also owned some clothing stores in Florida, both aided by startup capital from Herbert. Robert and Georgeanne had no experience in the clothing business, but they did their best and bought from the wholesale suit dealers in New York that Marty knew. Eventually, Marty began hustling Robert, selling him lime suits and overcharging for bogus advertising. Eventually, Robert and Georgeanne got so fed up, they secretly made recordings of their phone conversations with Marty to catch him lying. They then played the tapes to Herbert as proof Marty was cheating them. Herbert did nothing, but Robert remained bitter. After a few years, a Father's Day event forced them to reconcile in the hotel's bar.

The family clothing business, Dress for Success, never made real money like the hotel did. So Herbert, who owned one-third of the business, put pressure on Robert to kick Georgeanne out of the operation. The business had created all sorts of disputes between the married couple, so Robert was not slow to fire Georgeanne. The final straw came when Herbert disinvited Georgeanne from the hotel. Robert and Georgeanne's divorce came within a year, all because of the decisions made at Herbert's dinner table in Gramercy Park. Growing up, both my sister and I blamed "the store" for breaking our parents apart. But Herbert should have taken the real blame. My parents were not cut out for operating a business like he was. Eventually, the store was sold. My father went back to teaching as a full-time professor while my mother resumed her career as a social worker.

After the Father's Day meal, the family would often take a stroll in Gramercy Park. Herbert and Robert would sometimes walk together alone, away from the ears of the others. Later, I would understand this sparked jealousy among the other brothers—and his wife, Ruth.

In that warm June air, Herbert often blamed Madalyn for Steven's inability to make his own deals. In his mind, Madalyn's meddling interfered with Steven's ability to think clearly. Madalyn was on her deathbed, however, and Herbert's belief that there would be a benefit to her death was a cold way of viewing things. Once, he had written poetry to his lover. But then he discovered she had been having an affair, just like him. The scar from Frances's cheating decades ago had not healed, and Herbert continued to distrust women.

The other big piece of news to come from these private conversations was that our family was worth tens of millions of dollars. Herbert told Robert he would inherit $10 million. I couldn't believe how much money Herbert had accumulated. But in the end, most of it would disappear.

The Bar in the 1990s

Once, Herbert listened to an architect explain how a redesign of the hotel's bar, lounge, and lobby could free up some space and allow for more customers, i.e. more business. He leaned his head to one side and shrugged his shoulders. "You're crazy," he said, as if the man understood nothing. Herbert always believed places were better when they were crowded. He liked to put people close to each other. At the Gramercy, it was easy to meet people, whether they met in its slow elevators, at busy bar, or in the occasional obstacle course of luggage and guitar cases in the lobby. The focal point of this modern-day Agora was the bar and its adjacent lounge.

Though the Gramercy's bar was the house that Ruth built, by the 1990s, it had seen better days. The autographed Babe Ruth picture that had hung behind the bar was nowhere in sight. Still a popular meeting ground, it was frequently the scene of fading rock stars dolling out interviews to rock magazines. In 1990, Shane MacGowan of The Pogues turned up just after leaving this band. "I stopped being a human being," he explained to a journalist, reflecting on years of touring that included opening for Bob Dylan, among others. "It took me a while, but I'm human again." Like it was for others on the road, the hotel was a refuge.

MacGowan had become so exhausted that former Clash lead Joe Strummer had to step in his place and sing for The Pogues. Like The Pogues' ex-frontman, Strummer remained a Gramercy loyalist and gave interviews in the bar. But both MacGowan and Strummer were no longer drinking alcohol and popping pills like they had in the 1980s. Thankfully, the bar served coffee and espresso.

Another familiar face at the bar was Matt Dillon, a resident in the hotel. Usually, he came in to warm up before going out on the town. He was known for being friendly. Once, when he met my mom, he kissed her hand.

At fifteen, I regularly brought a friend from boarding school to New York. Though we didn't have fake IDs, the bartenders let my friend Jason Oberg and I drink at the bar. For my first real drink in a bar, I didn't know what to order, so I asked for a "vodka with ice."

"You mean a 'vodka on the rocks'?" the bartender asked softly, offering me a free lesson. I nodded and made it a double.

While my friend and I, in our Abercrombie & Fitch clothing, tried to blend in, a lot of cool shit was happening around us. Former screenwriter and director Harmony Korine (of *Kids* fame) knocked over a table and chased a German guest to the street, shouting, "Leave me alone! I'm only a kid, and I'm insane." Another time, his girlfriend and muse Chloë Sevigny sipped on a cranberry drink as she told the story of how meeting Korine underneath a tree in the West Village eventually led to her Oscar nomination for *Boys Don't Cry*. Add director John Waters and photographer Terry Richardson, who were always hanging around the hotel, and you had the full roster of the '90s cool kids.

With pianist Roy Bailey on the baby grand piano in the lounge, the jazz standards gave the bar a warm ambience that was inviting. Once, jazz pianist Jimmy Smith walked in and, inspired, played an impromptu session. Another time, Jewel played the piano and serenaded her date, Leonardo DiCaprio, with "Summertime." For many weeks in the early 1990s, Dave Pirner of Soul Asylum appeared nightly in the bar before his 8:00 p.m. studio call, occasionally pulling other musicians from the bar to join him in his sessions.

Once, a musician even missed his gig, thanks to the bar's allure. The story goes that Steven was drinking with Jerry Lee Lewis before Lewis's gig at nearby Tramp's. Just before Steven left the bar, he reminded Lewis (who remained behind) about his upcoming show. Sometime later, Steven arrived at Tramp's, but Lewis was nowhere in sight. The band started playing without him. Meanwhile, Lewis's manager frantically called his hotel room, looking for him, but there was no answer. Steven got an idea. So he called the hotel's bar and asked for Lewis, who, sure enough, had forgotten about the gig while drinking whiskey sours. Thanks to Steven, the "Great Balls of Fire" songwriter made it to the show by the third song.

Another time, David Carradine was drinking in the bar when he turned to a woman and said, "Madame, you have a face like an antique clock." The woman was very insulted. A scandal ensued, and the story was told for months afterward. Little old ladies were the bread and butter of the Gramercy Park Hotel.

In fact, whenever the bar was filled with just little old ladies, I had a hard time convincing my friends the place was cool. To them, it looked rundown, full of creaks with a permanent musty scent. Pests, too, were a problem. Once, when Steven put some magicians in the bar to stir things up, a cockroach ran across the bar in front of me during a magic show.

"Look, a cockroach!" I shouted. Ruth, who happened to be next to me, started shushing me.

"It was a mosquito," she said loudly and unconvincingly to the crowd, whose eyes were on the bar. *Oops*, I thought. Any child from a hotel family should know not to point out a cockroach.

Like the bar, the rest of the hotel was falling apart. In the 1990s, one reviewer pointed out that "the telephone appears to have torn cables, adding frisson to the competition between character and sheer seediness." That same author called the hotel "a bit seedy," a place they remembered for its "smelly rooms, rude staff, and dysfunctional romance." It also had "frayed pillowcases" and "scratchy towels," so thin you could almost see through them. Equally damning was a 1996 *New York Times* review that criticized the spelling mistakes on the menu and the carved initials in the elevator, among other shortfalls. When *New York Times* writer Sarah Lyall

Left to right: Tom O'Brien, Pinky, and Herbert, circa 1994. *Photo by David Weissberg.*

called the hair salon to ask what services were available, a voice angrily replied, "We're a beauty parlor!"

Alongside the critiques that highlighted the hotel's shoddiness were reviews that praised our rooms as being "very comfortable, friendly, and reasonable by Gotham's standards." Explaining how the hotel kept its business, art dealer Jeffrey Deitch said, "There is no good hotel downtown that has any style. Basically, the art world goes to the Gramercy, which is quite rundown."

In other words, certain factors that had little to do with the management were saving the hotel. The essence of the maintenance problem was that my grandfather Herbert would not live forever. After his death, there would be a large inheritance tax, which would force the sale of the hotel. Thus, spending a large amount of money replacing things would not pay back over the long run. Instead, Herbert took the profit from the hotel and invested it in the ever-growing stock market. Representatives from Goldman Sachs and Morgan Stanley often came to Herbert's corner table with offers. His days were spent watching CNBC's coverage of the stock market. While old men across the country bought Viagra, Herbert bought Pfizer. What he enjoyed talking about most, besides his stocks, was how his employees "loved" him. So he handed them wads of cash as a token of his appreciation for their loyalty. As for me, I got a $100 bill on every visit. Nothing about my stay in the Gramercy felt like a visit to an ordinary hotel.

Though it was deteriorating, the hotel still commanded respect. By the end of the 1990s, director Cameron Crowe chose the Gramercy as a location to film *Almost Famous*, an homage to the hotel's rock 'n' roll legacy. There were even songs written about the hotel by the Argentine duo Charly García and Pedro Aznar, Edwin McCain, and John Cougar Mellencamp. Even with its wrinkles, the hotel attracted many rock groups who wanted to imitate the bands who'd come before them.

With so many interesting people crossing paths and forming partnerships, there were also some misses. Evan Dando of The Lemonheads and his future wife, British model Elizabeth Moses, lived in rooms 921 and 1121, respectively, for eight months but never encountered each other. At the time, Evan was dating Courtney Love and a slew of other famous girls. So perhaps fate decided that the timing wasn't right.

No matter its shabbiness, the hotel could still draw people into its orbit, which brought financial independence for the Weissberg family. Like the slow and steady rise of the Dow, it was hard to imagine it all coming to an end.

8

BENIGN NEGLECT

1994–2002

The Gramercy Hotel Art Fair

While my family kept the museum running, it suddenly played a major role in the art world. In April 1994, the Gramercy Park Hotel became the birthplace of a new exhibit made entirely of Generation X art. The story goes that four downtown art dealers, Pat Hearn, Matthew Mark, Colin de Land, and Paul Morris, came together to rent rooms at the Gramercy so they could stage works. The idea was partly inspired by the "unFair" show in Cologne, Germany, and the Art Hotel fair in Amsterdam, but unlike these two fairs, in the Gramercy, the hotel's furniture remained and was incorporated into the show. For their groundbreaking fair, the group booked most of the rooms on the twelfth, fourteenth, and fifteenth floors (there was no thirteenth floor in the hotel), and the four-day Gramercy Park Hotel International Contemporary Art Exhibition began. Dealers came from Paris, Cologne, Berlin, Vienna, Milan, Los Angeles, Chicago, and, of course, New York. Thanks to the free admission perhaps, roughly five thousand people visited the first exhibits.

Since we didn't want anyone nailing their artwork on the walls, the dealers leaned pieces against the walls or placed them on the furniture. Despite the restrictions, the artists got clever. The rooms themselves became installations. Some rooms were stuffed with sculptures, photographs, and paintings. Perhaps for the first time, people could see what the works looked like inside a room with ordinary furniture. Other rooms were more adventurous and had art made out of trash piled up on the furniture,

furniture turned upside down, TVs hanging from the ceilings, floors and beds wrapped in artistic linen covers, old projectors playing films on the wallpaper, fake plants that spun in their vases, and all sorts of other weird and interesting things. In the men's lobby restroom, someone wrote "Marcel Duchamp took a piss here." Journalist Geraldine Norman described the exhibit as a reflection on "sex, death, and the shadow of AIDS." It was a scene, but it was also making history.

Among the artists who showed were Cindy Sherman, Takashi Murakami, Jeff Koons, and others. Artist Tracey Emin made her debut at the Gramercy show, brought to New York by the legendary British dealer Jay Jopling, the founder of the White Cube in London. Wearing a negligee in room 1515, Emin lay on the bed underneath a quilt that documented traumatic moments in her life. Along with the quilt were mementos and handwritten accounts placed in glass boxes; they included "My Abortion," a five-part work that included three watercolors, her hospital identification bracelet, and a handwritten account of what happened (she caught the fetus as it slipped down her leg in a taxi). The work sold for $2,000. Emin also had a three-part piece titled *My Future* that included an old tooth, a dentist appointment card, and an old passport, which sold for $1,250.

Over the next few years, the show grew in popularity, with some notable works on display. It also spread to other floors. In 1995, Jeffrey Deitch took over the rooftop to recreate the salon of the American painter Florine Stettheimer, based on photographs. In 1996, in room 402, the Korean artist Nam June Paik placed two TVs in the bathtub that broadcast two halves of a naked model gently turning on her back and butt, labeled by a critic as a "masterpiece of bathtub art." That same year, Tom Sachs transformed room 312 into a nail salon and called it "Sick Nails." Also among the items displayed (from the gallery Emmanuel Perrotin in Paris) was a medicine cabinet made by the artist Damien Hirst in room 510. (A decade later, after the hotel was redesigned by Julian Schnabel and Ian Schrager, another Damien Hirst medicine cabinet was installed on the rooftop of the Gramercy.)

"We were very naive," the fair's founder Morris once explained to journalist Tess Thackara. "At one point, David Ross, who had been the director of the Whitney, said, 'You guys have to charge an entrance fee, or people won't take you seriously'—which we really hadn't thought of before." The fair organizers later gave out a Gramercy International Prize, which included a free room for an artist at the fair. For many in the struggling art world, the show brought a ray of hope.

As if to recognize the Gramercy's own beauty, an artist removed the sink basin from their bathroom and displayed it as a work of art—or maybe there was just a plumbing problem. No one was quite sure. According to the *Wall Street Journal*, some employees of one of the galleries left their card game at a table unattended. Then some customers mistook it for a piece of art. They also reported that a maid ruined a display when she made an artist's bed. Were these stories true? I have no idea. But they were syndicated in newspapers across the country, fueling cynicism against modern art.

The show was so successful, it reappeared at the Chateau Marmont in Los Angeles and at the Raleigh Hotel in Miami. By 1999, the annual show had gotten so popular it was moved to a warehouse on a pier facing the Hudson River. It was then renamed The Armory Show, a nod to the 1913 art fair that had introduced Van Gogh and Cézanne to America. Today, the show continues as one of the biggest art fairs in New York.

Not every guest who brought art to the hotel was a dealer, however. Just after the Gramercy Art Fair departed, art thief Zion Morrally stayed in room 1509 with a stolen sixteenth-century painting, *The Annunciation*, by Italian painter Giovanni Battista Zelotti. The painting was worth $250,000 because of its unusual combination of the Virgin Mary with a phallic symbol. After stealing the painting from a house in the Hamptons and checking in at the Gramercy, Morrally thought he was on the way up. But he soon discovered he was on the way down. His buyer turned out to be an undercover cop.

The First Seeds of Tragedy: Michael and David

Of all my relatives who lived in the Gramercy Park Hotel, my uncle David was the one I saw the least growing up. To me, he was the "junkie" in the family. Admittedly, my view was heavily affected by my father, Robert. Because of David's drug use, my mother and the other wives of the family kept their children away from him. I usually bumped into him only when I was entering or leaving the hotel. One exception was, of course, Father's Day, when everyone in the family was required to eat lunch together in the dining room. On these occasions, David would show up late, pointedly underdressed. After he stopped showing up by the late 1990s, one of us would be appointed to go find him.

From the time I was sixteen, I heard about David's gun collection. There is no record of the guns David owned, though they included AK-47s, .357s, shotguns, machine guns, and assault rifles. Along with the weapons

Michael (*far left*), Jonathan (*sitting in the chair*), and David (*right*) at Jonathan's bar mitzvah in 1998.

were duffle bags stuffed with bullets. If someone attacked him wearing a bulletproof vest, David had hollow-tipped bullets that could penetrate the protective layer. Most of these guns were, in fact, legal and registered in the state of Florida. Many, however, were allowed only to be used by the military's special forces. As his collection began to fill several trunks, it was clear that he no longer bought the weapons to protect himself—he had developed a full-grown gun fetish.

By the 1990s, David's addiction had grown into a $500-a-day habit for speedball, a mixture of cocaine and heroin. His cocaine dealing fell short of what he needed to support himself, however. He offered his Florida connections, the Rastas, a deal. If he could reopen a popular nightclub that had recently been closed, they would give him 10 percent of whatever

Left to right: Steven, Jonathan, Herbert, and Michael in 1998.

business they conducted on the premises. Referencing his father's legacy as a hotel operator, he assured them he could bring customers into their operation. They agreed. David then proposed the whole operation to Herbert (leaving out many details, of course). He explained it as a way for him to follow in Herbert's footsteps. Frank Guma's son, Danny Guma, described his involvement:

> *David was down in Florida.* [Herbert] *called me. There was a club. Club Soda where all the wise guys hung out. The FBI shut this place down. David was obsessed with getting this place open. He flew me into the Gramercy Park Hotel and wanted to give me 50 percent of the nightclub and take care of David. I went down there. I met a ton of people. The FBI wouldn't let it open.*

David's failure to open the club caused his Rastafarian partners to threaten him with violence. According to Danny Guma, "it got ugly" and "people got hurt." It's unclear what exactly happened, but in a short while, David was back in New York City and didn't want to return to Florida. What hardly anyone knew at the time, however, was that when David moved all of his stuff from New York to Florida, he brought his weapons with him.

David still had big plans to increase his business. He upgraded his motorcycle to a Honda Prelude that had more places to hide things. In order to protect his car against any searches by law enforcement, he had his two Doberman Pinscher dogs live in the car for a day while he fed them through the window. His goal was to make the car stink. No dog, he believed, would be able to sniff through the Doberman scent to get to the drugs. Next, he made several contributions to police pension funds and other police-related charitable organizations, for which he obtained car window stickers. Seeing the stamps and official insignias, he reckoned, would encourage law enforcement to go easy on him during a pullover. Perhaps he got this idea from Herbert. If that weren't enough to protect him, David had a mechanic cut a hole in the floor of the car on the passenger side. This way, he could throw his coke on the highway if the cops were in pursuit.

Ruth and Steven at a table by themselves on Father's Day 1994. *Photo by Max Weissberg.*

Marty, Steven, and Herbert. *Photo by Max Weissberg.*

His other modifications were strictly personal. Unsatisfied with the car's overall power, he installed a Ferrari exhaust system and added a turbocharger to the engine. Then he tinted the windows and stuck a crown-shaped air freshener and the jaws of a baby shark on the dashboard. This probably gave him some legitimacy among fellow dealers who were put off by the police stickers. My family members and I called this vehicle the "Dope Mobile."

Despite his dope dealing, David remained separated from the hotel business. The hotel, his cameras, and a syringe were enough to keep him satisfied. Marty never wielded much control over David because David was hardly ever around. As his full brother, Steven saw David most and was the closest to him—partly because they never got in each other's way. The only authority David wielded was a business card in his wallet with "David Weissberg, OWNER" printed on it, along with the Gramercy's address and logo. This got him out of trouble (the local police had reason to be loyal to Herbert). David seemed unbothered by the concerns of anyone who judged his lifestyle. Not only was he open about his drug use, but he also told me that while visiting Amsterdam, he had hired a sex worker for the week. "She took me to all the art museums," he told me, like a restaurant critic giving his feedback after a meal. "Van Gogh. Rembrandt. And she didn't even charge me extra. She was cool. Real cool," he said, his mind floating back up to the clouds. A few minutes later, he retold the story as if he had forgotten that he had already told it.

Madalyn Dies

In August 1997, Steven's wife, Madalyn, finally succumbed to her cancer and died. At her funeral, Herbert said few words. He said he didn't like funerals and that he didn't like to speak at them. Madalyn's children, Jonathan and Michael, both preteens, were devastated by the tragedy. The family moved from their Upper East Side apartment into the hotel. Steven lived in the equivalent of five interconnected hotel rooms on the fourteenth floor, facing the park (1401–1405), while Jonathan and Michael lived on the fifth floor in rooms 501 and 502, next to Herbert and Ruth (Danny) (503–505). David, their uncle, eventually moved into room 512, just down the hall.

In the spring of 1998, Steven and his two kids went to visit David, who was then in a court-ordered rehab in Florida. David was allowed to accompany the group to Disney World, and both Michael and Jonathan enjoyed David's company. Later, they visited a shooting range, where David got to show off some of his expertise with machine guns. His wry sense of humor, his indifference to what the world thought of him, his love for Steven's children, mixed in with a touch of charm—these qualities endeared David to Michael and Jonathan. They did not find a replacement for Madalyn, obviously, but David did his best to fill part of that void.

Steven and his children returned to New York City, leaving David behind in rehab. It wasn't long, however, until David had had enough of rehab and fled the facility on foot. A warrant was issued for David's arrest in Florida, but he packed up his things into his car and drove off before they ever caught up to him. Banned from the state of Florida, David decided to make his home in the Gramercy year-round. Along with his clothes and his camera equipment, his pipes and his posters, there was his trunk of weapons. Some of the weapons he stored in a locker in the basement; the others he stashed inside the closet of his room.

I was sixteen the first time I smoked pot with David, which happened with Michael in the Hamptons. David had just gotten out of rehab for the umpteenth time and was nearly as thin as the African children shown in the Sally Struthers commercials. In between puffs, he explained how many of the Nazis had actually fled to Argentina after the war and developed flying saucer technology.

It wasn't long before we were seeing more of David than we were of Steven. While Steven dated young women and traveled the world to inspect hotels for purchase, Michael and Jonathan were back at the hotel being raised by David and the kitchen employees. I was in boarding school, far away from the anything-goes lifestyle, and visited the hotel only on breaks.

Because Michael liked David, he formed part of the circle that I hung out with in the hotel during those breaks. Instead of finding it cool, I found it odd. David had a way of creeping out the friends I brought to the hotel, some of whom were girls. But Michael and David were inseparable.

Michael and David soon started to look like each other. They wore cheap polyester shirts with beachwear patterns (decorated with tiny burn holes). Gold jewelry around their necks. Cheap, tinted glasses that covered half their faces. When they talked, you could hear the drugs. And you could smell them.

Like David, Michael was starting to believe in vast underworld conspiracies involving the Trilateral Commission. Gradually, the need to accomplish anything faded away for Michael. Perhaps this was inevitable living in a Manhattan hotel, where everything one needs to sustain their existence is given to them for free.

As Michael and David delved deeper into harder drugs, I became all-school president and captain of the wrestling team at my boarding school, Lake Forest Academy. I had also shed my dark views of humankind and renounced my atheism.

When Jonathan, Steven's younger son, had his bar mitzvah, I returned to the hotel for the occasion. Jonathan, at this time, was going through a tough time. Not long after his mother's death, Jonathan was diagnosed with a cancer similar to his mother's. Though he recovered, the effect his diagnosis had on the family was tremendous. Herbert decided that he would spare no expense for Jonathan's bar mitzvah. Hundreds of people were invited, including Herbert's lawyers, accountants, and investment advisors.

The religious ceremony was held in Temple Immanuel. In the middle of Jonathan's ceremony, David showed up in his tuxedo T-shirt, causing whispers among the relatives. David's body looked emaciated. It had been some time since many of them had seen David in public. He looked sky high.

The family returned to the hotel for the reception. Every room, it seemed, was filled with celebration. In the dining room, a small orchestra played Strauss. Later, four tuxedoed a cappella singers performed. In the lobby, a circus clown blew balloon animals. In the bar, a magician performed card tricks. The second floor became a casino, with blackjack, poker, and roulette tables, along with loose slots. A special currency with Jonathan's picture, redeemable for prizes, was printed for the occasion. In the Wedgewood Room in 50 Gramercy Park North, an emcee called up family members to stand next to Jonathan as he lit a candle atop a mammoth golden menorah.

Later that evening, I found myself in room 501, Michael's room, with David and his girlfriend, Barbara. Like David, Barbara was a hardcore drug addict. Her skin was lined with tattoos, bruises, and track marks. As we smoked weed, David and Barbara contemplated dropping some acid they had been saving. Something seemed odd about David's presence, as if he made everything okay from a responsibility standpoint. (I had just turned seventeen.) I didn't think much of it at the time, however, and went back to boarding school.

On another visit, Michael and a friend of mine from boarding school went to buy pot from a dealer. Perhaps to show off how much he knew, Michael went downstairs to use the hotel's pay phone. (We always felt the employees listened in on our phone calls.) A half hour later, the three of us were sitting in a sixth-floor walk-up apartment in Hell's Kitchen. There, Judy, a junkie with sapphire-colored veins and knotty gray hair, weighed ounces of marijuana from a giant Ziploc bag. The rotting floor creaked underneath us as we shifted in our spots on the floor. Behind Judy, a dark sheet hung from the ceiling, dividing the room. For $100, Michael bought a quarter ounce of weed.

After the deal was done, we sat and split a joint. I complimented the quality. I heard a cough behind the sheet. Someone else was here.

Back on the street I asked Michael how he knew Judy.

"She's kind of the family dealer." He smiled with pride. I then wondered what my high school friend thought of the Weissbergs now. After a while, David was getting ounces of weed himself and selling them off to whoever needed them, including relatives. It wasn't long before Michael and David started shooting up together. Many were aware of the situation, from the hotel's security, who observed their guests, to the room service waiters, who saw what was casually left out when they entered David's room.

Steven Marries Cameron

While eating lunch one day in a restaurant with Lionel, Steven saw a modelesque woman at a nearby table. Steven then sent Lionel over to offer her a free session with his friend, an expensive hair stylist. The woman, Cameron, agreed and got a $200 hair session with a few snips. Later, they started dating. Blond and blue-eyed, with a healthy amount of plastic surgery, Cameron had come to New York from Pennsylvania to work in the garment industry. She had been married once before under a different name, but they separated for personal reasons. After being laid off from the sinking garment industry, Cameron was almost broke and considered leaving New York.

Steven wanted to marry Cameron, but Herbert insisted on having a prenuptial agreement drafted by his lawyers. Dependent on Herbert, Steven agreed. The couple planned to have a ceremony in the Brotherhood Synagogue on the south side of Gramercy Park. But after the invitations cost a small fortune, Herbert halted the celebration. Instead, Steven and Cameron were married on Valentine's Day in 1998 in a brisk ceremony officiated by Mayor Giuliani, something he performed once a year.

"Steven was like my knight in shining armor," Cameron once explained. Though their values were not much different, Steven and Cameron often fought with each other, generating gossip in the hotel. Now married, Cameron spent the bulk of her time shopping, lounging in the Hamptons, and fighting with Ruth for control over Steven. Cameron and Ruth quickly developed a rivalry.

Steven, meanwhile, came up with one scheme after another to improve the hotel's business. In addition to the magicians, he wanted to install a pizza oven where the bar was. Another night, he talked about putting a mini zoo on the roof with peacocks. No idea lasted more than a week before it faded away.

Mayor Rudy Giuliani, Cameron, and Steven on Cameron and Steven's marriage day in 1998.

When the internet was in the news, Steven had a crowd of techies around him, eager for him to finance their next venture: a search engine that would go straight to a website after clicking instead of generating the typical list results. For all these ideas, Steven met with lawyers and businessmen over lunch at the Gramercy. You might think this lifestyle would get expensive after a while. It was: $6 million over a period of thirty years, excluding room and board according to Herbert.

David Marries Marilyn

While he was still with Barbara, David met a girl named Marilyn at a methadone clinic. According to Marilyn, they were introduced by a mutual friend, Bonnie, who told her, "I know a guy named David. He wants to meet a girl."

Marilyn had strawberry blond hair, butterscotch-colored skin, rotten teeth, and a listless, carefree personality that made her sound like a '60s flower child. According to Herbert's moonlighting NYPD officers, Marilyn had previously been arrested for prostitution.

David asked her to go to the movies. But she said she had food poisoning and just wanted to hang out (and do drugs).

For a while, David had two girlfriends. The older one, Barbara, gave David permission to be with Marilyn so she could "clean up the place now and then." David told Michael and me that he found Marilyn irritating, but she indeed cleaned up his room and he appreciated it. Eventually, David got rid of Barbara, and Marilyn became a regular sight in the bar and dining room.

David and Marilyn flew to Las Vegas with Michael. There, David and Marilyn were married in an Elvis Presley drive-through wedding chapel. "I had to buy glass shoes. Like Cinderella," Marilyn remembered. Eventually, she settled on clear plastic ones. "We were supposed to get married three times. Another time in a shul. Another time in Israel."

When they returned to the hotel, Marilyn instructed the staff to call her "Mrs. Weissberg." This minor request caused Herbert and Ruth tremendous embarrassment. Even though the wedding had already happened, Steven asked her to sign a prenup.

Concerned about Steven's sons, Herbert purchased a house for Michael and Jonathan in East Hampton in their name. As the family spent more time in Long Island, Steven's new wife, Cameron, insisted that David and

Marilyn not be allowed in the new house. So David and Marilyn stayed in a nearby apartment complex for the summer. But, imitating true rock 'n' rollers, they were kicked out for causing mayhem in the first week.

After he finished school, Michael started spending all his time with Marilyn and David. They even traveled together to Mexico. "We were like his parents," Marilyn remembered. "Michael hated Cameron. But he loved his dad. Every time he asked his dad to spend the day with him, Cameron would ask to go to the Hamptons or whatever. That really hurt Michael. And [Cameron] was pregnant. It was hard on the kids. They didn't like Cameron."

Eventually, Steven sent Michael to a remote boarding school for drug users. David and Marilyn flew in to visit, and once again, Michael was able to score. Then he was sent to another school. And so on.

One day, I hung out in Michael's room, 501, after he had returned from one of his special schools. He was in a very emotional state. In a broken voice, he revealed he had gone on a weeklong acid binge until he collapsed somewhere in the hotel. He sounded like he had seen many scary things. They took him to a hospital, he explained, and then returned him to the hotel afterward. Michael meekly handed me his journal to thumb through. Inside were poems and cryptic notes that, from the handwriting, looked like they were written by different people. Michael told me about the friendly nurses, about the bizarre hallucinations he had seen, and especially about how he was finished with drugs. Then he showed me a book he was reading called *The Art of Happiness*, by the Dalai Lama. I truly believed he had turned a corner.

Herbert Gets Sick, Steven and Marty Take Over

When Herbert caught a cold, the staff and residents used to say, the hotel would catch the flu. At the age of ninety, Herbert never changed out of his gray pajamas, perhaps a vestige of his former management style. Tending him was a staff of Caribbean nurses. Herbert's death would mean the end of hundreds of jobs in the hotel, so he was carefully attended to.

In 2000, Herbert suffered a mild stroke and lost his ability to speak almost entirely. Everything suddenly changed for the hotel. For Steven and his older half-brother Marty, it was their long-awaited opportunity to take over the Gramercy. Steven flew to Florida and tried hard to reconcile with Marty, with whom he had never gotten along. After agreeing with Steven to jointly run the hotel, Marty proclaimed that, at last, he had found a "true brother." In order to buy their brother Robert's allegiance to the new regime, they offered Nicole, age twenty-three, a job as a front desk clerk. (By this point, Nicole had worked in hotels in Madison, Wisconsin, and Sydney, Australia.) Nicole was eager to play a role in the hotel's management, but Robert refused the offer on her behalf.

Steven and Marty acted quickly. They fired the management and promoted a desk clerk to take their place. As Steven came up with plans to expand the business, Marty took over the website and the 1-800 number to pay himself a 30 percent commission on every room reserved at the hotel. In their frequent meetings, Marty vented his rage at the "lazy," "conniving" employees, while Steven sat silent. Unleashing decades of bitterness over his lack of power in the hotel, Marty insulted Pinky into retirement and started having an affair with the head of housekeeping (per Lionel). Sadly, Pinky died three weeks after his resignation.

Former manager Tom O'Brien gave his opinion of the changes:

> *There was no love or respect for the two of them* [Marty and Steven]. *They were running the show. They didn't have a clue—that's my opinion. Marty didn't come up with a lot of changes. His whole idea was computers and sales and travel agents. Supposedly, he had a whole staff in Florida dedicated to promoting the hotel. Steven wanted to convert the roof garden, make a huge nightclub. Steven was hard to deal with and would do things on a whim. I came back from vacation, and I was fired. Six months earlier* [resident manager] *Jack* [Vartebedian] *was fired. Steven did that on a whim.*

While employees openly complained about the new regime, thievery increased rapidly. One Chinese immigrant in the booking office (a young girl who had been a personal favorite of Herbert) set up a shell travel company and issued refunds, stealing $180,000. Meanwhile, Steven focused on recovering all the "stolen" Gramercy pens hidden in Jack's cubicle. Then he spent a small fortune replacing some of the hotel's air conditioners.

The gift shop, which still paid no rent to Herbert, also got greedy. As part of his marketing for the hotel, Marty developed package deals that included a bus tour of New York that was booked through the newsstand operated by a pair of Indian immigrants. Many guests didn't claim their tour, and in the confusion, the operators of the gift shop illegally pocketed more than $20,000. After they were caught, the operators couldn't return the money. So

Steven and Marty seized the gift shop's contents, and for the next few months, the family gave out "I love NY" mugs, pens, and playing cards; miniature Statues of Liberty; and handfuls of candy to anyone who wanted it.

Warning signs were everywhere. The elevator became filled with more scratch graffiti carved into the wood. The furniture in the rooms creaked louder. The maids did a worse job cleaning up, according to guidebooks and guests. Gone were the generous helpings of chicken wings in the lounge during happy hour, a minor detail that meant dozens of artists in the East Village were now starving. One of the hotel's most famous guests, Cyrinda Foxe, or "Syringa," moved into the hotel for her final resting place, in a suite paid for by her ex-husband Steven Tyler.

Nothing could be done to rescue the Gram, it seemed. As Herbert remained in a vegetative state, his official statements were now divinely interpreted by Ruth.

Michael Dies

In the summer of 2001, while a freshman at Reed College in Portland, Oregon, I went into the hospital for a pain in my abdomen and had emergency surgery. At the same time, five thousand miles away, Michael shot up a mixture of heroin and other drugs, a nineteenth birthday present from David. I was still unconscious when Michael died in room 512, David's room. After discovering Michael's blue-hued body, David and Marilyn spent the next three hours cleaning up their room before they called the police.

"That was the most horrible thing." Marilyn explained. "I remember yelling at David to dial 911. He was taking his time. He went downstairs. I don't know if he was trying to get a first aid kit. Then I dialed 911. The paramedics came."

With Michael in the hospital, Steven prayed that he would make it. But it was too late.

The news came to me while I was in the hospital. Of my cousins, Michael had been the closest to me in age, and we shared a lot of experiences and secrets together. The timing of his death with my surgery made me wonder—and it's one of those thoughts that makes no sense—whether one of us had to go.

I got some of the blame for Michael's death because Ruth thought that my nihilistic ideas and my casual use of pot influenced him. But most of the blame fell on David.

Three months later, two police officers showed up to David's door.

Marilyn remembered, "There was these two police officers. They were really nice. They said, 'You need to know that Steven is saying you murdered his kid.'"

Family Fighting

Though Steven was distraught and now had a grudge against David, he went on with his life. His wife, Cameron, gave birth to a son, Logan, weeks later. David, meanwhile, dug deeper into his biblical studies, with an emphasis on the mystic secrets of the Kabbalah. He contacted a rabbi at the Brotherhood Synagogue on the south side of Gramercy Park and sought biblical parallels to his story of shame and possible redemption. His drug use, rather than ebb, began to flow immensely. He was also getting sicker with liver cancer, for which he was taking interferon.

One day, while I was standing underneath the hotel's awning, I saw David come out of a cab with Marilyn. He had a fresh tan and looked healthy. In his stoned, nasal voice, he complimented my first beard. I thanked him graciously.

"I didn't want to, but they made me," he said in a throaty voice. I looked at him, confused. He then explained that Steven and Ruth had pressured him into firing Marty. The controversy over Marty's 30 percent booking commission had come to an apex. By firing Marty, David had done what Ruth and Steven could not. In his twenty-five years of living in the hotel, this had been his most significant contribution.

Marty filed for a conservatorship for Herbert, concerned that Steven was making crucial business decisions on Herbert's behalf. Marty then sent copies of the New York State law regarding illegal activities on the premises in reference to David's drug dealing. In bold letters, he mused what would happen if the hotel lost its liquor license. Eventually, the lawsuit ended with the hotel paying Marty a financial settlement, provided the hotel successfully renewed its liquor license. This money supposedly included Marty's liabilities related to booking advertising for the hotel. Ruth's lawyers responded by shrinking Marty's inheritance, and Marty began a letter-writing campaign denouncing everyone in the family, including Robert, who had tried to remain neutral. As part of the proceedings, Ruth was interviewed by the court and refused to let anyone speak with Herbert, though she maintained he made his own decisions. Several people falsely testified under oath, however, that Herbert was somehow capable of making his interests known. Though Marty's claim had merit and was truthful as far as I can tell, he lost.

Herbert's Will Altered

Other things occurred that were more worrisome. In Herbert's first will, he left his lawyer Paul Herman and his accountant Andrew Rubin as the executors of his estate. Then in a codicil dated December 2, 2002, (now former) Judge Charles E. Ramos became coexecutor of the estate, along with the octogenarian Ruth. Two important legal procedures were necessary to achieve this. First, Judge Ramos needed to be excused from the New York judicial rules that barred him, a judge, from participating in matters that came before the court. This was accomplished through a "highly unusual waiver" from fellow Judge Jonathan Lippman, who allowed for the measure because, he wrote, Ramos "had a longstanding relationship of trust and confidence with the Weissbergs going back thirty-six years." Second, Herbert had to sign off himself, which he supposedly did.

Herbert's signature on the revised will, however, has only one S in Weissberg. Nor does it appear to match his signature from years earlier. How Herbert could have managed to fill out the documents in his vegetative state is baffling. One of the witnesses to the signing even crossed out the words "of from any other mental impairment" on the affidavit and scribbled "with respect to aphasia" above. From at least the beginning of 2002 (well before the second will was drafted), Herbert was being treated by a doctor for aphasia and dementia. He could neither speak nor communicate with family members beyond giving a friendly smile. Yet somehow, important documents that gave Ramos enormous control over Herbert's finances were being placed in front of him to sign.

As for Ramos's relationship to the Weissbergs, I will say only that this was the first time either I or my father, Robert, had ever heard of him.

David on the Brink

While all of this was unfolding, the family talked only of David. Despite helping out the family by firing Marty, David must have experienced tremendous guilt every time he shot up in room 512, the same room where Michael had died. Ruth threatened to cut off the flow of money to halt David's drug use. David threatened to end his own life if he were cast aside financially. With the weapons he possessed, a shot to his head in the basement could have easily killed someone else in the lobby. David also had moments of rage. After David tried to kick in Herbert and Ruth's room 505 door during an argument, Ruth had an extra-thick replacement installed.

David's marriage also suffered. While David had tolerated Marilyn before, they now fought openly in all corners of the hotel. Not since Sid and Nancy's visit had the lobby heard so much screaming. Once, Peter O'Toole watched in the elevator as David and Marilyn argued with each other. Later, he commented to Steven approvingly, "It was marvelous. It just put so much passion in me." Later, Marilyn Gauthier, the former model and founder of the Marilyn Agency, recalled gossiping with other guests about the Weissbergs. When asked about the family, Debbie Harry answered only, "Well, you know the story, don't you?" To these people, it was theater. But few really understood the danger of having David around.

On March 13, 2002, I hung out with Jonathan in room 1401. Jonathan practiced on an orange Gibson guitar while I listened, and next to his Apple computer on the bookshelf was a picture of Michael, wearing sunglasses and a smirk, taken not long before he died. Jonathan had come close to death from brain cancer after Madalyn's death, but he had been lucky. More importantly, he resisted the lure of hotel life and did not become close with David as Michael had. He now had grown into a tall frame, with long, dirty-blond hair, and hazel eyes behind his glasses. He had the same nose as his father and had inherited a light olive skin tone from his mother. When he talked about his life, he ended every other sentence with a chuckle. Somehow, his experience with cancer had made him eternally light-hearted, not unlike our great-grandfather Max.

As I listened to Jonathan play, something was unfolding downstairs. Steven claimed that David had threatened to kill Marilyn and that she was pleading with him hysterically in the lobby. Then Steven called the police. Marilyn and my other relatives insist, however, that an employee had discovered David's weapons in a basement locker downstairs, where they had been stored uneventfully for twelve years.

In any case, Marilyn called David from the lobby's phone and told him to come down so he could be arrested. As she explained it, the detective said, "Supposedly, he was waving the guns." (This was something Steven probably made up.)

After the ordeal, Steven came to Jonathan's room. He was wearing a black Calvin Klein suit with no tie and was breathing heavily. "They got him. They came and got him." Steven said matter-of-factly, lying on the bed, his jacket collar crumpling against the wall. He was surprisingly calm given the circumstances.

Jonathan and I were confused. Jonathan laughed in disbelief.

"David. He had guns." Steven finally said. "In the basement. He had guns. And I mean *guns*. Rifles, shotguns, machine guns. He had a stash in the basement!" Steven added that only the special forces could get the guns David had. He then explained how hollow-tip bullets could penetrate a bulletproof vest. Steven seemed very knowledgeable about the weaponry.

David was sent to Rikers Island and was there for months. Marilyn and David felt that the Weissberg family–appointed lawyer was, in fact, working against them, trying to put David back in jail. Marilyn changed attorneys and got David out on a $10,000 bond, paid by Ruth.

"We had emergency money in the safe, but I didn't have the combination," Marilyn said. "It was a long combination. It was hidden. I went to see him. He was a mess. He looked different. He didn't have his medicine there. Couldn't believe it. He was hurt and very confused. He was just like, 'Wow. Where did that come from?'"

David made bail once again, and within days, he was back in the hotel, keeping his distance from the brother who had betrayed him. He visited Ruth and Herbert's suite. Marilyn recalled, "Herbert looked up and grabbed David and pulled his son to the bed and hugged him. That's how much he meant to Herbert."

Days later, the police came back a second time and found more guns, this time inside David's room. The employees and many guests privately worried if the police had found all of David's stash. David made bail once again, though Steven now tried to prevent him from returning. Ruth, however, once again insisted that David be allowed back to the hotel.

The family's descent was well covered in the press. The *New York Daily News* ran several stories underneath headlines like "Nab Hotel Boss in Guns Seizures" and "Guns Seized at Gramercy Hotel." Local newspapers quoted fearful Gramercy Park residents, who voiced their longtime suspicions about Herbert's operation. For David, hiding in a hotel room and quietly living off of room service was now impossible. The whole world seemed to be watching.

"There were private investigators," Marilyn remembered. "They were following me and David all over the place. It was David's birthday, and I was in a boutique buying a blouse. Then I see a he/she. And I saw him again at the hotel. David asked, 'Why don't you pull his wig off?' I went to smoke a joint on the bed. I looked up, and there was a camera. The whole suite was bugged. That's when David and I started make believe. We only talked when we were outside."

David thought the government was listening in on his phone lines, so he tore them out of the wall. That also destroyed his neighbor's phone connection to the front desk. The guest missed his wake-up call for his flight back home, causing the hotel yet another problem.

Marilyn Leaves

David faced a mandatory fifteen years of jail time for possession of illegal weapons, a result of New York State's "three strikes, you're out" rule. (David's prior convictions were related to his violent altercations with ex-girlfriends.) David had some hope that he could get a new lawyer and a better deal. He sold his motorcycle to raise money for a lawyer who had no connection to his brother. His goal was to get court-ordered rehab in a facility. David was also incredibly sick with liver cancer and didn't feel he had long to live anyway. No one in the family, including Marilyn, was aware of this diagnosis. David knew his days were numbered. His brother was already conspiring. David openly mused about killing himself. Adding to the tension, the interferon medicine David was taking for his cancer increased his suicidal thoughts.

According to Steven, David and the lawyers were working out a deal for him to return to a halfway house in Florida where he had lived years prior. But for Marilyn, this posed a huge problem. Again according to Steven, Marilyn had a bench warrant in Florida for failing to appear before the court over some legal matter. So she could not travel to Florida with David and instead wanted a divorce. Steven claims David told him all this, and to add insult to injury, David claimed she sold a bunch of his stuff while he was in jail and later denied it.

Marilyn described her own version of what happened next:

> *He wanted me to sign a post-nuptial—leaving me everything. He wanted to get back at his brothers. He knew I wasn't interested in money. I didn't sign because I didn't feel it was ethical. I wanted to sign in front of an attorney to be ethical. We went to an attorney to draw up the papers. The lawyer*

> *said, "This post-nuptial benefits her." "Do you really want to do this?" he asked. I never thought David was going to take his life.*

At one point, Marilyn confused a court date for an arraignment, which she thought was scheduled for a Friday, but it turned out to be scheduled for Wednesday. David was unexpectedly very angry.

"You lied to me," he told her.

Marilyn said, "What do you mean I lied to you? I didn't." But David was planning something.

It's hard to say what happened next. Some press reports indicated that Marilyn was planning to leave David at this point. Everyone in the hotel could see they were arguing. Marilyn had supposedly threatened to leave David, and David responded by threatening to kill himself. Marilyn insisted she was on her way to a weekend rehab facility to end a Xanax addiction and had no plans to leave David. In any case, Marilyn had packed her bags to go *somewhere*. It certainly seemed like an odd time to go to rehab.

Wherever Marilyn was going, she was headed out the door. David convinced her to go to the roof garden for some fresh air. She lugged her bags with her. On the eighteenth-floor terrace, David threatened to jump once and for all if she left him. She called his bluff. They argued some more. Marilyn decided to leave and went back to the elevator. Moments later, David looked over the ledge and watched as Marilyn rolled her heavy suitcases to the curb on Lexington Avenue. She waved for a cab.

David took off his gold jewelry and his emerald necklace and left it with the cash from the sale of his motorcycle. He rubbed his most precious item in his hands, a two-thousand-year-old Aramaic coin that was minted during the time of the second temple. He then climbed to the ledge and caught sight of Marilyn below. It was now or never, he must have told himself.

9

DOWNFALL

2002–2004

On February 9, 1933, at 6:45 a.m., a forty-five-year-old woman named Olive Rice walked into the Gramercy Park Hotel and checked in under the name "Mrs. A Bell." She carried no luggage, and the staff gave her a room on the fifth floor. Meanwhile, across town, her husband was in divorce court to fight her alimony claim. A moment after getting her key, the woman took the elevator to the rooftop. There, she jumped over the railing and landed on the seventh-floor extension. She died instantly.

Two years later, in 1935, a thirty-five-year-old woman named Miss Hazel Welo got locked out of her room on the third floor. Not wanting to pay a locksmith, she convinced the staff to let her into a storage room next door to her apartment. From the storage room, she climbed out the window and carefully walked along the ledge toward her apartment. Then she fell one story, fracturing her shoulder and suffering a brain concussion.

In the 1980s, a woman checked in carrying only a shopping bag. Pinky, the bellhop, showed her to her room, where the woman asked him to open the window for some air. Pinky cracked open the window.

"Can you open it more?" she asked. Pinky opened the window all the way.

As a tip, the woman handed Pinky ten dollars. Pinky turned to leave. "Can you give me five dollars change?" she asked. Pinkly complied and then went back downstairs. As he exited the elevator in the lobby, the doorman Phil rushed up to him with the news that the woman had jumped. Pinky immediately wondered why she had kept the extra five dollars.

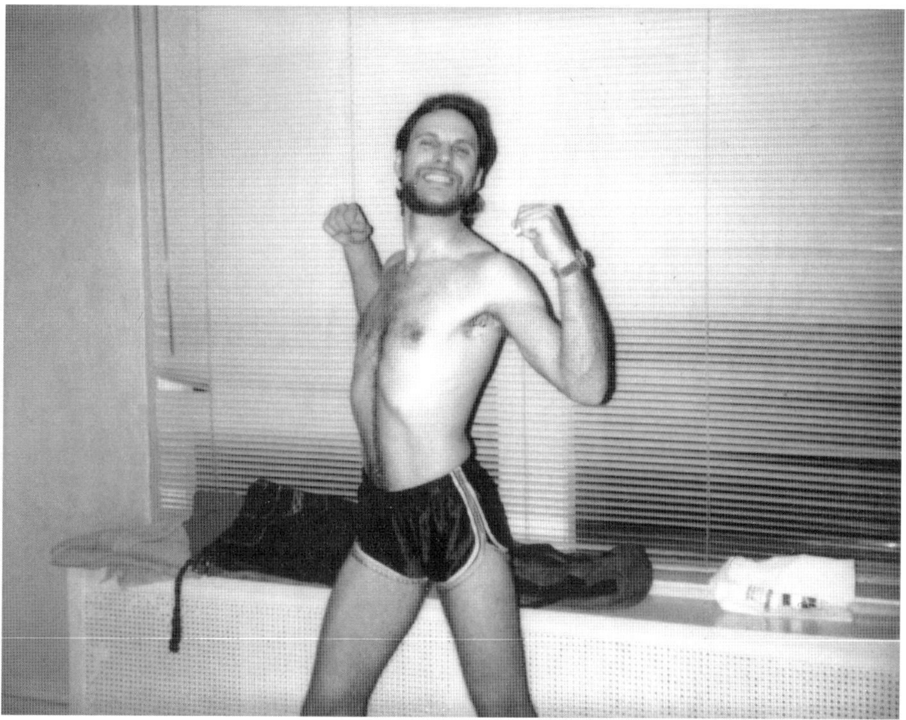

David Weissberg.

Then there was the time a man jumped and landed on Lexington Avenue without any shoes on. The body didn't have any wallet or an ID. So Steven and the maids conducted a room-to-room search before they finally found the man's shoes. And so on and so forth.

Now, it was David Weissberg's turn. He stood on the hotel's edge, feeling a cool breeze in the summer air. What is it that parachute jumpers always say? Choosing the right moment? Not now, but *now*, David thought. He stepped forward and, timing his jump perfectly, he landed in front of Marilyn with a bone-jarring thud. After he hit the pavement, according to witnesses, his whole body rattled for a moment. The Aramaic coin rolled down the street.

In a state of shock, Marilyn tried to touch him. For a moment, she thought he was still alive. He stared back, straight into her eyes. He wanted her to remember this moment forever. Then she began screaming hysterically.

Security showed up seconds later. Steven arrived on the scene, and then he returned to the hotel to grab a sheet to cover David's body. Instead of an ambulance, a CBS news van pulled up. Then ABC. By the time the medics arrived, David was dead. Whatever pain David felt didn't last long.

A postcard from the 1980s. Note the buildup of soot. *Photo by David Weissberg.*

Later, in David's room, Steven found his Bible on a bed, open to Deuteronomy 21, with markings on verses 18–21:

> *If someone has a stubborn and rebellious son who does not obey his father and mother and will not listen to them when they discipline him, his father and mother shall take hold of him and bring him to the elders at the gate of his town. They shall say to the elders, "This son of ours is stubborn and rebellious. He will not obey us. He is a glutton and a drunkard." Then all the men of his town are to stone him to death. You must purge the evil from among you. All Israel will hear of it and be afraid.*

The next day, the hotel and the Weissberg family were suddenly infamous. On July 8, 2002, *New York* magazine printed an article about David's death by suicide and informed the world about the chain of deaths in the family—first, Steven's wife from cancer in 1997, then his son Michael in 2001, and now David. In his interview, Steven speculated that the family curse had been inherited from the Kennedys, who had once lived in the hotel. The magazine effectively turned our family's ghost stories into banter on the cocktail party circuit.

The news was kept from Herbert, who by now was so sick that he was confined to two rooms in the hotel and unable to understand what was happening around him. When asked what Herbert knew, Ruth answered, "Daddy senses something's different." Perhaps Herbert, in his senility, still had enough awareness to notice his son no longer visited. Or maybe he saw it in the faces of his relatives and handlers, which carried somber expressions out of respect for the departed. But when I visited him, he seemed to have no reaction. If I or another family member tried to say something meaningful about our tragic losses, he merely grinned back as if he was oblivious.

Marilyn, meanwhile, went to a trauma center. By the time she returned, her dog Princess was gone. Steven had given the dog to Aerosmith musician Steven Tyler, who turned around and gave it to someone else. (Steven Tyler had recently been spending a lot of time in the hotel because his cancer-stricken ex-wife, Cyrinda Foxe, chose to spend her last days there.) When Marilyn returned, she found the same Bible passage that Steven had found.

Not long after David's death, Jonathan and I dug through a trunk filled with David's things. Inside were old cameras, a light box, and various electronics that no longer seemed usable. Buried along with everything was an old black notebook.

Inside, on yellow lined pages, were hand-drawn diagrams and descriptions of every piece of electronic equipment and camera David had ever owned. In blue ink, with no noticeable mistakes, the front and back panels were carefully detailed alongside notes on the product and warranty. The lines flowed between the pages to simulate cable connections, with the color of ink chosen carefully to avoid confusion. In fine block letters, David had written instructions on how to use one device with another. Everywhere were lines, details, and descriptions for equipment that had long since become obsolete. They were like maps to an ancient city.

The End of the Weissberg Reign

David's death turned Steven's anger into sentimentalism. Steven began wearing David's expensive Breitling watch and his sunglasses. A few days after David's death, the *New York Post*'s *Page Six* reported that Steven had attended a fancy charity benefit as if nothing had happened. Steven was livid. "What was I supposed to do?" he asked of anyone who would listen. Yet it was Steven who had created the legal headache for David in the first place, ratting him out for his guns, pushing him over the edge.

David's death increased the pressure on Steven and Ruth to find an outsider to take over the hotel's operations. In addition to facing a downturn in the New York hospitality industry, the hotel needed maintenance beyond what a family business could afford.

Several potential suitors recognized the hotel's value as a diamond in the rough and met with Steven. No one could doubt the hotel's prime location alongside a private park. In preparation for a sale, Steven fired the employees who worked in the dining room so their union contracts would not interfere with an outsider's plans to revitalize the restaurant.

Juanito, a waiter, described his experience:

> *We would always say, "Who's gonna take this place? Who will fit in their grandfather's shoes?"* [Robert] *looked the most like* [Herbert], *and we kept saying, "Someday they will." We always said that once Steven takes this place, it's gonna go down to the bottom. We always said that.*
>
> *We always had* [Herbert]. *We felt very secure that he was still there. And we said, "May God give him strength." But to* [Herbert], *I said, "You know, the minute God wants to take him away from this world, this is gonna go down because who's gonna be trying to get that spot there."*
>
> *Marty was trying to take over, and I don't know what happened. Marty stopped coming. Steven used to come and threaten us in the kitchen. "If you guys don't do what I ask you to do, I'm gonna close this place." And we were like, "Really? Who knows? He's the man now, so he probably will." One day, he came in and said, "I'm gonna close this place." The first thing he closed the complete food and beverage operations. He said, "I'm gonna close the door to you guys if you keep stealing my food." That's what he said, "stealing my food." So one day he got mad because somebody had left the ice machine in the kitchen open and all the ice got melted down. He said, "I know somebody did this, and if I don't find out, I'm gonna close this place." Nobody gave him an answer the next day, and the next day when*

Herbert and Nicole Weissberg, circa 1998. *Photo by Max Weissberg.*

> *we came in, the door was closed. And we thought he was joking. But it was closed, permanently closed the food and beverage department. He used the ice machine as an excuse. After that day, we never went back. The union went in to see him. He took care of us for one year medical to cover us for medical. But the feeling was like, "What was the hotel gonna do without food and beverage?" We were like, "What's gonna happen next?"*

Steven Greenberg Takes Over the Gramercy in 2002

As the courting continued, Steven enjoyed being wooed by famous hoteliers who (for once) bought him lunch. One of the first groups that made an offer was Sugar Enterprises, related to the rap act the Sugarhill Gang. They wanted to turn the Gramercy into a hip-hop hotel. As collateral, they offered two Mexican bonds from 1900 backed by JPMorgan, which they claimed were worth $160 million. Several affidavits from lawyers and financial advisors certified the bonds' value. Herbert's lawyers quickly determined the bonds were worthless, however, and the whole thing was dismissed as a scam. André Balazs, the Belgian owner of the Standard Hotel chain, also circled the Gramercy. Steven Greenberg, who had met Steven at the Roxy through Madalyn many years before, quickly emerged as Steven's preferred candidate.

Steven Greenberg looked just like Ben Franklin—if Ben Franklin wore $3,500 pinstripe suits, a $20,000 watch, and drove a $200,000 ivory Rolls-Royce. Greenberg had come a long way from the Roxy and Palladium, his two legendary nightclubs that were popular in the '70s and '80s. He had wisely invested in Commodore Computers (before they went bust), along with a handful of real estate properties. Later, he went through a series of stock-related scandals that led to SEC investigations and ended in lengthy court battles. Greenberg also invested in art, wisely collecting Andy Warhol and Jean-Michel Basquiat paintings, along with many important Art Deco pieces. Now in his late fifties, he was a regular fixture at trendy New York restaurants and had courtside seats for the Knicks. Greenberg was also known for his taste in women. His clubs invariably had pretty cocktail waitresses in black attire. Greenberg also had an Asian sex worker follow him wherever he went. He spent roughly $200,000 a year on sex workers alone.

For the first Father's Day after David's death in 2002, Greenberg treated Steven, Robert, and their children to a French bistro–style meal. Along with them was one of Greenberg's sex workers, who sat silently and smiled through the meal. Paying for everything, Greenberg held court. At one point, he gave a friendly, intimate nod to Lee Iacocca at the next table. Every story Greenberg told included the price tags, and he loudly announced what the bottle of wine on the table cost. In essence, he was buying our respect.

One evening, Robert got a call in Illinois. It was Lionel George, the Swiss barfly. "Greenberg has a hundred lawsuits going," Lionel explained emphatically, which turned out to be true. Lionel pleaded with Robert to cancel the impending deal. Clearly, Lionel had a stake in Balazs's success. Robert, however, had no desire to get involved in the negotiations.

Soon after, Greenberg was granted a fifteen-year sublease of the Gramercy for which he provided $1 million in cash up front. His contract stipulated that Steven would not involve himself in the hotel's management whatsoever. Steven was oddly also paid a handsome consulting fee for his services. Herbert's lawyers approved the contract, but according to court documents, Steven Weissberg's lawyer Andrew Schwab secretly agreed to a $1 million consulting fee (effectively a bribe) from Greenberg that was paid through a shell company. For this money, Schwab kept mum on a last-minute change Steven Greenberg made to the contract.

Unknown to Herbert's lawyers, the new contract included the right of first refusal, in the event that Herbert R. Weissberg was to sell his right to the hotel's lease. This meant he had to sell to Greenberg first before any other suitors, giving Greenberg effective control. Schwab himself presented the altered documents to Steven and Ruth. Thinking it was the same contract she had seen before, Ruth signed on Herbert's behalf. Then Steven Greenberg secretly paid the agreed-upon $500,000 to Andy Schwab and promised the rest after Herbert Weissberg's lease officially passed into his hands.

Now with the hotel's reins, Greenberg made several changes to give the place a more nightclub-like atmosphere. The dining room was made into an extension of the bar and decorated with French period furniture. Lit by candles, the new bar was staffed with "Greenberg girls" in black dresses. The old bar got new velvet couches and a velvet rope. The Wedgewood Room (an unused space in the annex and the site of Jonathan's bar mitzvah) became the Cobalt Club. Greenberg filled the place with Belle Époque furniture and put Karl Lagerfeld's old sofas in the women's bathroom. The club also had the Duke and Duchess of Windsor's old martini shaker, bought at auction for $45,000 from Christie's. Strangely, it was open only on Wednesdays, except when it was rented out for media launches.

In the lobby, Greenberg hung framed pictures of Babe Ruth, John F. Kennedy, and Humphrey Bogart, with captions tying them to the hotel's history. Though it was true that they had all been in the hotel, two of the captions were inaccurate. Babe Ruth's bandaged hand in the photo did not come from him drinking in the "famous" bar; instead, the image was taken just after he had surgery at St. Vincent's Hospital. And Humphrey Bogart wasn't married on the rooftop; he was married in one of the hotel's rooms.

Upstairs, Greenberg repainted the ninth floor's walls a burgundy color and installed gaudy rose-patterned carpeting. One guest remarked that it resembled a bordello. The other floors remained unchanged, however.

Greenberg saved his biggest development for the roof, where he installed the first bar on the hotel's rooftop since the 1940s. He called it the High Bar. There, a glass of wine cost fourteen dollars, a lot for 2002. The place quickly filled up with a young, good-looking crowd. It seemed the Gramercy was on the upswing, and the swanky hotspot attracted a new generation of loyal followers.

One of the largest parties to occur in this period came when Metallica premiered their new documentary *Some Kind of Monster*, which is based on the band's three years in therapy while they developed their album *St. Anger*. At the last minute, Jonathan and I were invited to the party and saw the rooftop transform to a space full of celebrities, photographers, and a bunch of black-clad Metallica fans. The fans seemed the most out of place. One told us he had earned his invitation by calling into a radio show. Girls in black T-shirts with the words "Some Kind of Monster" emblazoned on their chests served trays of mini hamburgers, tuna sliders, and chicken sticks. In the back room, actor Sean Penn, with his wife (at the time), Robin Wright, professed his love for Metallica as Traci Lords and Andy Dick mingled with the band. The bathroom was filled with people snorting cocaine. When I crossed through to the south side of the building, the photographers went into motion. One snapped a photo of me, just in case I was someone famous they didn't immediately recognize. Around two o'clock in the morning, a tipsy Jonathan and I left in style to his fourteenth-floor apartment accompanied by two girls in their mid-twenties (older than us at the time). Though he was only seventeen, Jonathan was now living the high life in the hotel.

It just so happened that Ira Gasman's room 602 was right above where I stayed (room 502, Michael's old room). In the last days of the old hotel, I remember waking up to the sounds of him having sex. He was so loud, the plumbing in the bathroom rattled. Ira was a man in his seventies and did not look like the kind of guy whose lust could make the pipes shake. Was the plumbing in the hotel really that bad and in need of replacement? Perhaps it was just part of a performance. After all, Gasman was famous for his musical *The Life*, about ladies of the night.

HERBERT R. WEISSBERG DIES

A year after David's death, on July 3, 2003, Herbert finally passed away. The estate sold his share of the hotel to André Balazs for $25 million. Steven Greenberg, exercising his right of first refusal, sold his share to Aby Rosen, a German real estate billionaire whose partner was Ian Schrager, the former owner of Studio 54. Suddenly, there were two groups of hotel "owners." Greenberg presented his doctored contract to the court. Herbert's estate lawyers threatened Andy Schwab with disbarment. An expensive legal battle ensued. Herbert's estate was successful in demonstrating Greenberg's deceit and Andy Schwab's double dealing. Aby Rosen and Ian Schrager emerged as the hotel's new owners, buying out André Balazs. In the legal battle, Greenberg also sued Steven Weissberg for interfering with the hotel's management (he had given instructions to a waiter) and won a settlement.

The person who came out best in the deal was André Balasz. For his troubles, he walked away with a quick $7 million profit on his investment. The ordeal also led to him dating Uma Thurman, who lived across the street and frequented the bar. Uma was now in the middle of a breakup with her husband, Ethan Hawke, who was spending more and more time in the Gramercy's bar as a result.

As for the Weissberg fortune, public documents in the New York surrogate court, filed by the executor, Charles E. Ramos, indicated that, as of March 31, 2005, the estate had collected $38,817,498.54 in assets for federal tax assessment purposes. My father, Robert Weissberg, who stood to inherit roughly 30 percent of the estate, was then given a trust account worth around $2.2 million. What happened to the rest of the money? The only person who can answer this is the will's executor, former judge Charles E. Ramos. When I asked family members to explain where such a vast amount of money could go, none could provide an answer—nor had they received an accounting from Ramos, despite repeated attempts.

Following Herbert's death, a blog called *Expose Corrupt Courts* created an online forum to discuss the case. Among its many pages devoted to Herbert's estate was one featuring a March 2010 letter from Franklin N. Brady (a stranger to the family) of "the Committee on Public Integrity" addressed to Preet Bharara, the United States Attorney for the Southern District of New York, and Joseph M. Demarest Jr. of the FBI. In it, he reviewed the mysterious circumstances of Herbert's second modified will and the "highly unusual" waiver Ramos received from fellow judge Lippman. Then he made the following allegations:

> *(1) Judge Ramos, in early 2003, filed papers within the New York State Court system containing knowingly false information, so to advance a scheme, in violation of various federal laws, where he would improperly, and financially, gain; and (2) Judge Lippman, since at least mid-2007, has been aware of the false presentation of information by Judge Ramos, and he has failed, and he continues to fail, to take appropriate action as required by law.*

Once again, I leave it for the reader to decide whether these allegations are true. If so, it would mean the Gramercy fortune was stolen.

Nicole Weissberg, Herbert's Granddaughter

Not long after Herbert died, I visited my sister, Nicole, who was getting her master's in business administration and hospitality at Denver University. Growing up, she had always wanted a career in hotels like her grandfather.

Her experience now included managing hotels in Australia, Wisconsin, and Portland, Oregon. She had proven her potential as a future hotelier, coming a long way from ratting me out for my mischief in the hotel.

By now, Nicole had thick chestnut hair, pearly white teeth, and a thin, athletic figure. Her cheeks carried a set of dimples, a trait inherited from her father and grandfather. Her face had a slight pinkish hue, a trait passed on from her grandmother Frances. Her upright posture manifested enormous confidence, perhaps the greatest gift she had received from Herbert. Like all good hoteliers, she loved to travel and easily made friends.

Though Herbert did not look fondly on the wives of his sons, he seemed to make an exception for his granddaughter. Growing up, the Gramercy Park Hotel meant as much to Nicole and the development of her character as it did to me. She listened attentively whenever an aspect of the family business was explained. She often went behind the front desk to see how it all worked. In the lobby, the two of us would play on the luggage carts together. Her brushes with celebrity included playing tag with Carlos Santana and a Central Park carriage ride with Paul Shaffer. She had her own special dishes prepared in the dining room and taught me how to properly order room service. After the hotel was no longer ours, she told me she wished to "one day" take it back. I heartily approved.

In December 2004, Nicole traveled through Asia while on vacation from hotel school. On Christmas Day, she stayed in a hotel in Khao Lak, Thailand, right on the beach. Gazing out on the horizon underneath a scorching sun, I imagine she must have felt she was in paradise.

The next day, a tsunami hit Asia. Two fifty-foot waves traveling at three hundred miles per hour slammed into the beach where Nicole was staying. Every bit of news confirmed the worst. Her boyfriend, Morgan, arrived in Thailand, as they had originally planned, on December 27. Nicole was not there to meet him. There were only stories of entire villages being buried under the sand and scattered survivors. Khao Lak was one of the hardest-hit areas. After he was unable to find her, Morgan returned and recounted his story on *Larry King Live*. Like Morgan, we refused to believe Nicole was gone. A few days later, Morgan went back to search with Lindsay, Marty's daughter. But again, they did not find her.

In my father Robert's New York apartment, producers called to get us on the *Today* show and other programs, but neither of us could handle that. One morning, as I ate my breakfast and thumbed through the *New York Daily News*, I saw a picture of Nicole and Morgan together with the headline "No Trace of Woman from N.Y. New Woe for Famed Hotel Family." The effect was gut-wrenching. The idea of a family curse, which was mentioned after David's death, seemed far more real now.

A week after Nicole's disappearance, I waited for Steven with Robert and my stepmother, Erika, in the National Arts Club in Gramercy Park. The former home of Samuel Tilden, the club was filled with Tiffany glass, nineteenth-century oil paintings, and mahogany furniture. The Gramercy Park Hotel was visible through the club's windows. A veneer of black soot now covered the hotel's façade. Steven arrived and gave Robert a copy of *Mourning and Mitzvah*, the same book a rabbi had given him after Madalyn's death. We were supposed to speak to each other about what was happening. We didn't know what to say besides the obvious. The tension was building every hour that went by without a phone call from the State Department saying Nicole was okay.

Steven took Robert off to speak while I waited in the living room of the club. My eyes wandered from the oil paintings to the urns on the shelves above, which supposedly held the ashes of former club members and their dogs. Robert returned. Privately, he told me they didn't end up speaking about Nicole. Steven explained instead that Cameron had discovered he had a girlfriend, whom he had gifted a pair of expensive earrings. Now that Steven's affair was over, he had an additional problem, as the mistress wanted the receipts for the earrings to return them. Yet Cameron was insistent that he shouldn't give them to her. Should he hand the girl the receipts? The story allowed Robert to forget about the tragedy, albeit momentarily. I didn't know if Steven was trying to humor his brother or if was just tone deaf.

When Nicole disappeared, I spent a lot of time in the hotel with Jonathan. Jonathan is a few years younger than me, but his experience of surviving cancer and the loss of his brother and mother made him seem older. Like me, he had an artistic nature, which he expressed through music.

Together, we climbed the "secret" tower of the Gramercy that led to the twenty-first floor. Though the tower visible from the street, most people were unaware this place even existed (the closest I've seen anyone get to it was a few pictures of Madonna on the nineteenth-floor rooftop). Jonathan and I discussed our memories of Nicole. She had just recently visited the Gramercy, and together, they had inspected the hotel's renovation plans.

Later, in room 501, I listened as Jonathan played the piano version of "Send for Water," a song about David and Michael in the hotel. The chorus goes: "Send for water, I'm dying, dying for some fire." I had heard the song before but never understood it. Jonathan explained the meaning: "water" was a euphemism for heroin, and in the song's other lines, "dead dog's souls and "something in the walls" were references to David and the eerie nature of the hotel. This was how it ended, I thought. Ghosts in the walls.

That night, we sat on the rooftop and listened to Jonathan's record play continuously on the bar's amplification system. Within days, the hotel was gutted for renovations. Herbert's legacy finally lay in ruins. Ruth, Steven, Cameron, and their young children, Logan and Alana, would be able to keep their apartments in the hotel, however, as they were not renovated.

Nicole never came back alive. By late February, people involved in the cleanup in Thailand had finally located and identified Nicole's body. She had probably drowned quickly. The hope of the Weissbergs one day retaking the Gramercy was lost.

Once again, the theme of a family curse was brought up in the newspapers and magazines. Something seemed too perfect about the chain of deaths leading from Madalyn to my sister, Nicole. There were times when I also thought about a curse, especially after discovering that the hotel's previous owner, Charlie Schwefel, had also lost much of his family around the time he lost the hotel. But ultimately, I refuse to believe in curses.

The role I had played was crucial. What if I hadn't introduced Michael to so many sinful things? Though David played a major role in Michael using drugs I never indulged in, Michael's first step had been taken with me. I made it all sound okay. Through me, he became easily infused by the philosophy of a dim-witted libertine, unable to see beyond his immediate pleasures. What was life in a hotel room but a life of corruption? It took me many books and many experiences to come to this conclusion. But by the time I did, it was too late for Michael. From there, his death put David in a corner, causing him to take the plunge. And then my sister, if she had not felt such a gaping hole in the middle of our family, would she have felt the need to take over the place? She seemed to want to wrap things up by traveling the world before she could return to focus on the thing she wanted most.

Trying to hold onto the memory of the hotel, I created my own hotel room at home with Gramercy Park Hotel glasses, dishes, postcards, menus, matchbooks, brochures, ashtrays, coat hangers, lamp fixtures, luggage stickers, furniture, a mirror, a doorknob, and a trash can. Every night, I slept on old Gramercy Park Hotel sheets and had dreams about the hotel. In my dreams appeared the cool guests, checking in from around the world, always in a hurry to the bar. There was Pinky and the rest of the Gramercy gang in their green suits, and the food in Le Parc tasted better than I remembered. All the chandeliers had their light bulbs shining, and the sound of telephones, piano music, and accented conversation hung in the air. And of course, there was my entire family, including Herbert and Nicole, and David, and Michael, and Lionel, too, all looking their best, in their best clothes, all with a golden gleam in their eyes. Never before did I appreciate the hotel so much as I did in those dreams, when I could only imagine what the hotel had been and what it would soon be.

10

RESTORATION

2004–2025

The Hotel Reopens: The First Reviews

I was there when the hotel reopened in July 2006. I arrived with an olive-green Army messenger bag. Inside was a three-ring binder filled with hundreds of articles about the old Gramercy Park Hotel. For some reason, I thought the new employees would find this interesting. My worldview had recently been turned upside down after a documentary crew started following me in the hopes that my mundane life might reveal something about the hotel's history. A year of this meant the hotel's reopening was super important—finally, a chance to see the new changes. Yet it was also a little heartbreaking to know the old hotel was finally gone. I mean, would I have to now pay for the drinks?

Every aspect of the new hotel had been carefully planned. The floor of the lobby was laid out in a clean black-and-white chessboard pattern, the same as it had been when the hotel opened. The sleek, black metal awning outside was also the same as it had been in 1925 (for a brief time), and the hotel's façade had been power-washed to restore its calming, beige-brick hue. But the similarities mostly ended there. Gone, once again, was the Ingersoll plaque. "[It's] in the basement," Michael Overington told me. Alongside the three-partitioned revolving doors was a new plaque with a squiggly "GPH" logo that Schnabel had designed.

Inside, I was instantly greeted by the smell of smokey wood and leather, a scent called Cade 26, custom crafted for the hotel by Le Labo, a local perfume house. The hotel also pumped its own custom playlist into the lobby, elevator, and bars.

Over the checkered floor was a lush velvet, ruby-colored carpet, topped by the hotel's new logo and accented with a regal lily flower design. The shade of the carpet instantly reminded me of the Oscars or a film premiere. At the far end of the room was a crackling fireplace. Replacing the chestnut paneling were four pillars of matte-finish "reclaimed" wood sourced from mushroom crates, which now rose to the third floor, as the renovations increased the lobby's height. Instead of a multitude of chandeliers, there was now a single, candle-style glass chandelier in the center of the room. Just off to the side was the concierge's desk, which was staffed by a heavily trained aspiring actress. The hotel had probably not had a concierge in seventy-five years. To put one in the middle of the room said everything.

Above the fireplace was a Fernando Botero painting of a chubby-faced woman, exactly the kind of person you wouldn't see in a place like this. Below the painting, Schrager included a piece from his own collection, a sparkling bullfighter garb, alongside a pair of ruby-red velvet couches. Cy Twombly's enormous *Bacchus (Untitled)* hung in the lobby's far corner, its heavy crimson paint strokes almost matching the carpet. Everywhere were plush leather and velvet armchairs.

Since the floor plan of the hotel had changed tremendously, the area that had been the lounge was now part of the lobby. The area previously occupied by the hotel's bar and dining room became the Jade and Rose Bars. The Jade Bar kept the same floor plan as the old bar, replacing the wooden stools with velvet, tassel-lined indigo chairs, matching couches, and jade-colored footstools for additional seating. The centerpiece painting was the silky *Blue Japanese Painting No. 3* by Julian Schnabel. Above the bar hung a Jean-Michel Basquiat diptych and, like in the lobby, the inward facing walls were lined with heavy curtains. There was no denying the striking elegance of the plush color combinations.

Next door was the Rose Bar, which had some of the same wooden pillars as the lobby, along with its velvet and leather armchairs and a sofa. As you entered, you immediately passed a charred oak pool table on the way toward the bar, which occupied one full side of the room. Like in the lobby, there was a crackling fireplace with a piece of art overhead, in this case, Schnabel's cubist-inspired *Suddenly Last Summer (Picasso Painting No. 2)*. In the far corner, over a dozen feet tall, was Andy Warhol's *Rorschach*, which vaguely resembled the Romanov coat of arms. In the near corner, close to the pool table, hung Schnabel's obnoxious *Teddy Bears Picnic*, a painting with "Teddy Bears Picnic" written on it, along with some smears of paint. A sawtooth chandelier, also made by Schnabel, hung above the bar, as if to ensure *everything* had some artistic flavor to it.

Later, I found myself at the Jade Bar. The Cade 26 scent was intoxicating. I flipped open my thick binder on the bar and yapped about what the hotel was like many years before. The gorgeous female bartender feigned interest in that polite way bartenders are so good at doing. At one point, Keanu Reeves popped in wearing a blank T-shirt and designer sport coat. He visibly gasped, mouthed "wow," then disappeared.

In the middle of my lecture, I started choking on my ginger ale. Perhaps my reaction to the soda was a warning sign. Just as I was recovering, the director of the documentary about the hotel, Douglas Keeve, showed up. We relocated to the Rose Bar and sat on a velvet sofa, observing the waitresses in black slip dresses circle the room. There was no doubt that everyone who worked in the new hotel was stylish and beautiful.

Doug ordered a twenty-dollar glass of Burgundy and left a ten-dollar tip. I asked Douglas why he tipped so much. He said it was good to make friends with the right people. Somehow I knew I would not blend in well in this environment.

Around evening time, I ran home to my apartment in the East Village to dispense my bag and come back in my coolest clothes. But when I returned, the doors were blocked, open only to those few who had a reservation. (My relatives had not moved back in yet and were staying uptown at the new owner's expense.) I called Wendy, the documentary film's producer, whose friend had booked a room, but they were unable to bring us through security. Then the Rose Bar held a party that we were not invited to—nor were those who had spent $525 a night and more to book a room. Our film crew was left out on the street.

We saw Ben Stiller, Winona Ryder, Jared Leto, Kanye West, Russell Simmons, and others on their way to the opening party. Clearly, the Gramercy was now no longer a place one would visit on the way up or down. It was a place for those at the top.

Ian Schrager and Aby Rosen's Takeover

The hotel's new owners, Ian Schrager and Aby Rosen, had bold plans for the Gramercy. Not only did they gut the lobby and rooms of the hotel, but they also transformed the hotel's annex at 50 Gramercy Park into a condo development.

Remaining in the hotel was much of the Weissberg family. The Weissbergs held onto rooms 501–505 and 1401–1405, which were to be kept until the expiration of the lease with Solil (Sol Goldman's estate, previously known as Avon Associates).

Thanks to the myriad housing laws of New York City, a dozen or so residents also kept their rooms and lived there through the construction. Thanks to Herbert's policy, they had all found it easy to become residents of the hotel but found it hard to leave.

Herbert Weissberg had once paid $400,000 a year to lease the hotel. But since the new owners had to renegotiate the terms, Solil now charged Aby Rosen and Ian Schrager $4 million a year, a 1,000 percent increase. Under the terms of the lease that ran to 2078, the rent increased every year, surpassing inflation.

According to newspapers, at least $210 million was put into the renovations. The 509-room hotel, spread out over two towers (with roughly 350 keys, including residents), was transformed into 190 rooms consolidated into one building.

The money-making part of the deal came with the condos. Over the preceding twenty years, few homes in Gramercy Park had opened for sale. This gave the new properties at 50 Gramercy Park North a mystique (or at least that's what the broker told me). The new brochures also emphasized that the apartments included a Gramercy Park key. The catch was that the condos were on seventy-five-year leases, meaning their value was certain to depreciate. Despite this drawback, the new owners of the hotel had no trouble finding customers for the properties. More on that later.

I was not there to see the very first chunks of brick and mortar taken out of the old hotel. Days after my sister Nicole's disappearance at the end of 2004, I went to St. Petersburg, Russia, as part of a planned study abroad program. When I returned to New York in the summer of 2005, the hotel was then in the middle of construction. It was devastating for me to see the hotel's rooms gutted when so many of them held important memories.

Almost immediately after my return, I was thrust into a documentary film about the hotel's history. The film's producer was Wendy Ettinger of 1 Lexington Avenue (across the street from the hotel), who originally produced *The War Room* (1993). Wendy is a thin, upbeat, liberal woman with tortoiseshell glasses and light, stringy hair. (I will add that my cousin Jonathan frequently referred to her as a "MILF.") Wendy had grown curious about the building that she saw through her windows and filmed some of the old hotel's final days. The film's director was Douglas Keeve, a tall, good-looking, gay photographer who was introduced to me as "one of Anna Wintour's favorites." After his *Vogue* stint, Douglas graduated to documentary filmmaking with *Unzipped*, a Sundance Film Festival Award–winning documentary film about designer Isaac Mizrahi, whom Keeve was dating at the time.

For *Hotel Gramercy Park*, Wendy gave me a camera and said, "Go film something." While loud machines tore into the body of the hotel, Jonathan and I traveled from room to room and smoked joints, telling various stories on camera. All around us, the hotel was being taken apart. We desperately tried to hold onto what was left.

One day before a round of filming (this was 2005, before the hotel reopened), I waited outside the Gramercy with Wendy. Jonathan was late. Ian Schrager was there at the corner of Lexington Avenue and 21st Street. Dressed in stonewashed jeans and a denim-blue collarless shirt, he looked like he had walked straight out of a J.Crew catalogue. With his carefully coiffed hair and camel tan, I mused that he had just flown in from the Hamptons by helicopter.

Then I heard him speak. He sounded like he had recently gotten out of prison. Schrager paced the street, cellphone in hand, saying things like, "Yeah, yeah." There was no voice on the other end. Was he or wasn't he on the phone? Wendy Ettinger tried to introduce us, and she briefly alluded to my pedigree. He offered me a limp handshake and quickly turned away to his nonexistent conversation. Wendy looked at me as if to apologize and reassure me he wasn't usually like this. That was the only time I met him. Strangely, he seemed afraid of me. Perhaps he lumped me in the category of those who are antidevelopment and antibusiness, of which there are many in New York.

I was concerned, however, that the hotel's six Stanford White fireplaces would be damaged in the reconstruction. So I informed Ian Schrager's team via email about the antiques. I never heard back from them. Months later, in the hotel's bar, Schrager's business partner Michael Overington informed me that my email had, in fact, been a revelation. Schrager immediately took four fireplaces for himself and donated one to the Gramercy Park Historical

Society. Only a single fireplace remained in room 1702. Eventually, this became the "White Room." Later, Schrager bragged about the find to the *National Post.*

"I haven't given them out yet," he said, dangling a carrot. "I don't know, John, if you want one?"

"Count me in." John Pawson replied, playing along. So five of the six fireplaces that had been in Gramercy Park for 150 years vanished without a murmur. Such was Ian Schrager's attitude toward history.

In that same interview with the *National Post,* Schrager outlined his thoughts: "The Gramercy Park Hotel is one of those sister hotels in New York that everyone thinks they own a piece of—the Plaza, the Chelsea, and the Gramercy Park. It will still have the same DNA, but we didn't want to look back in the past. We wanted to look forward. When we took it over, it was a dump."

Ian Schrager

A few words about Ian Schrager. Born in 1946, he grew up in East Flatbush, Brooklyn, with his Austrian Jewish immigrant parents. His father was in the shmata business and made coats for a living. He was also a known associate of Meyer Lansky. Unsurprisingly perhaps, Schrager's background mirrors that of former Gramercy owner Herbert Weissberg.

Supposedly, Meyer Lanksy was Ian Schrager's real father and Schrager's mother had an affair with the gangster—at least according to the theory of a lawyer whose name I won't reveal who played a role in managing Meyer Lansky's estate. This lawyer suspected that Lansky was Schrager's father because of some financial arrangement made in Meyer Lansky's will. I heard this information secretly at the National Arts Club in Gramercy Park. I do not believe this wild theory, but I share it here because it *could* be correct. In any case, Schrager's parents died when he was relatively young, leaving him to chart a path for himself.

In 1977, Ian Schrager, with Steve Rubell, opened the legendary Studio 54 inside what had once been a theater and later a CBS studio. Overnight, the disco club became a landmark of the 1970s dance scene. Andy Warhol, Michael Jackson, and Mick Jagger were regulars in the VIP room. One night, Bianca Jagger rode in on a horse (or just got on it—there is some controversy). Hundreds of people showed up to try to get in, and hundreds were rejected. To many in New York at the time, to be admitted into Studio

54 was a validation. Among those who got in was a young Steven Weissberg, who proudly claimed he got in because Steve Rubell had a thing for him.

In the club's first year, Schrager and Rubell had so much cash, they were stuffing it in the ceilings. After getting raided several times, however, the club was finally closed for tax evasion in 1980. Schrager and Rubell received short jail sentences. But to many club-goers, the two were heroes. After prison, the two decided to change businesses. In 1984, they opened the Morgans Hotel at 237 Madison Avenue, the first "boutique hotel" (a phrase Schrager coined).

By the time Ian Schrager and Aby Rosen took over the hotel in 2004, Ian Schrager was exiting his Morgans Group to start the Ian Schrager Company, whose first project would be the Gramercy. Morgans Group, which controlled eight hotels, soon went public on Valentine's Day 2006. Ian Schrager quickly cashed out $9 million in stock. But he remained at the company as a $2.25 million-a-year consultant. His perks included private jet travel, salaries for a full-time driver and secretary, as well as the ability for him, his family, and his associates to stay at Morgans' hotels for free. According to the *Miami Herald*, Morgans had posted a loss every year since 2001 and was $660 million in debt by 2005.

Despite Schrager's financial acumen, his hotels were developing a reputation for snottiness, particularly at the Hudson in Hell's Kitchen and the Delano in Miami. The Delano's ultra-modern interior was also not for everyone's taste. Like all Schrager hotels, however, the Hudson and Delano were filled with beautiful people.

One of the videos Schrager's own team produced shows him dressed in elegant denim in a fabulously expensive apartment next to a plastic model of the Gramercy Park Hotel. Speaking like the beat poet of the brokerage world, he repeats, "You *are* where you live." He then explains how the daily services of a hotel could change one's outlook on life. Either he was the oracle of Manhattan, or you wondered why they couldn't have found someone else to do the routine.

Something about Schrager's voice does not match his elegance, and no magazine or newspaper can quite capture it. To some, Schrager has the voice of a Brooklyn gangster. Nothing about his charisma or body language suggests he's a boxer or brute, nor do his words. It is that raspy Brooklyn intonation—the pronunciation of the street, not of the library—that marks Ian Schrager's voice, never mind that he has a law degree. Within that voice, one can gleam a sense of ownership and urgency to bend the will of other people.

Aby Rosen

The other new owner of the Gramercy Park Hotel was Aby Rosen, a German-Jewish real estate titan. I have never met him in real life, but he looks very much like the man on the Quaker Oats container. Long, white hair, brushed in waves like the familiar breakfast spokesman. His face often has a serious expression that even a smile cannot hide. Based on photographs, his uniform of choice appears to be a white or blue shirt, with the top two buttons (sometimes three) unbuttoned, with or without a suit jacket. He speaks in a soft German accent, one Americans would have trouble identifying if they didn't know he was German.

Rosen was born and raised in Frankfurt, Germany, the son of Jewish parents. His father was a survivor of Auschwitz, and his mother had fled the Nazis by hiding in a farmhouse in Belgium. Following the war, his father started a prosperous real estate business. Having suffered greatly, by now, he was wealthy enough to ensure Aby and his sister had a comfortable childhood. "We were brought up—it was about education," Rosen once described to Suzy Andrews of *Vanity Fair.* "It was about music. It was about culture. We went to theaters. I mean, it was like—it was all about embracing the good part of life, you know?"

In nursery school in Frankfurt, Rosen met his future best friend and business partner, Michael Fuchs, who also was the child of Holocaust survivors and the scion of a burgeoning real estate business. For a while in the 1980s, Rosen's family lived in Israel, but the young real estate prodigy had his sights set on New York.

"When I grew up, I always dreamed of coming to New York," he once told a writer for the *Daily News*. "Everyone wants to have a piece of the city." His partner, Fuchs, later described him as someone "always determined to become a captain of industry." For Rosen, it seemed, that could happen only in America.

In 1987, at the age of twenty-seven, Rosen arrived in New York and apprenticed at a real estate brokerage firm, Jones Lang Wootton. He soon became a whiz at selling properties to German clients and then started buying properties himself. Over time, his approach was that of an upscale bottom-fisher. Fuchs and Rosen bought cheap commercial buildings and hired famous architects to add in design and art elements that drew in higher-tiered clientele. They soon discovered the hype value from having a famous architect was worth more than the relatively small increase in cost.

The formula worked. Backed by German investors and banks, they went on a buying spree of properties in Chicago, Philadelphia, Miami, Las Vegas, Germany, Israel, and other cities. In 1998, they bought the twenty-one-story Lever House office building on Park Avenue, one of the world's greatest examples of modern architecture. Rosen was not even forty at the time.

In October 2000, Rosen and Fuchs's company, RFR, added to its holdings the famous thirty-eight-story Seagram Building for more than $375 million. Showing no signs of slowing down, that same month, the company paid $38 million for the Forbes Building on 5th Avenue. The company soon had six office buildings and was looking at hotels and shopping malls. RFR Realty was part of a trend in New York real estate, in which billions of German dollars were being poured into trophy properties; 80 percent of the foreign money coming into New York at the time was, in fact, German.

Aby Rosen's meteoric rise extended to the art world. Over his career, he built a solid collection of over seven hundred A-list pieces, including works from Jean-Michel Basquiat, Jeff Koons, Richard Prince, Keith Haring, and Damien Hirst. He also had a $15 million Francis Bacon piece and somewhere between eighty and one hundred Warhols (even he wasn't sure). Rosen knew many of these artists personally. To display all his pieces, he needed a lot of wall space and public rooms—more than his buildings could provide.

Not everyone was so impressed with his collection. "Why does Aby Rosen need 150 Warhol paintings?" Miami dealer Kevin Bruk once complained. "If you have 150 paintings by anybody, you're not hanging them. I don't care how big your house is."

I am not privy to the details of the deal between the Ian Schrager Company and RFR Realty. Ian Schrager himself referred to his share as "my half," which, if true, is incredible. Based on both of their backstories, it seems clear who was on the way up and who was on the way down. Nevertheless, all remained behind closed doors. As part of the deal, Ian Schrager brought in models, celebrities, and journalistic attention. To a real estate developer like Aby Rosen, that was something tremendously valuable. Perhaps Ian Schrager got his half without even putting anywhere near half the money on the table.

Photo by Cameron Weissberg.

Though New York was on the upswing after 9/11, there had been many hotels built over the previous decade that crowded the New York hotel market. On top of this, Hotels.com and other online booking sites were causing prices to race to the bottom, not to mention the sites added commissions that climbed as high as 30 percent. In 2000, it was nearly impossible to find a New York hotel room for under $200 a night, aside from some Bowery flophouses. By 2005, rooms could easily be found in Manhattan for half that amount. This made things challenging for the Gramercy.

The Gramercy Is Polished

For the makeover of the lobby and redesign of the rooms, Schrager hired artist and film director Julian Schnabel. Schnabel had a connection to the hotel and had been there during its Art Fair days. We had also crossed paths on the hotel's rooftop at the legendary Metallica party in 2004. Schnabel was hired at an incredibly busy time in his life, however, and I suspect he may have had some uncredited assistance. Before arriving, he had just finished shooting *The Diving Bell and the Butterfly* in Paris, which would eventually be nominated for an Oscar. He also had projects lined up for the rest of the year. But he was facing criticism. The *Evening Standard* claimed that Schnabel's works were fetching a quarter of their former value and that "his posterity is in question." Clearly, Schnabel had a lot riding on the renovations.

Our documentary crew captured Schnabel rearranging furniture in the lobby, changing his mind about where the couch should go based on the energy flow. With so many furniture movements, some of our film crew was called in to relieve the tired decorators as Schnabel continued with his orders. It was interesting to see him work, but like many artists, he was elusive in his responses to our questions.

Ian Schrager's PR machine labeled the hotel's new look "new haute bohemian," presumably aimed at those who appreciated the finer things in life. Initial write-ups were glowing. Like putting a can of Coca-Cola on top of a piece of furniture from Versailles, the eclectic pairings allowed visitors to see the various objects in a new and intriguing way. If I had seen the chandelier at a garage sale, perhaps I wouldn't have thought twice about it. But in a room full of world-class art, it stood out. The hotel was once again like a museum—less like the Tenement Museum (where I was then working) and more like MoMA.

Upstairs, the rooms were miniature versions of the lobby, with the same plush red carpet, heavy curtains, and indigo chairs. On the bed, the four-hundred-plus-thread-count sheets were noticeably luxurious, as were the towels and bathrobe. Perhaps to signal that the hotel was cool, each room had a Gibson music player, custom designed for the hotel.

Like a gift shop for the museum downstairs, everything in the room was for sale. Indigo pillow on the bed: $400. iPod: $750. "Privacy" tassel on the doorknob: $25. There were also designer T-shirts for sale from Narciso Rodriguez ($70) and Norma Kamali ($60). Inside the minibar, the Peanut M&Ms cost $5 and a Coke cost $6. God forbid you get a late-night junk food craving—it would cost you!

Up on the roof, Schrager resisted the urge to open yet another busy bar. Instead, he added a retractable glass roof and dining tables, making the space available for events. In the north-facing room, he added an eye-catching light fixture made up of hundreds of bulbs. The walls featured more pieces from Aby Rosen's collection, including a Warhol and one of Damien Hirst's pharmacy cabinets. Like the ground floor below, the rooftop had a chessboard tile floor, a fireplace, and stately-looking furniture.

As for the staff, the new Gramercy did not find its employees using craigslist or the wanted section of the *New York Times*. Instead, the management sent out casting notices to managers and agents that repped models and actors. Schrager's philosophy was that anyone could learn to serve a drink, but not everyone looks like a model. Taking no chances, however, the staff underwent intense training before the hotel's opening. Like a young Floyd Patterson, many of the new employees saw working at the hotel as a path to further their careers. In fact, some staff soon disappeared from the hotel after they booked gigs on the TV shows *Big Brother* and *Glee*.

Inside the Rose Bar

Guarded by the model-esque bouncer Damion Luaiye, the Rose Bar admitted only the crème de la crème of New York high society. Unless you were famous, you could not get in without a reservation. (It was not entirely impossible, but it was something that required spending lots of money.) It was so bad that once, Anne Hathaway was even turned away with her friends after Sean Penn entered with a party of eight.

Occasionally, some ordinary folk did get in. Among them was Tom Haines, a *Boston Globe* writer, who reserved a room for a few nights and fought his way into the Rose Bar. After seeing his promised 10:00 p.m. reservation get pushed back ("private party—just came up"), he waited in the corner of the Jade Bar as Michael Stipe, Heather Graham, David Spade, Russell Simmons, and Jim Jarmusch sailed past security inside. For another two hours, he listened to the bass and laughter spilling from next door as he sipped one cocktail after another. Then more celebrities showed up: Horatio Sanz, Molly Shannon, Bruce Willis, and Giselle Bündchen.

Finally, at midnight, Tom Haines got into the Rose Bar. It was Jimmy Fallon's birthday—all drinks were on him. (Oddly enough, I had been at Jimmy Fallon's birthday at the National Arts Club across the street the previous year, but that's another story.)

What Haines saw was two hundred or so people crammed onto soft couches and cushy chairs. Candles flickered as two models played pool. The DJ played "Tainted Love," "LA Woman," "New Year's Day." Supermodel Bündchen laughed and bowed before a pudgy man with wild hair. Stipe, head shaved, carefully followed a conversation with a group of guys. Willis appeared and said, "It is…claustrophobic in here." His eyes darted around the room. An eager young man at his back said, "How long are you in town for, Bruce?"

Outside the Rose Bar that night, Haines found a crowd of twenty waiting for four unisex bathrooms (one had to leave and come back through a side door to use them). Among the crowd was Claire Danes in an elegant black dress. "Pee faster. Or inhale faster. Or do whatever it is you're doing in there faster," she said as she started to dance about. Someone laughed. She continued, louder this time, "I'm a fast pee-er. I'm a good pee-er." Later, she returned to chat with Jarmusch, who had been sipping a glass of wine on the couch.

When Haines was back at his own seat, the girl sitting next to him leaned over. "There's, like, so many cokeheads in here," she said. He could smell the cocaine in other people's nostrils. By 5:00 a.m., Haines was back at the bathroom. This time, Willis was in line, smoking. A middle-aged, eastern European attendant told him to stop.

"Do you know who I am?" he said.

"Sir, you are a guest in the hotel. No smoking," she said. He continued anyway.

Such nights were typical.

Ironically, Ian Schrager started the Gramercy Park Hotel press tour saying that Studio 54 had been a Frankenstein monster he never wanted to repeat. Yet that philosophy didn't last more than a few hours after the hotel's unveiling, at least according to several British travel critics who stayed but could not get into the Rose Bar.

The Fashion Party Scene

The elite of New York City have three main party seasons: there's spring fashion week in February, the summer party season on New York rooftops and in the Hamptons, and the fall fashion week parties in September. The Gramercy could not wait that long, however. After its opening party, the hotel's first fashion party was a mid-July private dinner for Kate Hudson hosted by *Allure*'s Linda Wells. Then for September fashion week, *Vogue France* hosted a party attended by Paris and Nicky Hilton.

Two days later, Marc Jacobs, in a faded Mickey Mouse shirt and oversize glasses, hosted an afterparty for his fall show. There, Paris Hilton was famously not on the list and denied entry. But everyone else was welcomed in: Winona Ryder, Sofia Coppola, Eva Mendes, Dylan McDermott, Ashley Olsen, Kanye West, Jared Leto, Zooey Deschanel, Roger Federer, and so many more. The list of celebrities who attended was practically longer than Homer's catalogue of ships in the *Iliad*. As part of the presentation, Marc Jacobs set up an art exhibit of nude photography featuring famous models. In another corner, a booth, staffed by a good-looking coterie of young, gay models, sold T-shirts with photos of famous *naked* models on them. The T-shirts' text read, "Protect your largest organ" and "Protect the skin you're in." Something about having a room full of beautiful people and artwork with even more beautiful naked people really gets the senses going. It may have been the New York party of 2006, but it was just the beginning for the Rose Bar.

After Paris Hilton's rejection, the Rose Bar became a household name. The story filled the pages of gossip magazines across the country. Imitating the Rose Bar, other New York events started banning Paris as well. Even Ian Schrager weighed in on the matter: "People are really fed up with kowtowing to celebrities—celebrities making fools of themselves," he explained to a journalist. This from the man who created Studio 54.

A week after the Marc Jacobs party, *Vogue* and the Council of Fashion Designers of America (CFDA) threw a party that included, among others, Anna Wintour, model Karolína Kurková, Harvey Weinstein, and his wife designer, Georgina Chapman, who was up for an award (she didn't win). Milla Jovovich was also there as a contender for her Jovovich-Hawk line. Later, she returned to the hotel to throw not only a party for her fashion line but also her birthday party with *Vogue*. Then *Teen Vogue* threw a party for the Olsen twins in November 2006. It was like the publisher *Condé Nast* was vying to become the Gramercy's best customer.

Perhaps Anna Wintour was lured in by the Gramercy's red carpet and its "Oscar night" feeling. In subsequent years, she would cohost parties with Oscar de la Renta, Mulberry, and Cole Haan, among others. Also getting in on the action was *Vanity Fair*, which cohosted a Gramercy party with Tommy Hilfiger and held a dinner for writer Bob Colacello, with Calvin Klein and Diane von Fürstenberg.

The hotel was quickly leaving its mark on the fashion world. While admiring the Rose Bar's paintings and its "baroque divans," designers Domenico Dolce and Stefano Gabbana, i.e., Dolce & Gabbana, found inspiration for their upcoming 2007 gown collection. When viewing some of the dresses, it's clear the abstract patterns match the hues of the Rose Bar's art collection.

Once the hotel was "in," every fashion line wanted to associate itself with the Gramercy. Gucci and *Interview* magazine threw a party there. Donatella Versace showed up to help peddle *Allure* editor Linda Wells's new book. Giorgio Armani booked the rooftop and actor Josh Hartnett to promote a new fragrance. Dolce & Gabbana held a launch for their flagship Madison Avenue store, bringing in Anne Hathaway, Eva Mendes, and Kate Hudson to celebrate. Diane von Fürstenberg held a party, and fellow designers Calvin Klein and Nicole Miller showed up. Calvin Klein and Wilhelmina models hosted a surprise birthday party for model Gabriel Aubry, and it ended in a pool game between Aubry and actor Jamie Burke. And so on. And so on.

With so many fashion parties at the Gramercy, dueling parties were not uncommon. In the fall of 2007, Moët & Chandon and Marchesa hosted a party in the Rose Bar while, down the hall, Milla Jovovich and Carmen Hawk posed done-up models in their vintage clothing line set against a stylish 1960s-era backdrop. Another night, Victoria Beckham faced off against designer Zac Posen, with her on the roof and him at the Rose Bar. Unsurprisingly, the two ended up visiting each other's parties and talking all night. It was the kind of fast friendship that could only be found inside the walls of a closed-off kingdom like the Gramercy.

One of the hotel's largest new hosts of fashion parties was the Marchesa fashion line, run by Harvey Weinstein's wife. When I met Harvey, he was wearing blue jeans and a white wool sweater, and somehow, he wore everything in such a way as to look like a slob. He was on his way to catch a flight to Los Angeles, so maybe he was in relaxation mode. In addition to hosting the parties for Marchesa, he was one of the early residents of the Rose Bar. When writer Barry Avrich wrote a nasty book about Weinstein, *Moguls*,

Monsters and Madmen: An Uncensored Life in Show Business, Weinstein strangely offered to throw a party for the writer and his book at the Gramercy. Until the last minute, the author wondered if it was a trick. Yet it turned out not to be a hustle at all. Instead, the "usual" crowd showed up, including Petra Němcová, Dick Cavett, Martin Short, and James Earl Jones.

In 2007, Weinstein was at the Rose Bar when DJ Marcos Udagawa fell onto the girl sitting next to him. Supposedly, the DJ started groping the woman and, hearing the woman's complaint, Weinstein intervened. A fistfight ensued, an act of pure chivalry on Weinstein's part—or at least that's how Harvey Weinstein told the story to *Page Six*. That night, the crowd, including Heath Ledger, Uma Thurman, and Zach Braff, were all mum about the incident, perhaps unwilling to get into a conflict with Weinstein. Later, at a Rose Bar Halloween party in 2011, Weinstein bumped into actress Lacey Dorn, who he had seen earlier that evening at another event. She later said that he asked for her email, saying he wanted to talk about her career over lunch. In the subject line of a blank email sent at 12:26 a.m., he wrote her, "Great meeting you." As Lacey attempted to leave the Rose Bar, Weinstein grabbed her butt and crotch—this even though his own wife, Georgina Chapman, was at the party. Though photographers were everywhere, none captured anything. "I was so naïve, I didn't say anything. And he didn't say anything either," Dorn later told the *New York Times*. "I just got out of the party as fast as possible."

Weinstein continued to be a regular feature at the most exclusive Rose Bar parties. Often, he was seen pacing Lexington Avenue as he yelled into his cellphone about a film deal. Like an omen, Weinstein's wife, Georgina Chapman, once lost her wedding ring at the Rose Bar during a Marchesa fashion event. The loss sent her assistants scrambling, overturning furniture and pulling up the carpet as they hunted for the piece of jewelry. Later, however, an assistant called to report the ring was safely at home. After the #MeToo movement began and Weinstein was eventually jailed, the Gramercy Marchesa events became things of the past. Weinstein's presence at the Rose Bar, once a mark of prestige, became a grim reminder of the power imbalances that thrive in exclusive spaces like the Rose Bar.

THE FILM SCENE

As one would expect, many from the old rock 'n' roll crowd returned to the hotel. Both Jack White of the White Stripes and Weezer stayed for a while, auditioning new collaborators inside their rooms. Sting also came back to the hotel, and during his stay, a fan bugged him for performing his most recent concert in a Halloween mask. In the first few months of the New York leg of their tour, Aerosmith stayed at the hotel. When Jonathan Weissberg passed by their tour bus, the new doorman said to him, "Keep it moving." Alas, he didn't realize Jonathan lived in the hotel and knew Steven Tyler.

For the most part, the renovated hotel's famous guests were actors, models, and pop stars, not rock stars. Everywhere, it seemed, there were sightings. One night, Russell Simmons, Jay-Z, and Leonardo DiCaprio hung out at the Rose Bar together. The next day, the papers wondered if Leo was trying out to be the new Eminem. Russell Simmons, a nightly guest, explained to our documentary crew, "It's got to be one of the most beautiful places, if not most beautiful, in the city."

I remember regularly spotting a photographer hanging around outside with a hat on that said *The Daily News*, *TMZ*, or *Page Six*, the *New York Post*'s gossip publication. A symbiotic relationship formed in which celebrities came to the Gramercy partly to *make* the news. One night, the *Daily News* caught Justin Timberlake entering the hotel with a trio of girls. Another night, the same paper reported that Victoria Beckham (also known as Posh Spice) skipped singer Mel C.'s private solo show for one of the bar's signature cocktails. Jennifer Aniston also came to the hotel to show off her new boyfriend, actor/filmmaker Justin Theroux, to the tabloids. Her public appearance was perhaps a means to squash the rumor that she had recently met up with her divorced husband, Brad Pitt, for a 1:00 a.m. rendezvous on the hotel's rooftop.

I remember when I once encountered a celebrity inside Gramercy Park. After a short conversation, the celebrity left, and my friend explained, "That was the actor from *American Pie*. He was upset that you didn't recognize him." Before, celebrities wanted to be ignored at the Gramercy. Now they were disappointed not to be recognized!

Nevertheless, the growth in the hotel's business was emblematic of New York's continued success and rejuvenation. Led by Mayor Michael Bloomberg, business in the city was booming, thanks partly to low interest rates. Tourists were also flocking to the city, and its nightclub scene, led by the Box, Marquee, and the Rose Bar, was able to get away with charging thousands of dollars for bottle service. Though competition was increasing in the form of new faceless hotels that started popping up throughout the city, the hotel's bars and events were bringing in gobs of money.

The Gramercy, it seemed, was now the epicenter of extreme wealth and extreme beauty. One night, model Kate Moss, a regular in the old hotel, held a party in her suite and invited Cameron Diaz, Naomi Campbell, and singer Amy Winehouse with her husband, music producer Blake Fielder-Civil, whom Winehouse had just married a few weeks earlier. At some point in the party, the model asked the singer to get a ten dollar bill out of her purse to snort some lines. While digging around, Winehouse found a two-gram bag of coke, which she pocketed. Then she went to the bathroom with her husband and did all the blow on the sink, stopping periodically to have sex. According to the *Daily Mail*, Kate Moss hardly noticed her coke had been stolen.

Another evening, supermodel Gisele Bündchen got frisky with her dance partner while her husband, Tom Brady, was nowhere in sight. Then on another night, Tom Brady himself got wild at the Rose Bar, sans Gisele. Later, the two came together and attended a party, a spring fling event, with Naomi Campbell, Karolína Kurková, and Tyson Ballou attending. One wonders what role the Rose Bar played in their lives, considering how public these events were.

The gossip rags also caught "platonic couple" Diddy and actress Sienna Miller at the hotel getting very cozy, leading to rumors that they were in the middle of a honeymoon stage. Some years later, Diddy again chose the Gramercy when he was dating Cassie Ventura. A former desk clerk said, "[Diddy] would always rent the penthouse suite very last minute and would come very late at night. We automatically added an extra $500 cleaning fee because every time he would leave, every surface would be covered in baby oil—the curtains, the rugs, the pillows, everything. It really made the mind boggle. We used to joke that his fetish was to slather women in baby oil and just roll them around the room like a sausage." Diddy's "freak-offs" in the hotel would later be cited in court testimony against him. In the room, Diddy allegedly hired a sex worker to have sex with his girlfriend while he watched.

The band Arcade Fire were also troublemakers. During one of their many visits to the city to play on *Saturday Night Live*, they stayed at the Gramercy, keeping a tradition alive for bands that played on the show. Very late after the show, they arrived back at the Gramercy and drunkenly sat all over the floor of the lobby. The ground floor of the Gramercy suddenly became an obstacle course, with patrons having to move around or leap over the seven members of the band and their roadies lying all over the floor. The cuteness faded after a minute.

Because of the hotel's reputation and the unwanted attention it was receiving, Taylor Swift took no chances during her stay. She booked multiple rooms and parked her security in the hallway outside her rooms 24/7 as a safety measure. Not since David Bowie had the hotel seen a star with so much security personnel. When she wanted to eat at Maialino (the Gramercy's restaurant), Swift insisted on being allowed through the back offices via a hidden entrance rather than pass through the lobby.

But Taylor Swift was hardly as much of a hassle as Lindsay Lohan, apparently. A former desk clerk remembered:

> *Lindsay Lohan stayed for several days and wouldn't pay, insisting Oprah was supposed to pay. Got a call in the middle of the night. She got in a big fight with one of her friends—maybe it was an assistant—demanding that we move that person to a new room. We went up, there was chaos, and Lindsay was screaming, and we moved this person to a new room. They had more designer purses than I've ever seen in my life, and they didn't tip myself or the porter who helped move their rooms.*

At the time, Lindsay Lohan was filming a documentary series for the OWN channel in which she insisted to Oprah she was committed to sobriety. As part of the documentary, Lindsay's publicist badgered Cameron Weissberg so the two would hang out in the hotel's Weissberg suites. But Cameron turned her down.

At the other end of the guest spectrum was actor Jared Leto. Once, when "someone very sweet" sent forty white roses to Jared Leto's hotel room, his response was, "What are you going to do with forty roses in a hotel room?" Later, he gave them away, one by one, surprising guests of the hotel.

Not only did celebrities come to spend the night, but the hotel was also used as a backdrop for the TV shows *Girls*, *Gossip Girl*, and *Younger*. All found ways to incorporate the hotel into their storyline. For *Younger* (whose marketing I worked on at Paramount), the characters track down a missing person by identifying the Gramercy Park Hotel's famous Le Labo candle in an Instagram video. The Gramercy's candles were so zeitgeisty in New York at the time that the show's writer and creator, Darren Star, felt this story point needed minimal explanation. As for *Gossip Girl*, the cast lived in the hotel during production of the pilot and returned often.

50 GRAMERCY PARK

Alongside the new hotel was the renovated annex, which took its new name from the building's address. Initially, the space was to be designed by French architect Philippe Starck, but an early disagreement with Ian Schrager (details unknown) led to his replacement by English architect John Pawson. Pawson then designed a plan that created twenty-three apartments out of the former hotel's annex, filling in the space between the towers where Steven and David Weissberg had once lived with their nine dogs.

An important aspect of the apartments was that they were not truly *owned* by those who bought them. Instead, they were rented through seventy-five-year leases. Since Aby Rosen and Ian Schrager had negotiated only a lease with Solil that had built-in renewals, Solil was the real owner of the apartments. The triple net lease aspect of Rosen and Schrager's deal meant the condo buyers could be liable for the taxes on their properties, and they were responsible for maintenance and building staff costs. As a result, each condo's monthly maintenance fees were between $7,000 and $25,000. This type of lend-lease situation is found in roughly one hundred buildings in New York City. In such situations, the apartments typically cost 35 percent below the market rate.

At 50 Gramercy, however, the new apartments ranged from $4 to $16 million each. When I spoke to the real estate broker handling the sales (he tried to sell to me, not knowing who I was), he repeatedly emphasized how Gramercy Park real estate almost never came on the market. "Plus, you get the key to Gramercy Park," he added, by now questioning my ability to afford anything. Some buyers, like Karl Lagerfeld, who paid $6.5 million for 6A, purchased their apartments before construction was complete, relying on the miniature plastic model of the new hotel. The incredibly detailed replica was "made in Europe," Ian Schrager explained it, and he said it in such a way that it reminded you he was an ex-con.

The rapid sales caused some immediate reflection on the part of Ian Schrager and Aby Rosen. They decided to raise the prices. Not only that, but they also bought back a few of the recently sold condos at a premium and then resold them for a higher price. It was as if the hotel had become a microcosm of the snowballing mortgage crisis that would soon engulf America.

Another early buyer was Jón Ásgeir Jóhannesson, an Icelandic playboy billionaire businessman who had made a fortune in the retail store and grocery markets. In Jóhannesson's case, he ended up buying a full-floor apartment for $10 million. He liked it so much that a few months later, he bought the duplex penthouse with large terraces overlooking Gramercy Park for $14 million and spent $4 million to buy out the contract of another buyer. He paid for everything in cash. Then he hired an architect to combine the apartments with an inner stairwell.

By the end of 2005, only four units remained for sale (or at least that's what the brokers claimed). Presumably all the apartments were sold by 2006, mostly going to CEO types. At one point, a rumor was started that Jennifer Aniston had paid $8.7 million for 9B, a three-bedroom, 2,873-square-foot condo. Started by the *New York Post*, the story spread like wildfire. Unit 9B, apparently, was the *only* condo whose master bedroom had a view of Gramercy Park. The paper asked: Was this what it would take for the *Friends* star to finally find happiness? Once again, her reps squashed the rumor. She was only *looking*, not buying. Besides, she already had three apartments in New York.

Maialino

Ian Schrager had always imagined that his new upscale hotel would have a fancy Chinese restaurant. Initially, the restaurant was to be named Park Chinois, but visa problems for the desired head chef, Alan Yau, kept it from opening. So, for room service, the hotel initially offered a "greatest hits" menu, featuring items from local restaurants in the area.

After nearly a year, however, no progress had been made on the hotel's restaurant after an exhaustive search for a chef. Finally, in the fall of 2007, management decided to lease the restaurant space to Robert DeNiro's Nobu group. DeNiro was no stranger to the hotel, having made several movies there. He had also attended a recent rooftop party there for *Stardust*, along with costars Claire Danes and Robin Wright Penn. What resulted was a new restaurant, Wakiya, to be named after Yūji Wakiya, its new chef. Originally from Japan, Wakiya specialized in Chinese food and had won the *Iron Chef* television contest in Japan in 1997. A Japanese chef cooking Chinese food—what could go wrong?

In typical Schrager fashion, the hotel celebrated the restaurant's opening with a huge star-studded party, hosted by Robert DeNiro, Ian Schrager, and Japanese chef Nobu Matsuhisa (the "Nobu" in Nobu), on the roof. The event brought LL Cool J in a black New York Yankees cap, Molly Sims in a golden toga dress, and Aby Rosen in one of his unbuttoned dress shirts. Just to be clear which chef was the new guy, Wakiya wore a white chef's apron and spent most of the party standing at attention near the table. Next to him was a display featuring frolicking birds and dragons made entirely of carved vegetables. As the event reached its zenith, DeNiro and the two chefs poured boiling hot water over the food sculpture, simulating smoke from a dragon's mouth. Then DeNiro raised a glass to the new chef. "Let's do this. To the restaurant," he said. Camera bulbs flashed.

Almost overnight, the new reviews came in. The *Daily News* gave the restaurant one star, with the headline "Not the Finest China." *New York* magazine gave it zero stars, calling it a "bowling alley of a space" and noting that most of the $30+ dishes were no more than a few bites. The *New York Times* gave a more friendly "satisfactory" rating, comparing the cuisine to McDonald's with "nuggets no more tender than those you retrieve from many a drive-through window." Nevertheless, because it was the Gramercy, Wakiya hosted a Calvin Klein party the very next day. That evening, amid Wakiya's bordello-like ambience, nightclub queen Amy Sacco told actor Heath Ledger to *take it easy* during fashion week. How prescient that advice would soon be.

Despite regular celebrity sightings, Wakiya became known as a "failure." It closed of its own accord, giving the excuse that the chef needed to spend more time back in Japan. So Gramercy Park resident Danny Meyer took over in 2009 and hired architect David Rockwell to redesign the space as a Roman trattoria. Perhaps the most famous restaurateur of twenty-first-century New York, Danny Meyer launched on the scene in 1985 with Union Square Cafe, known for its model-esque waitresses and high-quality comfort food. He then followed with Blue Smoke, Gramercy Tavern, and the two-Michelin-starred The Modern at MoMA. On top of Meyer's commanding presence in the New York luxury dining scene, he founded Shake Shack, a burger chain that grew from a tin-covered burger and fry joint inside New York's Madison Square Garden into a four-hundred-plus-location chain.

At the Gramercy Park Hotel, Rockwell and Meyer transformed Wakiya's "catwalk" (plus its private dining areas) into a larger, lighter, more organic interior. In what was Herbert's old corner office, Danny Meyer installed an elaborate coffee and spirits bar. So nicely designed was the space that one felt comfortable there whether they were sipping an espresso or a glass of Chardonnay. Rockwell also removed the tinting on the windows, giving the guests clear views of Gramercy Park. Everywhere, there were chalkboards, comfortable chairs, wine racks, and slowly spinning fans overhead. For the first time, one truly felt they were dining in Gramercy Park, with all its brightness and greenery. I must admit, although I was sad to see my grandfather's office morph into a public space, the aura of the space could not be more welcoming.

Danny Meyer named the hotel's new restaurant Maialino, "little pig" or "suckling pig" in Italian. While studying abroad in Italy at the age of twenty (and working for his tour guide father), Meyer was nicknamed "Meyerino" by his Italian friends. After he developed a reputation for ordering pork, his nickname jokingly morphed into "Maialino." It's no surprise that one of the menu highlights at Maialino was the pork.

Heading the new restaurant was American chef Nick Anderer, who sourced many of the dishes' vegetables from the nearby farmers' market in Union Square. Instead of hiring models and influencers to serve guests, the restaurant hired ex-professors and people with graduate degrees. How much the Gramercy had evolved in such a short time.

New York magazine had little negative to say but gave the restaurant only one star. The *New York Times* said the pork "tastes great—pork at its best" but cautiously gave the restaurant two stars without a negative word. Perhaps the residue of Wakiya hung in the air. Whatever the critics thought, the place was a phenomenal hit with regular customers. Among them was President Barack Obama, who dined there with Valerie Jarrett and NFL wide receiver Ahmad Rashad in 2014. The presidential visit put the hotel in shutdown mode. Political advisor David Axelrod and ex-Mayor DeBlasio are also known to have been fans. As far as I know and have seen, everyone loved the place.

The Global Financial Crisis

It began with the collapse of Lehman Brothers in September 2008 and ended with a shakeup at the Gramercy Park Hotel. Before the crisis, the hotel was charging $525 a night for its cheapest room, the same as it had when it opened. But by 2009, that number had dropped to $420 a night. The hotel was also promoting weekend specials.

Aby Rosen's RFR Realty, meanwhile, was reshuffling $3.5 billion worth of debt. Eventually, the hotel was unable to pay its $140 million loan to Union Labor Life Insurance and defaulted. In an act of financial chutzpah, Aby Rosen offered to purchase the loan from the company for $90 million. According to the *Wall Street Journal*, the insurance company agreed.

The hotel's business problems caused Aby Rosen and Ian Schrager to have a massive falling out. "Honestly, the two of them just couldn't get along," an anonymous source told the *New York Post*. Reportedly, Aby Rosen was also fighting with his longtime partner, Michael Fuchs, and Peter Brant, a bigwig in the art world and Rosen's business partner in the Seagram Building. It was nothing personal, they insisted, only money.

Ian's exit package from the hotel included $20 million. His departure also meant the end of Nur Khan's reign in the Rose Bar; his job as "creative director" had been to stuff the place with models and celebrities.

Over at 50 Gramercy Park North, the residents filed a $3.1 million lawsuit against Rosen, Schrager, and Fuchs for sloppy maintenance and construction defects. Meanwhile, the residents were having their own crises. The Icelandic penthouse owner Jón Ásgeir Jóhannesson owed more than $1 billion to three Icelandic banks (via his companies), which added up to between 70 percent and 80 percent of the Icelandic GDP. So Jóhannesson put his apartment on the market for $25 million, a modest increase from the $24 million he had paid for it. Unable to find a buyer, however, he took it off the market and rented the bottom apartment for $320,000 a year.

The new tenant reportedly discovered IKEA cabinets in the kitchen and other cheap fixtures and sued their landlord. Apparently Jóhannesson had run out of money during the remodeling. Also in the $52,000 suit was a complaint that the billionaire had been dumping chewed-up chicken wings and other trash items off the balcony to land on the rental's balcony below.

Karl Lagerfeld also decided to sell his apartment for a loss at $4.5 million. A trend began. Many apartments at 50 Gramercy Park North were turned into high-end rentals or went back on the market at substantially reduced prices. It seemed the boom cycle in New York real estate had ended.

Rose Bar Sessions

As a sign of how bad business had gotten after the financial crisis, the hotel started letting me into the Rose Bar (accompanied by Cameron, my model-esque, trophy wife–ish aunt). With Cameron by my side, my streak of free drinks at the Gramercy continued. In another instance of lost revenue, some bargain-focused wedding specialists figured out that if you booked the Gramercy's rooftop for an "afternoon tea," you could avoid paying the hotel's exorbitant wedding fee. The scheme cost the hotel a small fortune. In an act of desperation perhaps, the hotel even licensed its name to Sears, which started selling the Gramercy Park Hotel sheet collection for $129.99 per piece. Clearly something big was needed to renew interest and bring back the high rollers who were willing to pay $1,000 a night.

The Rose Bar Sessions were the solution. Though the Gramercy had always been associated with rock 'n' roll and hosted countless rehearsal and recording sessions, it had never hosted a concert. That changed on May 23, 2007, when Velvet Revolver performed in front of the Rose Bar's limestone fireplace. The band, led by Scott Weiland from Stone Temple Pilots and Slash from Guns N' Roses, sold no tickets and made no public announcements beforehand. For the lucky few invited, they watched as Slash—in a backward cap and sunglasses—played the acoustic guitar as Weiland sang with an untied bowtie slung around his neck. Both smoked like chimneys throughout the session. Not only was the music cool, but there was also a forbidden fruit aspect to the show. The band broke up only a year later.

For the Rose Bar's second anniversary party, a slew of musical acts took to the fireplace stage to perform. These acts included the British group the Kooks, the "godfather of alternative music" Perry Farrell, and Dave Navarro of Jane's Addiction. Some months later, former hotel resident Evan Dando and the lead singer of the Butthole Surfers, Gibby Haynes, played a set. During the show, Haynes got so furious with the scene-y crowd that he yelled, "You cocky-ass motherfuckers can suck my fucking dick. Pay attention to Evan Dando!" The model-esque audience, which included Rose Bar regulars Jim Jarmusch and Clive Owen, merely shrugged their shoulders and continued sipping their overpriced cocktails.

After the financial crisis, the Gramercy gave its concerts a title: the Rose Bar Sessions. It helped brand the concept—and allowed the concept to be branded. DeLeon Tequila and SPIN signed up as sponsors. The first band to play was the Black Keys, who, ironically, had been banned from the hotel by Steven Greenberg back in 2002 for throwing beer cans and a Bible out the window.

The second Rose Bar Session on Valentine's Day 2009 featured Axl Rose sans Guns N' Roses. The night of the concert, the Rose Bar was absolutely jammed. Bar patrons rubbed elbows (literally) with Mickey Rourke and Ryan Phillipe. At 1:00 a.m., Axl finally took the stage in a brown fedora, unbuttoned shirt, and a giant golden cross that reached his stomach. Even behind the sunglasses, you could tell Axl had heavily imbibed. Moments after he began, a drunk fan lunged toward the stage with a switchblade knife hoping to stab Axl. But the crowd was thick and ex–Skid Row frontman Sebastian Bach tackled him to the ground. Security intervened. The knife-wielding man was tossed out. Then Axl Rose started singing "Sweet Child O' Mine" and a dozen other Guns N' Roses hits for the next ninety minutes. This was the first time Axl Rose had visited the hotel since 1987. Like before, his visit left a trail of violence, but his set also became the stuff of legend.

After Axl Rose, the next Rose Bar Session featured a much calmer Rufus Wainwright, who, like Axl, had a connection to the old place. Wainwright performed on the piano as Drew Barrymore and Scarlett Johansson listened in the audience. Then came a Sean Lennon concert, a Liza Minelli concert, and the Sleigh Bells for a special Lacoste L!VE branded event, all to star-studded audiences. It seemed like the concert-in-a-hotel-bar phenomenon was about to revolutionize the music scene. Perhaps the formula could work everywhere, generating interest in live music events and CD sales. In any case, the momentum ended with Ian Schrager's departure. With Nur Khan, Schrager's impresario, gone, the Rose Bar Sessions practically died.

By 2011, the new management had pivoted to showcase more jazz bands in the Rose Bar. Among them, playing every Tuesday and Thursday, was a band headed by trumpet player and singer Brian Newman.

One evening in May 2013, Lady Gaga was in the audience having just had hip surgery. The surgery and recovery had taken so long, Gaga ended

Logan and Alana Weissberg, children of Steven and Cameron, in the Rose Bar. The pair grew up on the fourteenth floor of the hotel. *Photo by Kari Otero.*

up canceling the remaining dates on her Born this Way Ball world tour. Suddenly, and without any prior notice, Brian Newman (then of the band the Dirty Pearls) invited Lady Gaga to the stage to sing. She sang "Someone to Watch Over Me," by George Gershwin. The audience was touched but also shocked to see her.

Soon there were Lady Gaga sightings throughout the hotel. Lady Gaga giving autographs to fans outside. Lady Gaga's eclectic costumes being wheeled by on clothing rocks. Lady Gaga in the elevator. Lady Gaga again at the Rose Bar, singing impromptu. My aunt Cameron Weissberg met Lady Gaga several times at the hotel, and she graciously gave my cousin Alana Weissberg (then a teenager) a few fashion tips.

For New Year's Eve 2015, Lady Gaga performed at the hotel's masquerade ball. In 2016, when Lady Gaga played Superbowl 50, the Gramercy's regular pianist Alex Smith accompanied her onstage. Lady Gaga's Rose Bar concerts continued until 2018.

The Weissbergs During This Time

One almost forgets that the hotel was still home to much of the Weissberg family. While the place was crawling with celebrities downing drinks and inhaling cocaine, Logan and Alana Weissberg, the youngest Weissbergs, were busy doing their homework. I visited them weekly. Often, we gathered to play Monopoly or Donald Trump's board game (one of his many ventures) on the fifth floor, in the same apartment where Debbie Harry of Blondie had lived. Logan had a knack for winning these games, a hopeful sign for the future.

Like a young Eloise, Alana and Logan made friends with the staff and carried out pranks in the hotel. Everyone knew them, and their modelish good looks helped them fit in easily. Logan, in fact, became a model for Ralph Lauren and the Children's Place, posing for magazine advertisements. But they did not grow up with the experience of being able to order room service for free simply by giving their last name. Now the hotel's staff hardly recognized me, and the older, rich, well-dressed clientele of the Rose Bar didn't interest me.

Instead, I was now focused on making movies. Among the many things the hotel had given me was a modest film career. Following the documentary on the hotel, I enrolled in the American Film Institute Conservatory to develop my skills as a director. For my AFI thesis film *Karaganda*, I hosted a fundraiser in my aunt Cameron's apartment on the fourteenth floor. The film, though set in a Russian prison camp, was inspired by the disappearance of my sister in the 2004 tsunami. At that time, I remember I prayed in room 502 that my sister would return. Then a voice in my mind strangely asked me what I would be willing to sacrifice in order to bring her back. *Anything*, I said to myself, begging for her life. Later, as I worked on the screenplay in Russia, I incorporated the theme of love versus goodness in the storyline, as the main character, a Soviet prisoner named Vladimir, is willing to do whatever it takes to find his wife, who is also imprisoned in the Karaganda region. Eventually, I wrote and directed the feature version, *Karaganda: Red Mafia*, which was released on Amazon Prime in 2025. Like so many others, the hotel was my muse and helped further my goals as an artist.

In October 2017, the Weissbergs finally vacated. It was the end of an era, though many of us still lived in New York and visited Gramercy Park often. Much of this book, in fact, was written atop Mark Twain's old poker table inside The Players, a Gramercy Park club where I am now a third-generation member.

The Hotel Changes Hands

In 2020, during the COVID shutdown, Aby Rosen fell behind on rent and closed the hotel. Perhaps it was an unavoidable situation, given how poorly hotels were doing at the time. The hotel had also accumulated a massive amount of debt.

A lengthy lawsuit ensued over the lease payments. According to press reports, Solil sued Aby Rosen for $80 million, though the judge ruled Rosen wasn't personally liable for the sum. Eventually, the Goldman estate, also known as Solil, took back control.

Just before leaving, however, Aby Rosen decided to liquidate *everything* in the hotel. The sale was a bonanza, sparking a frenzy for velvet furniture and anything with the hotel's squiggly logo. My aunt Cameron bought one of the hotel's paintings for $300. I tried to explain it was just a framed copy. My wife bought a pillow for $60, the kind you'd see at Target for $5. Like my relatives, many rushed to the Gramercy and walked away with furniture, sheet sets, bottles of lotion, bathrobes, slippers, ice buckets—basically anything and everything you'd see at a hotel. Many of the items later appeared on eBay at several times the original purchase price. All that remained in the hotel were the curtains.

In 2023, MCR Hotels, led by billionaire Tyler Morse, purchased the hotel's lease for $50 million with plans to reopen in 2026. The company owns Soho House, among other properties, and is known for its successful renovation of the TWA hotel at John F. Kennedy International Airport. For a hotel with such a legendary history like the Gramercy, the news of a new owner was an exciting development.

Final Thoughts

Sitting at the dining table of Le Parc as a kid, I never imagined myself to be the Livy or Thucydides of the Gramercy Park Hotel. I recorded this history only because someone needed to. It was not a labor of love. More like a twenty-year-long anvil of obligation.

Did I dream of running the hotel? As a kid, there were times when I imagined myself working in every department of the hotel for two weeks at a time, to learn its inner workings and to earn the respect of the employees. Somehow, I thought I could turn the Gramercy into a socialist workers' paradise, where the boss (me) treated everyone as an equal. That daydream obviously never came to fruition—probably for the better. Later, I saw that running a hotel is not as easy as it seems. Perhaps I would have lost myself in the hotel's abyss, just like many of my relatives. The hotel is in better hands now.

No matter who owns it, I think, every generation's immortals will continue to pass through the Gramercy's revolving doors. New stories will be told, and they will be better than the ones in this book. Its history lives on, and its legend will only grow. For many, it will remain New York's soul. For others, it will just be a place to get a good night's rest. As for me, it will always be home.

SELECTED BIBLIOGRAPHY

Introduction

Assayas, Michka. *Bono on Bono: Conversations with Michka Assayas*. Hodder & Stoughton, 2005.

Sloman, Larry. *On the Road with Bob Dylan*. Crown Publishing Group, 1978.

Chapter 1

Aronowitz, Al. *The Best of the Blacklisted Journalist*. 1st Books Library, 2003.

Blakley, Ronee. *Uncut*, June 2021.

Buell, Bebe., and V. Bockris. *Rebel Heart*. St. Martin's Press, 2001.

DeCurtis, Anthony. *Lou Reed: A Life*. Little, Brown and Company, 2017.

Ehrlich, Ken. *At the Grammys: Behind the Scenes of Music's Biggest Night*. Rowman & Littlefield, 2007.

Faithfull, Marianne. *Faithfull: An Autobiography*. Cooper Square Press, 2000.

Farren, Mick. "Motorhead: Scumbags Over USA." *New Musical Express*, June 6, 1981.

Gilbert, Pat. *Passion Is a Fashion: The Real Story of the Clash*. Da Capo Press, 2005.

Gray, Marcus. *The Last Gang in Town: The Story and Myth of the Clash*. Henry Holt & Company, 1997.

Harington, Kit. "High Flyers." *Esquire*, April 1, 2016.

Hughes, Rob. "The Clash in New York: 'De Niro Took Us Out Clubbing.'" *Uncut*, January 5, 2021.

Jones, Dylan. *David Bowie: A Life*. Crown Publishing Group, 2017.

Maggi Ronson. www.maggironson.com.

McCain, Gillian, and Legs McNeil. *Please Kill Me: The Uncensored Oral History of Punk*. Grove Atlantic, 1996.

McCormick, Neil. *U2 by U2*. It Books, 2009.

Perry, Joe. *Rocks: My Life In and Out of Aerosmith*. Simon & Schuster, 2015.

Porter, Darwin. *Steve McQueen, King of Cool: Tales of a Lurid Life*. Blood Moon Productions, 2009.

Sabotage Times. www.sabotagetimes.com.

Sandford, Christopher. *Bowie: Loving the Alien*. Da Capo Press, 1998.

Seymour, Corey, and Jan S. Wenner. *Gonzo: The Life of Hunter S. Thompson: An Oral History*. Little, Brown and Company, 2007.

Shaffer, Paul, and David Ritz. *We'll Be Here for the Rest of Our Lives: A Swingin' Showbiz Saga*. Knopf Doubleday, 2010.

Smith, Patti. *The Reader Is My Notebook*. www.pattismith.substack.com.

Sounes, Howard. *Notes from the Velvet Underground: The Life of Lou Reed*. Transworld, 2015.

Chapter 2

Devereux, Paul. *Earthlights*. Turnstone Press, 2005.

Garmey, Stephen. *Gramercy Park: An Illustrated History*. Balsam Press, 1984.

Chapter 3

O'Neil, Paul. "Meet the Next Heavyweight Champion." *Sports Illustrated* 4, no. 5 (January 30, 1956): 16–19.

Sperber, Ann M., and Eric Lax. *Bogart*. William Morrow and Company, 1997.

Chapter 4

Albelli, Alfred. "Hot Coffee Cooing Sends Mate Aboil." *New York Daily News*, October 4, 1951, C4.

———. "Wife Gets Children, and a Blasting." *New York Daily News*, October 9, 1951, C5.

Blake, Gene, and Jack Tobin. "Teamsters Loans in Deep South Analyzed." *Los Angeles Times*, October 23, 1962, 24.

Heimer, Mel. "My New York." *Record*, February 26, 1958, 12.

New York Times. "Puerto Rico Faces Teamster Threat." May 29, 1964, 20.

Ragano, Frank, and Selwyn Raab. *Mob Lawyer: Including the Inside Account of Who Killed Jimmy Hoffa and JFK*. Scribner, 1994.

Wilner, Norman. Norman Wilner interviews. *Brooklyn Daily*, October 23, 1959, 8.

Chapter 5

Angelo, Frank. "Buyer Dives into Revitalizing Hotel." *Detroit Free Press*, September 3, 1975, B2.

Sloan, Allan, and Ellen Grzech. "Businessman to Buy, Run Cadillac Hotel." *Detroit Free Press*, August 5, 1975, A1.

Chapter 6

Caldwell, Jennifer. "Sharing Your Man…and Accepting It." *Daily News*, October 2, 1983, 10.

Faso, Frank, and Paul Meskil. "Bonnie, Clyde, and the Boys Rob the Gramercy Park Hotel." *Daily News*, September 2, 1975, 19.

Gray, Tom. "Rock 'N' Roll Diary." *Atlanta Constitution*, September 28, 1980, 18.

Green, John. *Dakota Days*. St. Martin's Press, 1983.

Henke, James. "Squeeze Aims at US Market." *Philadelphia Daily News*, June 27, 1980, 10.

Michelini, Alex. "Slams Door in Crime's Face." *Daily News*, February 20, 1983, 37.

Robinson, Lisa. "Journey: Steve Perry Helped Push Group into World of Gold." *Green Bay Press-Gazette*, July 29, 1979, 14.

Schopenhauer, Arthur. *Essays and Aphorisms*. R.J. Hollingdale, 1851. Reprint, Penguin Books, 1970.

Chapter 7

Fletcher, Tony. "Still Alive and…?" *Newsday*, September 23, 1992, 14.

"News of the Weird." *Idaho Statesman*, May 31, 1995, 9.

Chapter 8

Norman, Geraldine. "In Bed with My Installations." *Independent*, May 15, 1994, 78.

Chapter 9

Bernard, Sarah. "Heartbreak Hotel." *New York Magazine* 35, no. 24 (July 8, 2002): 30–35.

Casimir, Leslie. "Guns Seized at Gramercy Hotel." *New York Post*, March 17, 2002, 14.

El-Ghobashy, Tamer. "No Trace of Woman from NY." *New York Daily News*, January 7, 2005, 4.

Expose Corrupt Courts. www.exposecorruptcourts.blogspot.com.

Mbugua, Martin. "Nab Hotel Boss in Guns Seizure." *New York Daily News*, March 14, 2002, 28.

Smith, Bob. "Judges Keep Quiet About Conflicts." *New York Daily News*, February 8, 2004, 22.

Chapter 10

Barbanel, Josh. "Trophy Homes on Offer." *National Post*, February 19, 2009, 12.

Beard, Alison. "Manhattan Project." *National Post*, July 9, 2005, A6.

Demetriou, Danielle. "Grand Designs." *Independent*, June 13, 2005, 33.

Freeman, Danyelle. "Not the Finest China." *New York Daily News*, September 11, 2007, 41.

Grant, Peter. "It's Apple of Their Eye." *New York Daily News*, September 18, 1995, 25.

Haines, Tom. "The Art of Money." *Boston Globe*, October 8, 2006, M1.

Hanks, Douglas, III. "Ian Schrager Returns to South Beach." *Miami Herald*, December 20, 2005, 42.

Huguenin, Patrick, and Laura Schreffler. "Bob Cheers, Fern Steers." *New York Daily News*, September 11, 2007, 16.

New York Post Wire Services. "Leo Wants to be Eminem?" *Spokesmen Review*, December 17, 2008, 36.

Piazza, Jo. "Fashion Dish." *New York Daily News*, September 12, 2007, 16.

Severson, Kim. "Decaf Coffee's New Buzz." *Springfield News-Sun*, March 16, 2010, Life 4. Reprinted from the *New York Times*.

Shanahan, Mark, and Meredith Goldstein. "A Busy Playmaker." *Boston Globe*, May 4, 2009, B12.

Weichselbaum, Simone. "Flash Mob Nuptials Whole New Twist on 'Something Borrowed.'" *New York Daily News*, January 12, 2011, 12.

Yancey, Kitty Bean. "Hotel Hotsheet." *Fort Collins Coloradoan*, September 17, 2006, 25.

ABOUT THE AUTHOR

Max Weissberg is a writer and filmmaker living in New York, New York. A graduate of the American Film Institute's directing program, Max Weissberg co-produced and appeared in the feature documentary film *Hotel Gramercy Park* (2008), which included cameos by Ben Stiller, Kanye West, Winona Ryder, and Karl Lagerfeld. He has also directed two feature films, *Summertime in New York* (2013) and **Karaganda*: Red Mafia* (2025), and has written for *Rolling Stone*, the *St. Petersburg Times* (Russia), *Pulse*, and *ICON: Grazia*, among other outlets. He is married to his wife, Ani, and they have two children, Athena and Sebastian.